IRVING
VS.
IRVING

ALSO BY JACQUES POITRAS

The Right Fight:
Bernard Lord and the Conservative Dilemma

Beaverbrook: A Shattered Legacy

Imaginary Line: Life on an Unfinished Border

JACQUES POITRAS

IRVING VS. IRVING

CANADA'S FEUDING
BILLIONAIRES *and the* STORIES
THEY WON'T TELL

VIKING

VIKING

an imprint of Penguin Canada Books Inc., a Penguin Random House Company

Published by the Penguin Group
Penguin Canada Books Inc., 90 Eglinton Avenue East, Suite 700, Toronto, Ontario, Canada M4P 2Y3

Penguin Group (USA) LLC, 375 Hudson Street, New York, New York 10014, U.S.A.
Penguin Books Ltd, 80 Strand, London WC2R 0RL, England
Penguin Ireland, 25 St Stephen's Green, Dublin 2, Ireland (a division of Penguin Books Ltd)
Penguin Group (Australia), 707 Collins Street, Melbourne, Victoria 3008, Australia
(a division of Pearson Australia Group Pty Ltd)
Penguin Books India Pvt Ltd, 11 Community Centre, Panchsheel Park, New Delhi – 110 017, India
Penguin Group (NZ), 67 Apollo Drive, Rosedale, Auckland 0632, New Zealand
(a division of Pearson New Zealand Ltd)
Penguin Books (South Africa) (Pty) Ltd, 24 Sturdee Avenue, Rosebank, Johannesburg 2196, South Africa

Penguin Books Ltd, Registered Offices: 80 Strand, London WC2R 0RL, England

First published 2014

1 2 3 4 5 6 7 8 9 10 (RRD)

Copyright © Jacques Poitras, 2014

Manufactured in the U.S.A.

Library and Archives Canada Cataloguing in Publication Data
available upon request to the publisher.

Print ISBN 978-0-670-06771-8

eBook ISBN 978-0-14-319303-6

Visit the Penguin Canada website at **www.penguin.ca**

Special and corporate bulk purchase rates available; please see
www.penguin.ca/corporatesales or call 1-800-810-3104.

FOR ROBERT PICHETTE

A newspaper is of necessity something of a monopoly, and its first duty is to shun the temptations of monopoly. Its primary office is the gathering of news. At the peril of its soul it must see that the supply is not tainted.

C.P. Scott, *The Guardian*, Manchester, 1921

CONTENTS

FAMILY TREE

KENNETH COLIN (K.C.) IRVING, 1899–1992

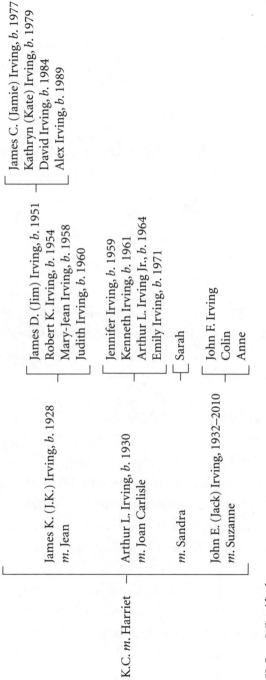

K.C. *m.* Harriet

James K. (J.K.) Irving, *b.* 1928
m. Jean

James D. (Jim) Irving, *b.* 1951
Robert K. Irving, *b.* 1954
Mary-Jean Irving, *b.* 1958
Judith Irving, *b.* 1960

James C. (Jamie) Irving, *b.* 1977
Kathryn (Kate) Irving, *b.* 1979
David Irving, *b.* 1984
Alex Irving, *b.* 1989

Arthur L. Irving, *b.* 1930
m. Joan Carlisle

Jennifer Irving, *b.* 1959
Kenneth Irving, *b.* 1961
Arthur L. Irving Jr., *b.* 1964
Emily Irving, *b.* 1971

m. Sandra

Sarah

John E. (Jack) Irving, 1932–2010
m. Suzanne

John F. Irving
Colin
Anne

K.C. *m.* Winnifred

CAST OF CHARACTERS

K.C. IRVING: Son of a small-town businessman and the founder of the Irving group of companies as it is commonly known. Father of J.K., Arthur, and Jack, who took over management of the various companies.

J.K. IRVING: K.C.'s eldest son, whose responsibilities include the forestry division, J.D. Irving Ltd., and the shipbuilding business. He is the father of Jim Irving and grandfather of Jamie. In 1971, he became co-owner, with his brother Arthur, of New Brunswick Publishing, publisher of the *Telegraph-Journal* and the *Times-Globe*. He is now the sole owner of Brunswick News Inc., which publishes all the Irving dailies and weeklies.

ARTHUR IRVING: K.C.'s second son, who ran Irving Oil; he brought his two sons, Kenneth and Arthur Jr., into the company. Arthur co-owned New Brunswick Publishing with J.K.

JACK IRVING: K.C.'s third son, who ran a variety of Irving companies including its construction businesses. Jack worked closely with Arthur building Irving gas stations. He owned Fredericton-based University Press of New Brunswick, publisher of the *Daily Gleaner*; and Moncton Publishing, publisher of the *Times* and *Transcript* newspapers (later merged into the *Times-Transcript*). Jack died in 2010.

JIM IRVING: J.K.'s oldest son, and the oldest grandson of K.C., has assumed responsibility for the group of companies run by his father. He is also the president of Brunswick News Inc.

JAMIE IRVING: Jim's oldest son, Jamie is the vice-president of Brunswick News, directly responsible for running the company.

KENNETH IRVING: Arthur's oldest son, he took over as CEO of Irving Oil in 2000 and ran the company until his abrupt departure in 2010.

JOHN IRVING: Jack's oldest son, he was the first president of Brunswick News after it was created in 1998. He left the company in 2005 to run Acadia Broadcasting. He took over the real estate and construction companies his father had managed after Jack's death in 2010.

THE NEWSPAPERS

The *Telegraph-Journal,* known at various times as the *New Brunswick Telegraph-Journal* and the *Saint John Telegraph-Journal,* is the flagship Irving newspaper, published in Saint John and distributed throughout New Brunswick.

The *Evening Times-Globe,* for most of its existence, was the daily afternoon sister paper to the *Telegraph-Journal,* sharing staff and offices but serving a local Saint John readership.

The *Times-Transcript* is based in Moncton and primarily serves the southeast part of New Brunswick, though it is distributed in the northeast as well. Until 1983, when they merged, the *Times* was the morning paper and the *Transcript* was published in the afternoon.

The Daily Gleaner is the daily newspaper based in Fredericton, New Brunswick's capital.

AUTHOR'S NOTE

I worked at the *Telegraph-Journal* from 1993 until 2000, and for the Moncton *Times-Transcript* for three earlier summers during my university years. This gave me a more nuanced view of the Irving ownership issue than either the rosy perspective of the family's defenders or the robber-baron caricatures of its critics.

In 1997, as the *Telegraph*'s Ottawa correspondent, I covered the ceremony when J.K. Irving was invested into the Order of Canada. Afterward, we chatted briefly. It was the first time I met him, and I thanked him for the newspaper's support of me and three colleagues when we were sued for defamation by a disgraced politician. It would have been easy, and tempting, for the newspaper to agree to a cash settlement, but Mr. Irving allowed the newspaper to defend the case in court. We won at trial, and I wanted him to know I was grateful.

Still, I felt the need to avoid giving Mr. Irving special treatment when I filed my story that day. I gave equal play to the day's other investee from New Brunswick, Sarah Anala, a Saint John woman who worked as a counsellor to aboriginal offenders. For the sake of transparency, I mentioned in my story that Mr. Irving owned the newspaper I worked for.

All of this is to say that I have written this book neither to praise nor to condemn the Irvings, their newspapers, or their employees. Many of my friends have done excellent work at the papers. Several still do now. There is, however, a broader story of how the worlds of industry, media, and politics influence each other. In New Brunswick, a small province often desperate for private-sector investment, it can be especially difficult to tell that kind of story candidly—even when it is a very good story, as this one is.

BEHAVE YOURSELVES

Fred Hazel knew something had changed the moment he saw the front page.

Hazel had stepped outside his modest shingled house on Duchess Street, in Saint John's west end, to pick up his copy of the *Telegraph-Journal* sitting on the doorstep. It was the morning of Wednesday, August 18, 1993; Hazel had retired from the newspaper the previous year after more than four decades as a reporter and editor, including twelve years as editor-in-chief. Still a newsman at heart, he unrolled the bundle of pages to see the big news of the day on page one.

In a lifetime spent in the Saint John newsroom, Fred Hazel had seen a lot of front pages, but this headline, the photos, the very subject matter were like nothing he had seen before. "I thought it was unusual," he recalls now, with his typical soft-spoken understatement.

Hazel's reaction was shared across Saint John—in fact, across the entire province of New Brunswick. The word *sensational* is

1

used too often in the media business, but this story *was* sensational: rarely had a *Telegraph-Journal* article provoked such a unanimous reaction. "People were really shocked," says one prominent community leader. "They were surprised."

The newspaper had obtained the last will of K.C. Irving, the billionaire industrialist whose vast, diverse enterprises made up the single largest private-sector economic force in New Brunswick. His forestry mills kept entire towns alive; his oil refinery accounted for more than half the province's exports. His power and influence were constant topics of conversation, especially in Saint John, the heart of his empire. Those who admired him and those who feared him agreed on one thing: K.C. Irving, once listed as Canada's richest man, was a singular figure, endlessly fascinating and famously secretive.

Irving had died the previous December, at ninety-three, during a Christmas visit to Saint John. He had made Bermuda his primary residence in 1972 to protect himself from Canadian taxation. Now, the *Telegraph-Journal* was breaking the news that Irving had left control of his multi-billion-dollar empire not in the hands of his three sons, J.K., Arthur, and Jack, who still ran the various companies from Saint John, but under the ownership of an offshore trust in Bermuda, run by three non-Canadian trustees, including K.C.'s widow. His sons—"the Irving boys," as they were still known in their sixties—were managing the enterprises, but could have no say in running the trust unless they, too, took up residence outside Canada. "Irving's Last Will Bequeaths Foreign Exile for His 3 Sons," blared the headline dominating the front page above photos of J.K., Arthur, and Jack. "Control of 'Entire Estate' Linked to Non-residency," said a subhead. A small sidebar, placed next to a severe-looking photo of the dead patriarch himself, reproduced the text of the relevant section of the will so readers could peruse it for themselves. "Like Father, Like Sons?" the headline asked. "K.C.'s 'Canada Clause.'"

In the coming days the *Telegraph-Journal* would run more stories on the will. One reporter quoted an economist comparing the offshore trust to tax-dodging cross-border shopping. Another profiled—without the benefit of an interview—Winnifred Irving, K.C.'s former secretary, whom he had married after the death of Harriet, his first wife and the mother of his three sons; Winnifred was now a trustee to an empire worth an estimated $8 billion. The most revealing piece, headlined "K.C.'s Will Tells Heirs to Behave Themselves," suggested that by keeping the empire out of his sons' Canadian hands, K.C. ensured it would not be taxed—a bill that might total $1.5 billion, according to one analysis. The trust would expire in thirty-five years, unless the trustees dissolved it sooner, but the will was silent on how its assets were to be divided; this suggested, one story noted, "that Irving did not want any of his descendants to take anything for granted."

For the time being, family members could draw on the trust for funds, but only if the trustees approved. K.C. instructed them, through one clause, to act "as I might do with respect to such property if I were living"—a phrase that extended the patriarch's extraordinary penchant for control beyond the ninety-three years of his mortal lifetime.

For three days the *Telegraph-Journal*'s journalists probed the document's implications, relying on experts after the Irvings themselves rebuffed interview requests. The coverage, though often speculative, was compelling, even gripping. "These people are very prominent in New Brunswick and they're bound to make news no matter what they do," Hazel says now. "They employ so many people and they're involved in so many industries. But I thought it was a little unusual to have that kind of story."

Unusual, shocking—for one important reason: the newspaper breaking the story that morning, the Saint John–based *Telegraph-Journal*, was part of the very empire it was reporting on. Like all the English-language daily newspapers in New Brunswick, it was owned by the Irving family, and had a reputation for not digging too deeply into the family's business. Long before the creation of Bell Globemedia and Quebecor, New Brunswickers had grasped the concept of the concentration of media ownership.

"We didn't have instructions, written or verbal, that I was ever aware of, on how to handle Irving stories, or not to do this or not to do that," Fred Hazel says. Yet the papers rarely went beyond the most superficial reporting on their owners. Yes, as Hazel points out, they covered stories like smog from an Irving smokestack becoming trapped over Saint John, or dust from an Irving mill settling on hundreds of cars across the city. These stories did not reflect well on the family, but these were highly visible events that could not be credibly ignored. Investigating what lay under the surface, the stories that required time and effort and courage to expose, like the provisions of a will: that was rare.

However, a new editor had arrived at the *Telegraph-Journal* and its sister newspaper, the *Evening Times-Globe*. Neil Reynolds, a man with a track record of award-winning investigative journalism, had been promised—by J.K. Irving himself—the freedom to turn the two publications into great newspapers. His arrival was not widely known outside the *Telegraph* building over on Crown Street, but that front page was a signal that a new editorial posture was in place, one that would scrutinize even the newspaper's proprietors—who happened to be the most

4

powerful family in the province. "No editor ever put his head into a toothier lion's mouth," a Halifax columnist would later write admiringly. "There was a lot of excitement," Philip Lee, a reporter at the time, remembers of that day. "People were talking about the paper again, so that was good. There was a lot of buzz."

In the newsroom that morning, Gerry Childs, an old-school veteran who oversaw the editorial page, "was visibly shaken" by the will coverage, Lee says. Reynolds had not made a splash since his arrival in the spring, "and then suddenly he comes in and says, 'We're doing *this*.'" Childs, Lee, and other editors gathered with Reynolds in a glassed-in little office in the corner of the old wood-panelled newsroom for the regular morning story meeting. "Before we get started," Childs said to Reynolds, "I just need to know: where did you get this document? Where did it come from?"

There was a long pause. Reynolds had hired a freelancer in Bermuda to pick up the document at the probate court and mail it to him, a routine transaction. He sensed, though, as he sat back in his chair, the tips of the fingers of one hand resting in his trademark fashion behind the buckle of his belt, that the moment called for a touch of the drama he favoured in his journalism.

Reynolds leaned forward. He slapped his hand palm-down on the desk with a theatrical thump and declared, "I bought it!"

Then, to break the tension, he gave a laugh—a deep laugh punctuated with a toothy smile—and the meeting moved on. "He was clearly in charge," Lee says. "He was very clear that newsrooms are not democracies, and the best you hope for is a philosopher-king, and you had one with him. He was definitely going to be in charge. And I was so happy at that moment. I knew my life was going to change."

Many lives began to change that summer, including the

5

owners'. "It was news, I guess. That's the way it works," J.K. Irving says of the coverage of his father's will. "Did I like it? Not really. But that's the business."

That front page is still electric to look at twenty years later, because it opened a window into the Irvings' world. The public glimpsed what J.K. and his brothers already knew: their empire was facing great transformation as they set out to manage their holdings for the first time without their father's counsel. Reynolds's scoop marked the beginning of two decades of upheaval for the family—a new chapter in one of the most remarkable stories of Canadian entrepreneurship.

The newspapers would eventually falter in telling that story, because they were inextricably part of it. Next to the other Irving operations—pulp mills, the oil refinery, logging operations, trucking, shipbuilding—the papers were tiny. But K.C.'s death, Reynolds's arrival, and the popularization of the internet would transform them, to the point that they would prove contentious themselves when the empire began to fracture. As rivalries and resentments grew among the next generation of Irvings, one of their own—a great-grandchild of K.C.—would take direct control of the news business for the first time. This in turn would revive the debate about editorial control, even as a rift in the family grew wider.

By 2013, it was clear that K.C. had failed, with his will, to impose unity and harmony on his family—that he had failed, as the 1993 had headline put it, to make them "behave themselves."

By then, the front page that so shocked Fred Hazel was a distant memory. The window had closed again, and the story of the Irving split—the tale of one of Canada's richest families divided by jealousy, discord, and competing visions—was a story no Irving newspaper would tell.

1

BECOMING K.C. IRVING

▼

Here is a story about K.C. Irving.

Long before his name became synonymous with industry, long before he was hailed as one of Canada's greatest entrepreneurs, long before he was lionized by many of his fellow New Brunswickers and demonized by others, K.C. Irving faced a choice. Upon that choice hinged not only his own destiny but also that of the province he called home.

In the summer of 1921, Kenneth Colin Irving was jammed with hundreds of other young men into a grimy, overcrowded CPR train chugging west across the broad expanse of the Canadian prairie. He and his friend Addie McNairn had left their hometown, the tiny village of Bouctouche on New Brunswick's eastern shore, to join the harvest excursion. This was a rite of passage for many young Maritimers, a migration west at the end of each summer by thousands of young men to harvest wheat on the prairies—to fill labour shortages and make good money.

For twenty-two-year-old Kenneth Irving, the cash was, as it always would be, a short-term goal: a means to an end. Irving and McNairn planned to push farther west after the harvest, to Vancouver, and then to secure passage by ship to Australia. There, far from Bouctouche, Irving would find a new frontier where he could establish a business and build his fortune.

Kenneth Colin Irving was a born entrepreneur. On the harvest in Saskatchewan, "the cook fell ill one day," says Joan Carlisle Irving, who heard the story from Irving himself, "and he signed up for the job of cook, because the cook made more money."

K.C.'s father was an entrepreneur, too, one of the leading citizens of Bouctouche. James D. Irving ran a sawmill, a gristmill, three farms, and a general store. "He knew what hard work was," K.C. would remember of his father. "He knew how much a man should do and he knew how to fix a piece of machinery. And if he didn't know, he would learn very quickly. I suppose I am a bit like him in many respects. I always liked machinery and that sort of thing. I like to see wheels turn."

When Kenneth was eight years old, his father bought one of the first cars in Bouctouche; the boy, fascinated, took it apart and rebuilt it. Three years later, he secretly bought his own automobile, a Ford, for eight dollars. His father discovered the purchase and commanded him to sell it immediately. Kenneth complied— but only when he found a customer willing to pay the higher resale price he was demanding. "He tried to buy it for less," K.C. remembered in a rare interview for a 1981 National Film Board documentary, "but I wouldn't drop the price below eleven dollars." Irving chuckled at the memory of his three-dollar profit.

The born entrepreneur soon developed his own ideas of how to grow his father's businesses, but found his commercial ambitions stifled: Kenneth was the son of James Irving's *second* marriage, and had an older half-brother, Herbert, from his father's first marriage. Herbert lacked Kenneth's drive: in 1919, when Kenneth returned from Europe after the end of the First World War—he had arrived too late to see action—he was alarmed to find the general store faltering. Eaton's had established a mail-order warehouse in nearby Moncton, and sales were suffering at general stores like J.D. Irving's. Without consulting his father, K.C. ordered a two-hundred-and-fifty-gallon gasoline tank and installed it out front, digging the hole himself. "I'm darned sure we're not going out of business," he told his father when the older man arrived on the scene. The Irving general store became the local agent for Imperial Oil, selling gasoline to the growing number of automobile owners. But half-brother Herbert, fourteen years his senior and well-regarded around town, wasn't sure about the gasoline tank. He proposed closing the store in the face of the Eaton's threat—giving up, in other words. "We had different ways of doing things," K.C. said in a typical under-statement. But the brothers were bound together: their father planned to turn ownership of the store over to the two of them, a shared responsibility, with Herbert in charge of the day-to-day running of the company.

This, according to Joan Carlisle Irving, was the decisive moment.

Joan was K.C. Irving's daughter-in-law from 1957, when she married his son Arthur, to 1980, when they divorced. During the marriage, says a family acquaintance, K.C. was "quite smitten by Joan." Despite being the daughter of a small-town barber in Sackville, New Brunswick, she possessed a touch of movie-star glamour. K.C. allowed her to record interviews with him about his early life, and eventually permitted her to tape conversations with his relatives, his childhood friends, and his parents' acquaintances. She developed an intimate glimpse of his formative years—including an early example of what would become his trademark brinksmanship.

When K.C. learned that his father would force him to share ownership of the store with his half-brother, Herbert, Joan relates, he was furious. She quotes him from memory: "I told my father, 'If you think giving me half the company with Herbert running it is giving me a gift, you're giving me *nothing*! ... I'm going to go west and join the harvest excursion.... Then I'm going to take a boat to Australia and I will go and earn my own fortune in Australia!'"

There are different versions of what happened after Irving and McNairn reached Vancouver to find a ship. K.C.'s authorized biography, by Douglas How and Ralph Costello, says that while he was visiting a relative, "a wire came from his father, urging him to come home. The family ties proved too strong." Irving himself told *Maclean's* magazine in 1964 that he and McNairn stayed with a friend of J.D. Irving, Bob Brown, and, "I have a feeling Uncle Bob might have gotten in touch with my father about this Australian thing." In this account, McNairn stalled on booking their trip, then suggested they do logging in northern British Columbia; K.C., always in a hurry, declared that if he were going to work in the woods, he might as well return to New Brunswick.

Joan Carlisle Irving says K.C. told her a different story, a tale that suggests a young man so canny, he bluffed his father by leveraging his mother's affection. James Irving's second wife, Mary, "was absolutely devoted to her Kenneth," Joan says, recalling a neighbour's account of Mary pretending to feed chocolates to a photograph of her son on the mantelpiece. "He was very, very closely connected to his mother," Joan says. "All the work ethic, he inherited from her." It was Mary Irving who taught him, "If you are going to do something, do it right."

In Vancouver, K.C. chose to make his banking arrangements for Australia with a banker originally from Richibouctou, a village fifteen miles north of Bouctouche—knowing, Joan says, that the man would contact his father. "And meanwhile back home his mother was exerting her pressure on J.D. Irving," Joan says. The banker's call was apparently the tipping point: before long, the man summoned K.C. to his office for a long-distance telephone conversation with his father. "And J.D. Irving said, 'Kenneth, come up. The company is yours, a hundred percent.'" Herbert lost his stake in the general store: K.C. Irving had won control, not for the last time.

Joan says K.C. told her this story himself; it does not appear in any other accounts of his life.* "I think," she says with a soft laugh, "he was a pretty shrewd cookie."

A decade later, after K.C. moved to Saint John to expand his oil business, J.D. Irving died, leaving his lumber business, J.D. Irving Ltd., to his wife, to his two daughters, Lou Dorothy and Marion, and to Herbert and K.C. Though K.C. inherited only 50 of the company's 394 shares, the family agreed he should run it. For several years he scrimped along, resisting buy-out offers, refusing to sell wood at a loss, scraping to keep the enterprise alive through the Depression. Then, just as he began to turn it around, he persuaded his mother to turn over controlling interest to him.

---

* Joan Carlisle Irving's account of K.C. Irving's early days is based on her memory of their taped interviews. She did not make the tapes available to me. Her recollections of other events, however, including her divorce from Arthur Irving, are corroborated by court files and other documents.

K.C.'s move alarmed his sisters, according to Joan Carlisle Irving's account of her interviews. "Dorothy told me that when this happened, her sister Marion, who was a doctor in Halifax, called her and said, 'Dorothy, get up here. We need to take action against Kenneth.' And Dorothy said, 'Oh, I can't go up there and fight against Kenneth. You know who will win.'" And with that, K.C. Irving had won control of the lumber business that became a cornerstone of his empire.

Even in those early days, what would become known as the Irving Way was emerging: Kenneth Colin Irving was bold, decisive, unsentimental—willing to use the threat of departure to win, willing to play so hard that others saw no point in taking him on. On this foundation was built one of the greatest industrial empires Canada has ever seen.

In 1981, a National Film Board documentary about K.C. Irving opened with a shot of him at the window of his company jet, scanning the terrain below. "Today, when K.C. Irving looks down from his plane, chances are he owns whatever he sees," the narrator said. This image of Irving assets as far as the eye could see became a trope for journalists. John DeMont opened his 1991 book on the Irving empire with a similar *tour d'horizon* from high above Saint John: "When he peers out from the penthouse atop the Irving Building, K.C. Irving finds many of his prize assets spread before him, most branded with his name." Fifteen years later, *The Globe and Mail's* Gordon Pitts applied the same motif to K.C.'s second son: "On a clear day, 76-year-old Arthur Irving can stand on the hill beside his big white mansion, at one of the highest points in Saint John, and survey an urban industrial landscape that should, in reality, be called 'Irvingville.'"

It was literally true, and still is, that the Irving presence is everywhere in Saint John, New Brunswick's largest and most commercial city. K.C. himself always insisted it wasn't greed that drove him to such dominance. "Of course, money is a necessity," he told Giles Walker, the director of the NFB film. "But outside of taking care of your needs and that, it's only good for what you can do with it." And what Irving did with it was keep buying and building. "You've got to keep going," he would say. "Expansion is the thing. The trouble with many businessmen is that when they have made some progress they sit back and take a rest. We can't progress while standing still." This is the drive that would define not only his life but also the lives of his heirs.

Almost a century after K.C. Irving began constructing his vast, seamlessly integrated industrial machine, it's easy to assume that the pieces fell into place inevitably. After all, each new enterprise sprang from an existing venture and was interlocked with it, as surely as one generation begat another in the Old Testament.

In the beginning, there were cars. Kenneth Colin Irving loved cars; he began selling Fords from the store in Bouctouche not long after his return from Vancouver. Cars required gasoline and maintenance, and by 1924 Irving was offering both at a service station across from the general store. He was so good at it that other Bouctouche merchants complained to Imperial Oil, whose fuel Kenneth sold, that they were in effect being forced to buy from their competitor. When Imperial pulled his franchise and handed it to another businessman, Irving ordered a larger storage tank and found another supplier: if he was too successful for Imperial, he would take them on with his own company, Primrose Oil, the forerunner of Irving Oil.

Ford Motors also found Kenneth too good a salesman. He opened a second car dealership and service station in nearby

Shediac in 1925; when he began attracting car buyers from Moncton, the urban centre of southeast New Brunswick, that city's Ford dealer complained he was losing sales to an interloper. Irving refused Ford's request to back off but, as a compromise, agreed to leave Bouctouche to run the Ford franchise in Saint John, the province's largest port and a bustling, sometimes seedy city of opportunity. Car sales were brisk, and more cars required more fuel and more repairs: by 1930, he was a businessman of regional consequence with twenty service stations in New Brunswick and Nova Scotia. He started a construction company to build them, an early sign of his impulse for vertical integration.

During the Depression, he went after consumers who couldn't afford cars: he bought up small, local motorcoach carriers, transforming them into New Brunswick's largest passenger bus and freight truck service, SMT Eastern Ltd. He bid to run Saint John's municipal bus system and found himself battling another bidder, a Nova Scotia company, on three fronts: at City Council, in the courts, and before committees of the New Brunswick Legislature in Fredericton. When it appeared the Saint John council would award the contract to his competitor, K.C. Irving fumed that such a move "certainly would discourage anyone from increasing investments or establishing new industries in Saint John." The implicit threat—an echo of his vow to move to Australia—worked: the councillors hesitated, Irving held on long enough to resume the battle, and in 1948, twelve years after his initial bid, he emerged as the winner.

Running a bus company required buses, and K.C. Irving built them himself through another of his companies, Universal Sales Ltd. Rather than buy supplies from Thorne's Hardware, a Saint John retailer, he bought the company. The buses used hardwood veneer—thin slices of wood cut into panels—from Canada

14

Veneers, a Saint John company Irving had acquired when it hit hard times in 1938. His timing was, as usual, perfect: Irving used his connection to another New Brunswicker, Lord Beaverbrook, Churchill's minister of aircraft production, to supply veneer to the British air force for its lightweight, all-wood fighter plane, the Mosquito. By the end of the war, Canada Veneers was the largest supplier of aircraft veneer on the planet, and Irving was flush with cash to fuel even more expansion.

He was getting big now, very big, but more important, his companies remained privately held: there were no investors, no shareholders, no directors to answer to. "When you go public," he explained once, "you have certain rules you have to go by. Those may not make it the most convenient way of accomplishing what you set out to do." Perhaps Herbert's diffidence still haunted him. "You can take a calculated risk," K.C. said, "if you only have to account for yourself."

The success of Canada Veneers begat more: Irving had already bought a Quebec company, d'Auteuil Lumber, to supply veneer logs and pulp logs for a mill he bought in Dexter, New York. But the d'Auteuil lands were far from Saint John, so—with his wartime profits—he picked up 1.6 million acres of timberland held by the defunct New Brunswick Railway Company, making him one of the largest owners of forest land in New Brunswick. This heralded a buying spree that included a lumber mill in Keegan, Maine, across the international border, and, with U.S. paper company Kimberly-Clark as a minority partner, a pulp mill at the Reversing Falls in Saint John.

In 1951, he expanded the pulp mill, renamed it Irving Pulp and Paper Ltd., and won concessions from the city and the province, including a fixed property-tax assessment, immunity from nuisance lawsuits, the right to dump waste in the river, and the right to expropriate additional land for future expansion. When some members of the legislature hesitated over such a complete surrender to industry, a representative from a Saint John constituency reminded them the mill was "the biggest industrial plum that has fallen our way for some time." New Brunswick could not afford to be choosy when it came to its industrialists.

The expansion of the mill spawned another Irving enterprise: after a legal dispute with the supplier of steel panels for the pulp mill walls, K.C. decided to make the panels himself, founding Ocean Steel Construction. He later established Strescon, a maker of pre-stressed concrete. Now he was spreading out laterally, each company spawning more and more spinoffs: to avoid what he considered unfair CNR freight rates, he launched a shipping company, Kent Lines, to distribute oil to his growing network of service stations; then, in 1958, he acquired a past-its-prime shipyard to build and repair his boats.

It had already been a breathtaking and rapid expansion. Then came the grandest manifestation of his ambition—the single largest physical monument to K.C. Irving's desire for domination.

Imperial Oil had been his nemesis back in Bouctouche, but business was business: the company still supplied much of the refined fuel to Irving's service stations. When he pushed his chain deep into Quebec, however, Imperial threatened to cut him off— another outrageous example, he concluded, of being punished for success. No longer would he allow anyone to deny him the freedom to grow, he vowed. He decided to build his own refinery in Saint John and process crude himself.

K.C. Irving loved machines—he loved "to see wheels

turn"—but a refinery was no early-twentieth-century car. The technical expertise required to build and run an oil refinery was beyond him. Though it went against every instinct he had, K.C. would not have complete control. He would need a partner—but on his terms: when British Petroleum (BP) insisted, on the eve of signing an agreement, that it have the right to buy out Irving Oil upon K.C.'s retirement or death, the industrialist walked away and recruited a more accommodating partner in Standard Oil of California. (Three decades later Irving Oil bought out SoCal's stake, finally gaining 100 percent control.)

The refinery spawned more growth. Other Irving companies lined up as subcontractors, and the already ubiquitous chain of service stations expanded again, even before the refinery was finished. "They needed to expand the retail network, so that when the refinery was done they would have an outlet for the product," says Pat Darrah, who worked with K.C.'s son Jack in the late fifties to build more gas stations. Irving was not responding to anticipated demand but instead was building service stations— he had three thousand by 1970—to *create* more demand for his own product. "That," Darrah says, "is what made him different."

The completion of the refinery in 1960 was not the last expansion of Irving's reach, but the basic architecture of his empire—the refining and selling of fuel and the cutting and processing of wood on an industrial scale—was now in place. And more than any other single asset, the sprawling refinery complex in east Saint John, with six giant storage tanks each bearing a single letter that together spelled out I-R-V-I-N-G, symbolized his imprint on the New Brunswick economy.

The refinery also brought into relief how governments had learned to fear his wrath. In 1958, the city agreed to build a new waterline to the pulp mill for a fixed annual charge of only thirty-five thousand dollars. Then the city realized Irving's bill would cover only a tiny fraction of the city's cost; the balance would be passed on to residents in a rate increase. City Hall sought a way out, but K.C. stood firm: a contract was a contract. So when the refinery missed the first payment on its lease of municipal land, the city moved to cancel the lease and repossess the property, hoping this leverage would force Irving to renegotiate the pulp mill's water deal.

Instead, Irving hinted he might take his investments elsewhere. "You can't do business with people who want only to oppose and attack you," he said. He had pledged $100 million in new investment in his Saint John operations if Ottawa would help fund the Chignecto Canal, a fanciful scheme for a waterway—a shortcut for his ships—across the isthmus linking New Brunswick and Nova Scotia. Now, Irving withdrew the pledge. "It would be ridiculous," he said, "to consider new agreements with a city which, apparently, is more anxious to break contracts than to see progress." The city backpedalled, and Irving kept his generous water deal.

The refinery bedevilled federal tax authorities as well. Irving and SoCal developed a novel scheme that saw SoCal's crude, which was extracted abroad, sold not to Irving in Saint John but to an offshore subsidiary, Irving California Co. Ltd., incorporated in Bermuda. The price would match the cost of production and shipping. The Bermuda company, known as Irvcal, would then sell the crude at the higher market price to Irving Oil in Saint John. The crude itself would not pass through Bermuda en route to the refinery; only the dollars would come ashore, landing in Irvcal bank accounts on the tiny British island. This way, Irvcal made its profits in Bermuda, and they were paid to Irving as tax-free dividends under Bermuda law. The higher price paid in

Saint John, meanwhile, lowered the refinery's profits, keeping its tax bill low as well. The Canadian government challenged the arrangement, but while the eventual court ruling conceded it was "a tax avoidance scheme," it was perfectly legal. "Everybody is entitled to reduce taxes, as long as he stays within the law," the judge wrote.

The Irvcal case revealed a fundamental contradiction in the Irving Way: though he sheltered his fortune offshore, K.C. Irving professed undying loyalty to New Brunswick and the Maritimes. He built his refinery where he did "because I live in Saint John," he told an interviewer. His empire would spread through the Maritimes, then into Quebec, Ontario, and down the eastern seaboard of the United States, but its foundation—the refining of fuel and the cutting of trees—remained in New Brunswick. The province's other billionaires, the McCains, to whom the Irvings are often compared, decentralized their global frozen-french-fry empire, with operations on six continents and a head office only nominally in New Brunswick. The Irvings, though, clung stubbornly to home. "I didn't want to live in Alberta," K.C. said when asked why he passed on a chance to invest early in western oil. "This is where I wanted to live. It's nice to stay home. You couldn't get a better place than the Maritimes."

The down-home patriotism carried an edge: when a rival Ontario company claimed to be the only Canadian-owned oil firm operating in the Maritimes, Irving corrected the record publicly—and added, "Let's not forget that in some cases Upper Canadians are the worst type of foreigners." And when national union leaders flew in to organize a strike of his refinery workers, he said he had "more interest in local labour and advancement of local labour than any of these people who come to Saint John determined to force their will on the people of Saint John." He also questioned, during the same labour dispute, whether all his work building the refinery "wasn't worth the effort," another example of the perpetual asterisk on K.C.'s professions of loyalty to his roots. "Too much of this thinking," he said once when a government didn't move fast enough to accommodate him, "can cause New Brunswickers to become outsiders."

By the 1960s, no one doubted K.C. Irving's dominance of the province. Though he was "the essence of civility" personally—an assistant to the province's premier recalled him holding an umbrella for the politician "like a zealous butler"—public officials were afraid to criticize him on the record. "We haven't got a democracy in New Brunswick in the ordinary sense of the word," one such anonymous official told Ralph Allen of *Maclean's* in 1964. "In nearly all matters pertaining to the public affairs of New Brunswick," Allen wrote, "what K.C. wants K.C gets." The scale of his success, it was sometimes said, scared off other businesses from establishing themselves in the province.

In their scathing 1971 portrait, *K.C. Irving: The Art of the Industrialist*, Russell Hunt and Robert Campbell wrote that Irving was "a lot more than just a man. K.C. Irving is a social phenomenon on the same level of importance as a revolution or a war.... There is hardly a pie in New Brunswick worth having a finger in, in which you won't find an Irving digit." In *Maclean's*, Allen was in awe of "one of the most unbelievable business empires and one of the most astonishing men in the history of the Maritime provinces, of Canada, and quite conceivably of the modern business world anywhere."

Oddly enough, what finally stirred the first truly public debate about his influence was not the scale of his forestry operations, nor the centrality of his refinery to the province's economic output. No, what would put K.C. Irving under the public spotlight, to his everlasting fury, was one of the smallest, seemingly least consequential assets of his empire, "almost incidental to the scope and value of his vast holdings," his biographer would write—an operation he would claim not to understand and would struggle to explain: his newspapers.

2

A LOCAL OIL COMPANY

▼

K.C. Irving became a newspaper owner in 1936, when he bought a small Saint John weekly publication, the *Maritime Broadcaster*, a listing of local radio programs, and turned it into a daily newspaper called the *Citizen*. The populist *Citizen* urged readers to buy New Brunswick products and touted, among other ideas, the expansion of Saint John's port and the construction of the Chignecto Canal, two ideas close to its owner's heart. According to journalist Charles Lynch, who worked there, it also provided "a safe outlet" for stories reflecting Irving's side of the battle for the city bus franchise. "It quickly became clear that we had an editorial axe to grind," remembered Lynch. "All of the Irving interests were sacred cows."

The *Citizen* lasted only three years. In 1939, Irving sold it to another local businessman, Howard P. Robinson, who closed it and absorbed some of its staff into his existing newspapers. Robinson had bought up many of the dozen or so dailies that had competed in Saint John in the late nineteenth century, combining them, under the auspices of the New Brunswick Publishing Co. Ltd., into just two: the *Telegraph-Journal*, published in the morning, and the *Evening Times-Globe*, which appeared in the afternoon.

In 1944, the two entrepreneurs reversed roles. Robinson, in the twilight of his career, sold New Brunswick Publishing to Irving, the up-and-comer, in a deal that included Robinson's radio station, CHSJ, and—symbolically—his large home on Mount Pleasant Avenue overlooking the city. K.C. Irving always said his goal was to keep the newspapers in local hands, but Ralph Costello, later the publisher of the *Telegraph-Journal* and the *Times-Globe*, acknowledged Irving's brief ownership of the *Citizen* was politically motivated. "He was deeply involved in politics, in the Liberal party," Costello wrote years later, "and a friendly newspaper was a necessary tool of a political party, *because*, and this is important to understand, that is the way things were done in those days." While Costello acknowledged it was reasonable to ask whether Irving bought the Robinson papers for the same reason, he argued there was no evidence he had used them for propaganda. The motive, says Joan Carlisle Irving, was "the integration of everything"—the same impulse that drove all his acquisitions. "The shipyard made ships that carried the oil for Irving Oil that would supply J.D. Irving, and it would get all its equipment from Thorne's Hardware, and the newspapers would buy the paper that the pulp mill produced, and it made the whole system a totally integrated product."

Irving purchased the Robinson papers quietly. Shortly after joining the *Telegraph-Journal* in 1949, rookie reporter Fred Hazel was in a boat on Saint John harbour with a group of visiting parliamentarians. "How do you like working for K.C. Irving?" one of them asked Hazel. "I don't work for K.C. Irving," replied the startled journalist. "I work for the newspaper." Hazel wrongly believed Robinson and a consortium of other businessmen still owned New Brunswick Publishing. Irving himself would refuse to discuss it, and well into the 1950s, many Saint John residents presumed Robinson remained the proprietor. Irving was equally stealthy in 1948 when he bought the two daily newspapers in Moncton, the morning *Times* and the afternoon *Transcript*. He made no announcement, and kept the previous owner in the job of publisher.

Word got around, of course, and there were whispers that K.C. Irving had bought the papers to keep bad news about his companies from getting out, an accusation that continues today. The Saint John newspapers, the *Telegraph-Journal* and the *Times-Globe*, were scrutinized most closely because their coverage area included the head offices of most Irving operations. According to author John DeMont, Tom Drummie, Irving's first publisher in Saint John, decreed that, if there were a spill or similar mishap involving Irving Oil, the *Telegraph-Journal* and the *Times-Globe* were to identify it as "a local oil company." Drummie also instituted a policy that K.C. Irving's photograph was never to be published in the papers. "Those were the days when advertisers, the establishment, the owners had a lot of influence," Drummie's successor, Ralph Costello, acknowledged years later. The newspapers covered the news but avoided controversy.

The papers improved in 1961, when Drummie retired and Irving installed Costello as president of New Brunswick Publishing Co. and publisher of the two Saint John papers. Costello had started at the papers as a part-time sportswriter in 1940 and rose through the ranks as sports editor, provincial editor, city editor, columnist, and managing editor. As publisher, he modernized the design, hired better reporters, and demanded a new level of professionalism. "The *Telegraph* changed the day Ralph took over," says Jim Morrison, a veteran editor. "It changed for the better. Better staff, better layout, better everything."

Costello did not, however, bring a new approach to covering K.C. Irving. The publisher grew up in poverty in the south end of Saint John and had worked his way to the top of the company, says Michael Camp, who worked for Costello as a reporter in the 1980s. "He's the ultimate shop-floor success story." This gave him the classic working-class conservatism of a blue-collar, industrial city: a skepticism of government and a healthy respect for the hard-driving entrepreneur who provides people with an honest day's work. Costello "never had Irving trouble," Camp says, "which was a sign of two things. First, I think the Irvings clearly trusted Ralph not to embarrass them. And two, Ralph would put out a paper that suited what the Irvings thought a paper should do."

It is impossible to measure empirically exactly when and how often Costello's papers reflected the company line. News judgment is subjective. Any editorial decision, any story, can, in isolation, be explained by random factors: a short-staffed newsroom on a given day, bigger stories competing for attention, a missed phone call, a looming deadline. Once, critics leapt on the *Telegraph-Journal* for burying on its inside pages a story about a consultant accusing the pulp mill of dumping millions of gallons of waste in the harbour; the editors pointed out it had been on the front page of the previous day's *Evening Times-Globe*. "Costello used to say that his only instruction from K.C. was to put out the best newspapers you can for the community," Fred Hazel says. "There's always a suspicion that, you know, the Irvings owned the newspaper, so you don't say this, you don't say that. We never had any instructions on that, written, or verbal, at all."

And yet journalists in the Saint John newsroom would recall trouble over a story about an Irving tugboat running aground, because it was bad for the company's insurance rates, and the spiking of a piece about a shantytown for refinery labourers, because it might cause them to demand better conditions. Union leaders complained about no coverage of their positions during labour disputes with Irving. The papers editorialized for months against a proposed toll bridge across the harbour, echoing arguments by a "citizens' committee" that it would be costly for business; the committee was run by one of K.C.'s sons and an Irving lawyer.

Jackie Webster, a retired reporter, remembers being assigned a story in the early sixties explicitly to make K.C. Irving happy. An icebreaker built by his shipyard returned to Saint John for maintenance, and a colleague filed "a perfectly adequate story." The next day, however, Webster got a note "that Mr. Irving was very unhappy with the coverage.... He thought it was inadequate. And I was assigned to do a make-good story." Her story ran on the front page, complete with a photograph of the captain and crew. "It was a straight case of Mr. Irving interfering." Other times, no explicit instruction was necessary, Webster says. One night she was on duty when the newsroom took a call that an oil truck had hit a Volkswagen in Grand Bay, near Saint John—a typical spot-news photo for the city section. "I did exactly what any Irving employee with any brains would have done," Webster says. "I called the police to find out what oil company it was." Learning the truck belonged to Imperial Oil, she sent a photographer. "Now had it been an Irving Oil truck, I wouldn't have bothered," she says. But there was no directive. "It was osmosis," Webster says. "I don't remember ever being directly told, but there are things you learn, things you pick up."

Fred Hazel, who eventually became editor-in-chief, has just as many examples that he says prove the papers were free to report stories that didn't reflect well on the Irving companies. A huge front-page headline shouted "SMOG" one day when weather patterns trapped emissions from the Irving plants in the air over the city. He also recalls stories on citizen complaints about their cars being coated in residue from an Irving mill. "That was the story and we did the story," Hazel says. "We didn't bury it or hide it." Those stories, however, affected hundreds of people in a public way and could not be credibly ignored—a distinction that would be important for decades in the Irving newspaper-ownership debate.

If K.C. Irving was dictating editorial policy, "it was a very closely guarded secret," says Joan Carlisle Irving. "He would always come out with explanations like, 'Oh, I don't know why they think I control it. Look at that terrible picture of Jack they put in the paper last week. My goodness! I have no control over what they're doing!'" Even Russell Hunt and Robert Campbell, in their 1973 book that portrayed K.C. Irving as a manipulative industrial monster, admitted that, while the quality of journalism was poor, "whether or not … it is the ownership of the news-papers that has produced that situation is an immense and complex question." More persuasive was the argument that monopoly ownership meant there was no incentive to improve.

And while a newspaper can be seen as a public trust with a duty to clear-eyed candour, it is a private enterprise: its owner is at liberty to publish what he or she wants. In a 1980 essay called "What About the Irvings?" the celebrated New Brunswick poet Alden Nowlan, once a night editor at the *Telegraph-Journal*, blamed the paper's journalistic weaknesses on its typical small-market newsroom, with a constant turnover of young journalists in a hurry to leave for bigger cities, and a coterie of "lifers" who "may sometimes err on the side of excessive love" as uncritical hometown cheerleaders. These were functions not of Irving control but of life in a small province. Nowlan wrote: "A reader who is unhappy with the *Telegraph-Journal* is probably unhappy with New Brunswick."

Nowlan was on to something, but he was also disingenuous, rationalizing the papers' flaws by pointing out they were as mediocre as other similar-sized newspapers. David Folster, a one-time staff reporter who left to freelance and write books, once pointed out that nothing prevented K.C. Irving from aspiring to be a news-industry leader, as he was with his constant upgrades and modernizations of his refinery and his mills. "What they really ought to do is take one of those newspapers and just make it a super paper," Folster said. "One could certainly say they have the wherewithal, they have the corporate ability, to do that."

Nowlan's most famous rejoinder in his essay was his assertion that critics would be satisfied "by nothing short of the Irvings mounting an editorial campaign against themselves"—but this ignored another possibility: that somewhere between uncritical acquiescence and an all-out anti-corporate crusade, the papers might offer a higher quality of journalism, carefully researched and diligently reported, that provided fair, accurate analysis of the Irving industries, rather than simply react to random events like a coating of mill dust on cars.

But this was not the kind of newspaper Ralph Costello was running. "I mean we weren't crusading for the environment, but I don't think anyone was in that era," Fred Hazel says, his bent, gnarled fingers the legacy of a life spent in front of a typewriter. "The environment wasn't a word that was used at all.... [We] actually had some anti-Irving employees in the newsroom, guys who believed that we should be investigating conditions on the ships that came in.

"Well, you know, we weren't really into that."

Michael Wardell was the very opposite of the taciturn, frugal K.C. Irving. Brash and flamboyant, prone to overspending, Wardell favoured the screaming headlines and the editorial crusades pioneered by his Fleet Street patron, Lord Beaverbrook, who was raised in New Brunswick and brought Wardell to Fredericton, the provincial capital, to keep an eye on his interests there. Wardell possessed one quality, however, that made him a perfect fit with the Irving Way: absolute servility. His entire life was defined by his deference to one powerful patron or another, from his friend Edward, Prince of Wales (later King Edward VIII), to Beaverbrook himself, who hired him to work at his *Evening Standard* in London, England, in 1925. In 1950, Wardell was persuaded by Beaverbrook to buy the Fredericton *Daily Gleaner*, the only daily newspaper in the province not owned by Irving. The press baron orchestrated the move after executives at his *Daily Express* in London—where Wardell had landed after the war—threatened to quit if Wardell didn't go.

Michael Wardell's patrician bearing and his eye patch, the result of a fox-hunting accident, impressed the small political elite of Fredericton, the genteel provincial capital a hundred miles upriver from bustling, entrepreneurial Saint John. Borrowing a page from Beaverbrook's sensational *Express*, Wardell brought a taste of Fleet Street to Fredericton, launching *Gleaner* editorial crusades against the fluoridation of the city's water supply and in favour of liberalizing the province's archaic liquor laws. "It turned into quite a paper," says Jim Morrison, who was lured there from his job at the *Telegraph Journal* in Saint John. Wardell "spent, overspent, a lot of money. It was good. It brightened the paper up." Fred Hazel looked on with dismay from Saint John. "He certainly turned the *Gleaner* around and made it a different kind of newspaper, but it wasn't an example I would like to follow. He was colourful, but he was not my own cup of tea."

Wardell's free-spending ways got him in trouble. Harry Bagley, an advertising salesman at the *Gleaner*, remembers Wardell making a trip to New York where he "spent a fortune" on a completely new darkroom, purchasing the very best in new equipment. Against Beaverbrook's advice, he added a commercial printing press, book imprint, and stationery business to his operation of the *Gleaner*. This lack of discipline, Bagley says, led to "a constant fight with Beaverbrook for money, begging for money, looking for money somewhere." In 1957, Ben Smith, a Wall Street financier who had helped Wardell raise capital, came looking to cash in his shares. Unable to pay, Wardell called on K.C. Irving. The industrialist said he would take a minority stake in the company, University Press of New Brunswick Ltd., if Wardell agreed to a voting trust in which the two men would always vote their shares together. The agreement would also give each man the first option to buy out the other. Wardell would lose sole control of the *Gleaner*, but he had no option. He agreed to Irving's terms.

In the years that followed, with Beaverbrook in failing health and Irving now an equally vital patron, Wardell, though still fawning over the press baron in print, also showered Irving with praise at every opportunity. In a single 1959 issue of *The Atlantic Advocate*, a magazine he added to his holdings, Wardell published a ringing endorsement of the Chignecto Canal project, which would boost Irving's shipping businesses and his planned refinery; a skeptical assessment of the St. Lawrence Seaway, which Irving considered a threat to the Maritime shipping industry; and a glowing profile of Irving himself. Penned by Wardell and bearing the headline "The Amazing Creator of Millions," the profile credited Irving's success to "a combination of character and genius" and noted in passing his ownership of the Saint John and Moncton newspapers, "capably conducted with moderation and impartiality." The piece concluded by reporting, uncritically, Irving's assertion that he remained in New Brunswick because he loved it. "It is as simple as that," Wardell concluded. "K.C. Irving *is* New Brunswick."

There was no mention in Wardell's profile of Irving's 1957 acquisition of his minority stake in the *Gleaner*, the moment the paper came under Irving's influence. "To avoid knowledge of the transaction here," Wardell had told Beaverbrook in a letter, Irving suggested "that it should be worked out with his lawyers in New York."

It took another eleven years, and his buyout of Wardell's majority stake, for K.C. Irving's control of the *Gleaner* to become known to the people of New Brunswick.

When it did, it happened in spectacular fashion.

3

HIS PRESENCE IS THERE

▼

William Hoyt still remembers the last leg of the journey, the flight that took him from New York to Bermuda in June of 1972. "It was the first time I had flown in a 747," he says. "I was quite impressed with that." Hoyt, described as "boyish" by *The Globe and Mail*, was forty-one years old. He had a "successful though not spectacular" private law practice in Fredericton, the *Financial Post* reported. "Mild mannered and academic in appearance, he hardly seems the type to charge head-on against Canada's only billionaire and his family compact." But Hoyt was charging: the federal government was prosecuting K.C. Irving under the Combines Investigation Act for his ownership of all of New Brunswick's English-language newspapers, and it had hired Hoyt to make the Crown's case.

Hoyt went to Bermuda for the testimony of K.C. Irving. The industrialist who had professed his love for New Brunswick, who had said he never wanted to live anywhere else, had abruptly left the province a few months earlier to avoid—it was said—a new

32

estate tax that threatened his plan to hand over his empire to his sons. "At that time he wasn't coming back to New Brunswick at all," Hoyt says, "so if we took his evidence, it was going to have to be there." Hoyt, the judge, Irving's lawyer, and a court reporter all converged on a hotel meeting room in Hamilton, the capital of Bermuda, to hear what Irving had to say about his newspapers.

K.C. and his wife, Harriet, were living in a small house near the Southampton Princess Hotel, a modest home he would eventually tear down and replace with a $2.5 million white stucco mansion. Though he avoided the dinner party circuit of Bermuda's moneyed elite, Irving was open to visits from fellow Maritimers. Not long after his arrival, he invited to lunch a young TV journalist from Halifax, Andrew Cochran, who was profiling east coast expatriates on the island. Though K.C. politely rebuffed Cochran's request for an on-camera interview, they had a wide-ranging conversation. "He was interested to know what was going on at home," Cochran says. Years later, another visiting New Brunswicker, Peter Wright, "got it into my head that I'd really like to meet that guy" and called him. Wright spent two hours with K.C., who was warm, polite, engaging. "If I didn't know who he was or how much money he had," he recalls, "I wouldn't have dreamt that he had accomplished what he'd accomplished in life."

The industrialist was equally civil with Hoyt—"Mr. Irving was the epitome of politeness and courtesy," he says—but the hearing "was very strained. You could tell that he was most uncomfortable and didn't want to do it. But he was very polite." Hoyt faced a challenge: his case could be proven only through the testimony of Irving and Ralph Costello, requiring Hoyt to call them as Crown witnesses—and that prevented him from asking them leading questions. "It put us in a hell of a position," Hoyt says. "It was very hard to frame questions to get the answers that you wanted."

So William Hoyt got very little that was useful out of K.C. Irving that day in Bermuda—nothing more, he says, than "the fundamentals that he was the ultimate owner."

But in the case he was prosecuting, Hoyt would argue in court, that should be enough.

A Liberal senator from New Brunswick, Charles McElman, was the first to make a public issue of K.C. Irving's newspaper monopoly. On March 11, 1969, McElman gave a speech in the Red Chamber in Ottawa in which he revealed Irving had recently bought a majority stake of the Fredericton *Daily Gleaner*. The industrialist had exercised the option he had secured in 1957, adding Wardell's 55 percent stake to the 25 percent he already owned. Irving now controlled all of New Brunswick's English-language daily newspapers.

The sale had been a secret until Wardell revealed it to a friend of McElman's he ran into during a trip to the United Kingdom. "I have nothing but commendation for Mr. Irving and his corporations, for the great faith he has displayed in his native province by continually expanding investments," McElman told the Senate. But his ownership of the newspapers, and of the CHSJ radio and television stations in Saint John, "cried out for corrective action," the senator said, given the breadth of Irving's industrial holdings. "I suggest that balanced news coverage might suffer." He would support a motion by Senator Keith Davey to strike a committee to study media ownership, he said, and would also file a complaint with federal investigators under the merger and monopoly provisions of the Combines Investigation Act.

Two days later, the *Gleaner* published the official announcement of the transaction it had ignored when it took place.
"There is nothing secret" about it, K.C. said in a statement,
adding that it was mentioned in a brief he was submitting
that very week to the Canadian Radio-Television Commission.
McElman was waging "a personal campaign" against him, he
added, insisting he had never been involved "in either the editorial or business operations" of his newspapers or broadcast
stations. "Senator McElman has implied that there is something
wrong with New Brunswickers owning and building businesses
in New Brunswick," Irving wrote, though McElman had said
nothing of the sort. He had received many offers for the papers
over the years, he said, but he preferred they be owned by New
Brunswickers, "not by some company with a head office in
Toronto or some foreign country." In an accompanying article,
Wardell said he himself continued to exercise "control of policy
and full direction of the newspaper."

Irving had his reasons for suspecting that Charles McElman
was not exactly dispassionate in raising the alarm. Before his
appointment to the Senate, he had been a senior advisor to the
premier of New Brunswick, Louis Robichaud, whose policies
prompted a series of angry confrontations between the government and Irving.

Louis Robichaud became premier in 1960. At the age of
thirty-four, he was the first francophone elected to the job, and
at first it appeared that, like his Liberal and Conservative prede-
cessors, he would be willing to adjust government policy to
help Irving grow. As opposition leader, Robichaud had attacked
Tory premier Hugh John Flemming for reneging on a promise
to give Irving the first option on a ninety-acre piece of public
land he wanted in Saint John. Flemming had opted instead to

sell it to Rothesay Paper Company, a consortium of Canadian and foreign forestry companies looking to build a pulp mill, and offered similar concessions to those granted to Irving. In the 1960 election, Irving backed Robichaud, contributing thirty-five thousand dollars to the Liberal campaign, a huge sum at the time and well beyond legal limits later placed on campaign donations.

Once in office, Robichaud saw the Rothesay mill issue differently. If the province didn't keep its promise to Rothesay Paper, other potential investors might avoid New Brunswick for fear of running afoul of K.C. Irving. Irving got the site, but Robichaud found another parcel of land for Rothesay—a sign that while he recognized Irving's power, he resisted becoming beholden to it. The premier, his advisor Ned Belliveau would write, was "by temperament a reformer, ebullient, easily roused, more dedicated to the people's welfare than he himself then understood and wholly outside Irving's world of commerce and industry." A showdown was inevitable.

The relationship deteriorated further when Robichaud decided to revive a stalled mining development in the province's economically deprived north. The developer, Jim Boylen, convinced Irving to invest $3 million. But the project was fraught with problems, and Irving and other investors repeatedly sought extensions on the provincial government's loan guarantees. Robichaud was accused of pushing the project forward too fast so he could score political points. At the same time, Irving was suspected of slowing it down to create more business for his engineering and construction companies at the site. Irving attempted a buyout, but Boylen and Robichaud blocked him by bringing in Noranda as a new investor, marginalizing Irving as a minority shareholder. "For the first time, the government had imposed its will on K.C. Irving," writes Robichaud's biographer, Michel Cormier.

The industrialist was furious, as Robichaud would soon learn. "I so wanted industrialization in the province that I did not understand this concept of absolute monopoly so important to Irving," Robichaud would remark years later. "When he saw that he was losing control, he turned against me."

It is an article of faith among many New Brunswick francophones and Liberals that during the 1967 provincial election campaign, "the Irving newspapers" set out to destroy Louis Robichaud, publishing anti-French bigotry to ensure his defeat and block the implementation of his Equal Opportunity Program, the signature reform of his time in office. The reality is more complex. The *Telegraph-Journal* editorialized against the Equal Opportunity Program, but its news coverage was straight. Wardell's *Gleaner*, not yet controlled by Irving but in his thrall, was indeed vicious, but not *during* the 1967 campaign. The venom was published mainly in 1965 and early 1966, when the program was debated in the legislature. And the *Gleaner*'s nasty hyperbole reeks of Wardell's personality, not Irving's; if the industrialist had been directing the editorial campaign, it is odd that the most pronounced attacks were not in his own newspapers.

Irving would be one of the obvious losers after Equal Opportunity. The goal of the program was to equalize the uneven quality of public services provided by county councils by abolishing the councils and having the province absorb their functions, including the assessing and levying of property taxes. The goal was social justice, but the reform would also prevent municipal governments from giving tax concessions—like those

Irving had received—to businesses. "No government in its right mind would dare go forward with such a series of measures," K.C. said when he appeared before a legislative committee in December 1965. Trembling with rage, according to some witnesses, K.C. scanned the faces of the elected members in their seats. "We are alarmed that anyone would propose legislation which would deprive industries of their contractual rights," he said. His paper mill was still not profitable and would not have survived without concessions, he said. "Do you really think that the government will help the New Brunswick economy by abolishing the tax breaks of this mill?" And he issued his now-classic threat: "Surely the province does not expect to attract new industry, or even retain existing industry, under such terms?"

The dramatic performance rattled the government, which had waffled on whether the legislation would repeal existing local tax concessions or simply prohibit new ones. Now the municipal affairs minister, Norbert Thériault, scrambled to clarify: "The government believes it has a moral obligation to honour those agreements," he declared that evening. Irving had won a key battle. "It was the first time I ever saw power being manifested in such a personal way," Richard Hatfield, a young opposition member and future premier, would recall.

Meanwhile, Wardell gave Robichaud the full Fleet Street treatment in the *Gleaner*, running cartoons portraying him as a Louis XIV–type monarch, part buffoon and part authoritarian. The paper published unsubstantiated stories, later debunked, about Robichaud's supposedly lavish Fredericton home and extravagant trips to Europe. When a Protestant minister used his sermon to claim that Robichaud had secretly amassed a fortune of up to $2 million, the *Gleaner* treated it as news, forcing the premier to release his personal financial statements to refute it. "I thought the *Gleaner* was really out of line," says Fred Hazel, who watched the spectacle from the *Telegraph-Journal* newsroom in Saint John. The *Telegraph* editorialized against the legislation, but without Wardell's flamboyance. Still, it made its own inflammatory contribution to the growing tension when it published a letter to the editor under the heading "Robbing Peter to Pay Pierre," implying Robichaud wanted New Brunswick's English majority to subsidize its French minority. (Poor, rural anglophone areas stood to benefit from the Equal Opportunity Program as well.) The phrase captured the ugliness behind some of the anti-Robichaud sentiment. One day there was a bomb threat at the premier's office; another time one of his assistants was confronted by a man with a gun. Robichaud agreed to police protection for the first time. A psychologist compared the mood to that in Dallas in 1963.

The legislation took effect on January 1, 1967, making the election held later that year the last chance to repeal Equal Opportunity before it took root. Irving made his vast resources—"Irving money, Irving cars, Irving employees," according to Ralph Costello—available to the Conservative campaign. It was widely believed he recruited and bankrolled the new PC party leader, a former Irving employee named Charlie Van Horne. "Whatever K.C. Irving had said about his lack of involvement in politics," Russell Hunt and Robert Campbell would write, "there was no politics in New Brunswick without him."

Still, Robichaud was given fair, uncritical coverage *during* the campaign. In Fredericton, Wardell's *Gleaner* ran anodyne stories about the Liberal platform and the party's local candidates, often with front-page photographs of the beaming premier. No Louis XIV cartoons appeared. But as has often been the case with the Irving newspapers, the real question was what was left out:

from the day after Irving's appearance at the legislature in 1965 though the election in October of 1967, there was no mention of his opposition to Equal Opportunity or his impact on the campaign. Robichaud himself had to call out his nemesis. At the final Liberal rally before the vote, in Bouctouche, he articulated the stakes: "This man, who had his home not far from here, this man wants to run the province," he roared. "If he wants to run the province, let him, like me, present himself before the people and seek election." When Robichaud won his third majority the following Monday, it was said to be the first time K.C. Irving had lost an election.

A postscript came thirty-seven years later, in January 2005, when Louis Robichaud died at the age of seventy-nine. By then he was revered as an icon, his reforms lauded across New Brunswick's political spectrum. The day after his death, an editorial in the *Telegraph-Journal*—then run by K.C.'s great-grandson Jamie Irving—did something newspapers rarely do. It renounced the editorial posture it had adopted decades earlier. The newspaper had raised "grave concerns" about Robichaud's historic reforms, it said. "We were wrong."

Newspaper editors are fascinated by stories about newspapers and editors. Within weeks of Charles McElman's Senate speech revealing K.C. Irving's takeover of the Fredericton *Daily Gleaner*, and the launch of both the Combines Investigation and the Senate Committee study, a journalist named Kenneth Bagnell arrived in Saint John to write a piece on the Irving press for *The Globe and Mail*'s weekend magazine.

The reaction from the Irving papers to McElman's speech had been predictably critical—"scurrilous," "garbage," pronounced the *Telegraph-Journal* in Saint John. In Moncton, the *Times* demanded McElman document real abuses or shut up—but Bagnell was in the city to do real reporting. He made his way to "the fringe of downtown Saint John," the corner of Union Street and Crown Street, to "a low, grey building," the home of the *Telegraph-Journal* since 1963.

Bagnell had heard from a salmon anglers' group about pollution in the Saint John harbour, and he asked Fred Hazel, then the managing editor, if the paper had reported on it. "I know of no such incidents," Hazel told him. Bagnell asked, "What about water pollution?" He pointed to the *Telegraph*'s extensive coverage the previous summer of protests in Centreville, a tiny village more than a hundred miles away, where angry residents dammed a river carrying pollution into the community from the American side of the border. "I can't find a thing on pollution in the Saint John harbour, right in your own city, where Mr. Irving is alleged to be a big polluter," Bagnell said. "How come?"

"Because something happened in Centreville that all the media could cover," Hazel explained. "There was a public protest. There hasn't been in Saint John." The paper's job, he said, was "to cover the news that happened, and in my recollection nothing has happened in Saint John." Costello made the same point to Bagnell, but more succinctly: "If someone dams the Reversing Falls, we'll cover it." When Bagnell asked why the paper didn't analyze water samples itself and report on the results, "Costello didn't answer right away. He just looked at me." After an awkward silence, he told Bagnell, "I think we'll leave it right there for now."

What Hazel and Costello described was an approach not unusual in small-market newspapers: report news that erupts in public and can't be ignored—but don't do time-consuming digging for information or context that is otherwise hidden.

Bagnell also met reporters, however, who knew what *not* to do: no stories on pollution from the refinery, no stories on house fires caused by oil furnace explosions. A former reporter told Bagnell that an editor once advised him, "Let's think ahead of them, because we don't want any Irving boys down here interfering in the operation." Whether Irving himself meddled didn't matter, Senator McElman told Bagnell. "His presence is there. His publishers and managers are aware of his involvement. That's all that's necessary."

This was the image of the Irving newspapers—incapable of properly covering their owner, the largest industrial player in their market—that was taking shape in the political, media, and business consciousness of the country when the Senate committee chaired by Keith Davey began its study of media ownership in the autumn of 1969.

Irving appeared as a witness on December 15, alongside Costello and Wardell. Seen from today, it is a singular moment: at the acme of the Pearson–Trudeau era of Liberal state intervention in the economy, a branch of Parliament in a modern, Western democracy was asking why the state shouldn't have the power to decide who owned a newspaper. Fred Hazel remembers being "mad as hell.... They say that it's questionable for an industrialist to own newspapers, but it's far more questionable for me for a government to be running newspapers or harassing them." Irving made the same point to the committee: "You have asked whether it is socially desirable for conglomerate corporations to include among their holdings interests in the communications media," he said. "It is my contention that no individual or company or group of companies should be denied the right to publish a newspaper or a group of newspapers in a free society."

Irving revealed that he held 25 percent of the voting shares in K.C. Irving Ltd., with members of his family owning the rest. K.C. Irving Ltd. in turn controlled New Brunswick Publishing Co. Ltd., which published the two Saint John papers. Its subsidiary, New Brunswick Broadcasting Co. Ltd., owned CHSJ, while another subsidiary, Moncton Publishing Co. Ltd., published the two Moncton papers, the *Times* and the *Transcript*. K.C. Irving Ltd. also owned a majority of shares in University Press of New Brunswick Ltd., which published the *Gleaner*. He had bought all the papers, he explained, because he didn't want them falling into the hands of out-of-province owners. No one in the Irving family, including K.C. himself, drew any salary from these assets, he said, and no dividends were paid: all profits were reinvested. And, he added, he never spoke to anyone at the papers about editorial content, only about business decisions.

As an entrepreneur in a small province, Irving explained under questioning, he had two choices: expand his core businesses nationally and lose his New Brunswick roots, or diversify within the province. "I prefer diversification," he said. "Call it conglomerate or what you will. In New Brunswick it contributes to survival." It might look "peculiar" to people elsewhere in Canada, "but it is the only way I know to get along in New Brunswick and in the Maritimes, and to retain control of at least some part of the activity." That was what interested him. "I have purchased companies and started companies to create activity, not necessarily to make money. They might never make money but they would create a certain amount of activity." Irving was befuddled, however, when senators asked him what he meant by "activity" with the newspapers: "You know, that is pretty hard to answer." Authors Russell Hunt and Robert Campbell suggested he genuinely couldn't articulate why he had bought the papers because he had never put the concept into words before.

Costello testified next, admitting the newspapers weren't perfect but insisting quality journalism cannot be created "by any form of government legislation or regulation." He accused McElman of pursuing a vendetta over the coverage of Robichaud's Equal Opportunity Program. Wardell went further, calling the Senate investigation the latest chapter in a long campaign by Robichaud to destroy him. The coverage in the next day's New Brunswick newspapers emphasized the attacks on McElman.

But Davey got the last word: the committee's report, issued a year later, called Irving's newspaper monopoly "about as flagrant an example of abusing the public interest as you're likely to find in Canada." The report, titled *The Uncertain Mirror*, lamented the state of small-market newspapers across the country, deriding their coverage of "the local trout festival," their "Chamber-of-Commerce boosterism," their unwillingness to probe deeper, to right wrongs. Irving was singled out because he was "by far the most important economic force in the province" while controlling 92.7 percent of English-language newspaper circulation. But, the report conceded, it was "at least arguable that the province is better off with a home-owned media monopoly than one controlled from Toronto or Winnipeg."

At times the report seems bewildered by, or hostile to, the premise of free-market capitalism. Passages lament "very generous" newspaper profits that were not reinvested in better coverage. "This is what, in contemporary parlance, is called a rip-off," the report said. The news, it said, was "as a public resource, like electricity"—a sector where government-run utilities were the norm. The committee said newspapers ought not to be rewarded or punished for what they printed, but it recommended a Press Ownership Review Board that would assume any future media mergers were "undesirable and contrary to the public interest—unless shown to be otherwise." The only concession to the industry was a recommendation that the board not have the power to retroactively break up existing chains.

The Irving papers editorialized against Davey's report. The Moncton *Times* called it full of "prejudices and preconceived ideas." In his biography of K.C. Irving, Costello disputes the report's suggestion that the *Telegraph-Journal*'s journalism amounted to civic boosterism—but the only editorial crusade he cites was the one against Equal Opportunity, a cause it shared with its proprietor. "The Senate Report was now part of the public record," he wrote in a resigned tone. "Protests from the aggrieved newspapers would do nothing to change that."

Costello was right. The Davey report articulated a clear vision of the news media—not a free-market vision, but one that gave Canadians, particularly New Brunswickers, a new way to think about their newspapers. Its impact on the business, however, was slight. Ottawa chose not to create a Press Ownership Review Board, though newspaper owners set up press councils to hear complaints from readers. And the newly created broadcast regulator, the Canadian Radio-Television Commission, would restrain Irving from further dominance of radio and television.

None of this, of course, changed K.C. Irving's existing newspaper holdings whatsoever. That would require another mechanism: the criminal prosecution led by William Hoyt.

In April 1971, RCMP officers and federal investigators raided the newspaper offices in Saint John, Moncton, and Fredericton, and the homes of K.C. Irving, Michael Wardell, and Ralph Costello, seizing almost four thousand documents. "What we were looking for," Hoyt says, "was some sort of memo from Mr. Irving or one of his family to Mr. Costello, or from Mr. Costello to one of the editors, saying 'Don't print this' or 'Maybe you should give this story a little more prominence.' A so-called smoking gun was what we were looking for."

The pickings were slim. There was evidence that the *Telegraph-Journal*, as a charter subscriber to a nationally syndicated Saturday insert called *Weekend Magazine*, had exerted its right to block a competitor in the same market—a French-language daily newspaper in Moncton, *L'Evangeline*—from offering the insert's French counterpart, *Perspectives*. "We felt that was some example of trying to stifle competition," Hoyt says. There was also a handwritten observation by Costello in a small reporter's notebook: "The ownership of all English-language newspapers cannot be defended," it said. "Dedicated respected newspaper editors and publishers will not agree that it is in the best interest of the province or people."

Costello would testify this was a devil's advocate position he had used to prepare himself for his appearance at the Davey hearings. "It could also show what he felt himself," Hoyt says. "I thought it could be both." But it was hardly proof. So the investigators analyzed phone records, where they spotted a high volume of calls from Costello to the Fredericton and Moncton papers. "We tried to suggest that could show Costello was guiding all of them, which was a bit of a reach," Hoyt says, "but which we felt we had to do to compensate for the lack of a smoking gun."

A prosecution counting on proof of K.C. Irving or Ralph Costello dictating the content of all the papers was doomed. The Moncton newspapers, outside the twin orbits of Saint John's business elite and Fredericton's political insiders, had in fact been "more restrained" in critiquing Robichaud on Equal Opportunity, *The Globe and Mail*'s Kenneth Bagnell acknowledged. "Their reports were fair and their editorials reasonable," according to Ned Belliveau, the former aide to Louis Robichaud. And despite sharing an owner, the papers competed with each other, stalling on filing their stories to Canadian Press to prevent the others from picking them up. "We thought we were the top newspaper and we wanted to be ahead of Moncton and Fredericton," says Fred Hazel. "We were trying to get stories that other people didn't have."

This reality forced Hoyt onto more abstract, theoretical ground. "Total ownership of a commodity in a defined market is itself a detriment," he says, summing up his argument at the time, "and you don't have to prove actual detriment or give an illustration of it." Seized financial records showed that the morning papers in Saint John and Moncton, the *Telegraph-Journal* and the *Times*, were losing money: Irving owned them only to block others from coming into the market, the prosecution alleged. Expert testimony from prominent Canadian newspaper publishers rounded out the theory. St. Clair Balfour, president of the Southam chain, recounted how, shortly after he had become publisher of *The Hamilton Spectator*, a lot of navy stories began appearing in the newspaper. "We thought you'd like that, sir," said an editor, referring to Balfour's wartime navy service. This anecdote, Hoyt argued, showed how "the staff *anticipate* the owner's wishes."

It was not an easy case to make. For all its ethical codes and its mantra of objectivity, journalism is a highly subjective business: any two reporters or editors, both entirely professional, can come to opposite but reasonable decisions about how, or whether, a story is covered.

47

So, too, can a proprietor. "Have you been treated any better than any other business or enterprise in New Brunswick?" Irving was asked during his testimony in Bermuda.

"I would say a little worse," he answered.

"Why would you say that?"

"I think they lean over backwards to put me in black ink just to keep their skirts clean," he said. This seemed like a ludicrous assertion—but how could a judge rule definitively that Irving was right or wrong to feel that way?

K.C. Irving's abrupt departure from New Brunswick, in the midst of the investigation, was accompanied by a restructuring of his newspaper companies. Irving's youngest son, Jack, bought Moncton Publishing and Fredericton's University Press of New Brunswick Ltd. outright, and sold his stake in K.C. Irving Ltd. His two older brothers, J.K. and Arthur, each purchased 40 percent of New Brunswick Publishing, which published the two Saint John papers, with K.C. Irving Ltd. retaining 20 percent. Hoyt argued that this changed nothing: these nominally autonomous companies were still under K.C.'s effective control.

The Irving papers covered the seventeen-day trial by publishing Canadian Press reports rather than assigning their own reporters. Costello testified for five days, entering into evidence several stories that, he said, showed the papers didn't go easy on the Irvings: a report naming the pulp mill as a heavy polluter, and a series of stories about the sinking of two Irving-built fishing boats. But he also said that "it was not their function to harass people." Their responsibility was "to keep their readers informed of all developments." This seemingly reasonable distinction defines the gap between investigative journalism—the unearthing of news that may make some people uncomfort-able—and conventional reporting, which merely reacts to events.

For Hoyt, the case was even more basic. "No one is suggesting that K.C. Irving should be muzzled," he told Judge Albany Robichaud, "but there should be other voices in New Brunswick. By the existence of this monopoly, other papers are prevented from coming in."

The judge accepted Hoyt's argument even though there was no evidence Irving had interfered. The papers, the judge found, "have complete editorial autonomy and the owners have never cast over their columns any editorial shadow whatsoever." But "the potential was always there," Robichaud wrote. Irving, he concluded, had established a monopoly with a goal of "the prevention or lessening of competition," which, on its own, was "to the detriment or against the interest of the public." The real stunner was the judge's remedy: on top of paying $150,000 in fines, Irving was ordered to sell the two Moncton newspapers within a year.

Irving appealed. His lawyer, J.J. Robinette, argued any monopoly had ceased to exist when K.C. turned over the papers to his sons. Jack Irving, who now owned the Moncton news-papers, could hardly be ordered to sell them when he had not been convicted of anything. And, Robinette said, without evidence of actual detriment, the Crown had failed to show the monopoly was against the public interest. The New Brunswick Court of Appeal agreed: the Combines Investigation Act did not say a monopoly automatically harmed the public interest, nor was it intended to regulate "ideas, editorial comment, or editing of news." Seventeen months later, the Supreme Court of Canada upheld the appeal court ruling. Chief Justice Bora Laskin avoided the issue of editorial content, but agreed that without factual evidence of actual detriment, the conviction could not stand. The Irvings could keep their newspapers, and the Combines Investigation Act was eviscerated: with such a high burden of proof on detriment, it was unlikely the legislation could ever be used against media monopolies. "It was game over," Hoyt says.

A decade later came a sequel, the Royal Commission on Newspapers, better known as the Kent Commission. Responding to the simultaneous closure of the Southam chain's daily in Winnipeg and Thomson's in Ottawa—which left each company with a monopoly in the other market—the Trudeau government asked Tom Kent, a bureaucrat and former journalist, to head a commission that would reopen the issue of media concentration. Kent, citing the "last rites" administered by the Supreme Court to the Combines law in the Irving ruling, proposed a more interventionist "press rights panel" with the power to break up newspaper chains, including Irving's, that controlled two or more papers with 75 percent of the circulation in their market.* "They could be and should be diverse voices," Kent wrote of the New Brunswick newspapers, "correcting and balancing one another, competing for influence." Newspapers owned by conglomerates would be forced by law to hire, on fixed-term contracts, editors answerable not to the paper's owner but to an advisory committee with newsroom and community appointees holding a majority of seats.

The Trudeau government, reluctant to adopt such provocative measures, opted instead to strengthen the competition law, but its amendments died in Parliament when the 1984 election

---

* Combined, the five Irving dailies sold 125,000 copies per day in 1980, a commanding position in a province of fewer than 700,000 people, one-third of them French-speaking.

was called. With the arrival of the pro-business Progressive Conservative government of Brian Mulroney, any prospect of newspaper regulation died, too.

By then William Hoyt was a judge. Occasionally he ran into K.C.'s son Arthur Irving, who had been a friend when they both started at Acadia University in Nova Scotia in 1948. "We were cordial until this paper thing came up," Hoyt says. "For a long period of time after that he was very cool towards me. On a couple of occasions he went out of his way to not have to speak to me." Eventually Irving softened, and as chancellor of Acadia presented Hoyt with his honorary degree in 2001. They have never discussed the Combines prosecution. "Arthur's a very emotional person," Hoyt says, "and in his mind it was a bit naughty of me to take a case like that."

As a justice of the New Brunswick Court of Appeal, Hoyt watched jurisprudence in corporate cases evolve. Though governments have become more averse to media regulation, Hoyt suspects today's courts might have upheld the original Combines conviction. "I have a hunch they would take a more expansionist view on detriment," he says.

After retiring as chief justice in 1998, Hoyt was appointed by the British government to a three-member international panel of inquiry that spent twelve years investigating the Bloody Sunday events of January 30, 1972, when British soldiers shot twenty-six unarmed protesters in Derry, Northern Ireland. Apart from that historic process, "the Irving case was the highest-profile case I ever had, and intellectually one of the most interesting," he says. "A lawyer should never get too wrapped up in the case because you lose some of the objectivity required, but I think I got quite wrapped up in this case."

Today, sitting on his enclosed porch overlooking the Saint

John River in Fredericton, Hoyt still believes the Irving newspaper monopoly, which has now acquired most of the province's weekly newspapers as well, is a detriment to the public interest. "I feel it's wrong for a number of reasons," he tells me, "one of which I think a lot of people forget: they're really writing the history of New Brunswick. A hundred years from now, researchers will be using—as we all do—old newspapers as contemporary records.

"Maybe I'm more sensitive to that than other people because of this case," he adds. "But even at the present time—I always wonder what's *not* in the newspapers."

4

STRAIGHT ROADS

Not long after the release of the report of the Royal Commission on Newspapers in 1981, Tom Kent, the commission chair, came to Saint John one weekend to give a speech. Michael Camp, a reporter and the son of the legendary political strategist and columnist Dalton Camp, was assigned to cover it for the *Evening Times-Globe*. "I was kind of fired up about it," says Camp, who had just started at the paper. "I was looking forward to writing a big anti-Irving screed." Instead, Kent's speech focused on the need for newspapers to hire better reporters. In an interview after the event, Camp couldn't get the prickly former commissioner to go much further. "Look, put it this way," Camp recalls Kent finally telling him. "Free-market capitalism just isn't working for the average New Brunswicker when it comes to journalism."

Camp got back to the newsroom around ten thirty. It was a Saturday night, and with no paper the next morning, the place was empty. Then he looked over to the corner. "There were Ralph's galoshes outside his door." It was odd for Ralph Costello, the publisher, to be there on a Saturday night. "I knew Ralph had pulled in just to see what I was going to drop in the story file."

Camp wrote his story, giving prominence to Kent's remark about the free market not working for New Brunswick newspaper readers, and left the typed pages in the bin for incoming copy. The story made it into the paper unchanged, but the image of the publisher's galoshes stayed with the young reporter. K.C. Irving had left New Brunswick for Bermuda in 1971, but a decade later, Costello was still carefully attuned to how the paper treated the Irvings—and how it treated the question of how it treated the Irvings. The patriarch was absent, but his power and influence were still present, channelled through his three boys and their management of the family companies.

The papers were now operating under the structure the industrialist had set up before his departure: K.C.'s oldest son, James K. Irving, known as J.K., and the second-oldest, Arthur, shared control of New Brunswick Publishing Co. Ltd., which ran the Saint John papers as well as New Brunswick Broadcasting Co. Ltd., operator of the CHSJ radio and television stations. "I intend to keep it forever," Arthur had told the Kent Commission. "It is our privilege to own it, and nobody in this God-given room is going to take it away from us." The industrialist's third son, John, known to everyone as Jack, owned Moncton Publishing Co. Ltd., which put out the *Times* and the *Transcript*, and University Press of New Brunswick Ltd., which published the *Gleaner* in Fredericton. Jack had testified to Kent that he had no interest in editorial content, only in the balance sheets and the physical plants of his newspapers. "The only terms of reference which I have given my publishers in Fredericton and Moncton are: one, to publish the best possible newspaper, and two, to be as competitive as possible."

To J.K., the papers were something of an oddity. "Up until that point in time, I was busy cutting wood or making pulp or something else," he says. "I had nothing to do with the newspapers whatsoever. It was a big shock to the system, one day, to find out you've got to look after a newspaper." And no wonder: he and his brothers had been groomed all their lives for bigger things—for taking over the large industrial holdings, the mills, the refinery. "There was never any question about what we were going to do," Arthur told the CBC in a 1998 interview for a documentary series, *The Irvings: Unlocking the Mystery.* "We were going to go to work."

Their first business was selling eggs. As young boys in Bouctouche they bought 145 hens and started their first business. One New Year's Eve, before the family moved to Saint John, K.C. came home at eleven thirty at night to find two cartons of undelivered eggs on the kitchen table. What happened next became part of Irving family lore: K.C. woke J.K., who explained the eggs were for a Mrs. Carter. "I was going to deliver them, but I forgot and I'm going to take them up first thing in the morning." No, K.C. answered, you are taking them over there right now. And so the boy got dressed and walked the eggs over to the Carter home, interrupting a New Year's Eve party. "When I got home my father wished me a Happy New Year—and I never again forgot that work came first, no matter what."

For the three Irving boys a typical weekend family outing involved them and their mother climbing into K.C.'s Ford to tag along as he went out to inspect gas stations, sawmills, or other parts of his business operations. "A lot of times we ended up on a trip with him up in the woods to see what was going on," Jack once recalled. "That was the only time he had to look around. He was very busy in those days." Arthur's ex-wife, Joan

Carlisle Irving, remembers a story K.C. told her once about a family road trip to Goldboro, Nova Scotia, where he had bought a gold mine. "Arthur didn't want to go, so he was kicking up a racket in the back seat," Joan says. The five-year-old wanted to return to Bouctouche. So, K.C. told Joan, "I stopped the car and put him out and drove off and left him there." Eventually K.C. turned around to retrieve Arthur. "He was standing beside the road, white as a ghost and shaking all over," K.C. told Joan. "I always regretted doing that." Joan adds: "You know, a child's most important thing is security and trust.... And I think that breach of trust really affected Arthur's life."

K.C. remained an unforgiving taskmaster as the boys became men and took on greater roles in his companies. The pressure was unrelenting. "It was definitely a push, push, push," Joan says. J.K. was taught the importance of building straight logging roads in the woods, for efficiency, no matter how many rocks, streams, and stumps were in the way. Once, flying with his father over central New Brunswick, he proudly pointed out a logging road that ran straight for six miles—but K.C. noted a slight curve at the very end. "I had to go back and re-survey it," J.K. would recall. "It wasn't good enough." Years later, Arthur's own son, Kenneth, reportedly told friends he was relieved his four children were girls, because they would not bear the same weight of expectations he had. "Much is expected of the men in this family," he said.

"Oh, I suppose we should spend more time at home," J.K. said in 1998. But, he said, "my wife did a good job bringing the children up. I guess in hindsight, going back, we should have spent more time doing some of the things that we should have done."

As the first-born son, J.K. Irving faced particularly high expectations. After playing rugby and managing the hockey team at Rothesay Collegiate School, a private boys' school in the suburbs of Saint John, he enrolled at Acadia University in Wolfville, Nova Scotia, but didn't finish his degree. He loved the woods and gravitated to the forestry business. "I quit school on a Friday," he once said, "and Monday morning I was two hundred and fifty miles north of Saint John, helping move Irving logs down the Saint John River." Work was everything, his wife, Jean, recalled in a rare interview in 2008. "My father had said, 'If you marry him, you'll always have to put him first,'" she recalled. "Well, that was true, but it was true of everyone in those days. He was away a lot, and I had the kids, but it worked."

J.K.'s first job was running J.D. Irving Ltd.'s logging camps in northwest New Brunswick. Like his father, he made quick decisions, and was prone to firing people on the spot if they weren't making an effort. But he would also seal a deal with a handshake and live by it. "He was an honourable guy," says Abel LeBlanc, a former head of the longshoremen's union at the port of Saint John, from which Irving's pulp was shipped. "He was up front, honest.... He told me what he wanted and what he expected, and you had to respect that." One night, J.K. Irving called LeBlanc at home. It was snowing heavily and LeBlanc's men were loading toilet tissue onto a ship; Irving wanted plywood on the ground to keep the tissue dry. LeBlanc hurried to the wharf to find J.K. laying down boards himself, a violation of union rules. "Mr. Irving, you can't do our work," LeBlanc said. "You have to pay somebody." And Irving did pay. "He paid an extra man for the work he did until I came. That's the type of guy he was."

"There is nothing that he thinks cannot be done," his wife told an interviewer. "He was always that way. And he's still going." Even in his eighties, J.K. exudes a hardy, man-of-the-woods physical strength. He describes himself as a conservationist and funds a variety of environmental projects around New Brunswick. He speaks of his love for the province and the need to keep its economy and the Irving businesses chugging along in tandem. "The reason we're here is because we live here," he tells me, echoing his father, K.C., and tapping the table for emphasis. "We run our mills and we're around and we see them. And the money we have gets invested here. If you had a public company, you couldn't do it. They'd fire us because we weren't getting a big enough return. But we live here, and our job is to run things and try to keep it going. All we ask for is support from everybody in the province to keep the wheels turning here. That's all."

J.K.'s seemingly banal comments, the very essence of Irvingness, reveal how completely his father's world view was passed down. Perhaps they represent a genuine, if simplistic, belief that the province prospers when the Irvings do; perhaps they are carefully calibrated to convey homespun sincerity and humility. Either way, it is a rhetorical style that pervades the family. J.K.'s son Jim uses a more blustery version of it to this day. J.K.'s brother Arthur deploys it regularly, as in 1998 when he told an interviewer, "We want to be successful, we want to have a sense of accomplishment and [do] a good job. We're not in it for anything else." It is a way of thinking—black and white, lacking in nuance or introspection—that has allowed them to carve a corporate empire out of a small, impoverished province on the periphery of the continent.

Arthur, K.C.'s second son, bursts with the same energy as his older brother, J.K. A hockey and rugby player at Rothesay Collegiate, he was the smooth-talking one of the Irving boys. The 1981 NFB documentary shows him jetting to New York and Washington to cut deals. "Arthur has a personality that is completely charming," says Joan, his ex-wife. "He could mesmerize anyone and made a terrific salesman." He was a carouser at Acadia, where, like J.K., he did not finish his degree. As a young Irving Oil executive, he drove a BMW and wore snappy clothes, coming closer than any other Irving to the image of a flashy tycoon. But he was just as relentless as his older brother in pushing for more growth and more market share, as he assumed responsibility for Irving Oil. A circular logic took hold: a 1998 analysis by CBC News concluded Irving Oil's push into New England was essential, because only dominant market share there would create enough sales volume to run the refinery at full capacity—and only full capacity, and the efficiency it would create, would keep the export price low enough for the Irvings to stay competitive in the United States.

Arthur's love for duck hunting led him to become the Canadian president of Ducks Unlimited, a wetlands conservation group, burnishing his environmental credentials. He also enjoyed long canoe trips in Canada's northern wilderness. But his drive never waned. He grew animated and his voice rose as he barked out his vision in that 1998 interview. "We want our employees to be proud of us, we want to be proud of them and we want to keep going down the road and making this part of the country a better place to live." He jabbed the air for emphasis. "That's our drive, every day. Every day. *Every day!*"

In his 1991 book about the Irvings, John DeMont suggested Arthur's 1980 divorce from Joan Carlisle created the anger he seemed to carry into middle age. The split was a legal epic, long and bitter. "It took four years to get a divorce, seven years for a chattel battle, twelve years for a child support case," Joan says. Arthur said in court filings that Joan made "irresponsible, extravagant and impulsive expenditures"; she responded that she was sentenced to "many, many lonely evenings and weekends" because Arthur was so consumed by work.

The proceedings revealed a curious aspect of Irving domestic life: Irving Oil owned many of the contents of Arthur and Joan's home, including rugs, antique books, a pine desk, a china set, a 1926 Ford car, and paintings by A.Y. Jackson, William Kurelek, and Jean Paul Lemieux. This lowered the value of Arthur's personal assets, and thus his financial obligation to Joan—though Joan remembers an incredulous judge asking, "Isn't that your oil refinery down the street?" Arthur acknowledged during his examination that he had moved millions of dollars into a trust in 1976 to protect them from "mismanagement" by his wife. "I didn't think that I wanted her relatives, friends, lawyers, and her own lousy judgment to squander what rightfully should belong to the children." Joan, he said, "will get what she is due"—but not a penny more. "She has to face reality that she has to get by in this world like the rest of us."

The divorce settlement—reportedly ordered by K.C., aghast at the potential publicity that would come with a public trial—set aside $1 million for the children and provided Joan with $500,000. She had no claim to the five-bedroom house that sat on a hundred acres of land on the Kennebecasis River outside Saint John, the ski chalet in Whistler, and the yacht—because none of it belonged to Arthur. "Everything," Joan says, "was owned by the company." Like the divorce itself, this insight into one of New Brunswick's wealthiest men went unmentioned in the Irving newspapers.

Jack Irving, K.C.'s third and youngest son, was close to Arthur, but in many ways his opposite: quiet, bookish, reflective. "Jack would have made a marvellous farmer, always philosophical, thinking things out," says Joan. Though he, too, played rugby, as well as basketball, and was a school chess champion, he was considered the least confident of the Irving brothers. In their 1998 interviews for the CBC, Jack let J.K. and Arthur dominate the conversation; at one point he leans forward to interject, then visibly decides against it. "I know I can never do the sales, or the credit or that, because it's not my side," he said haltingly, later in the same interview, "and so I'm quite content to do the best at whatever I can do." Jack's nervousness in public was often attributed to his kidnapping in front of his wife and daughter in 1982. Bound and blindfolded, he was driven around Saint John in the trunk of a car until the police captured the abductor.

Jack ran the construction side of the empire, erecting the ubiquitous Irving gas stations. "Jack helped build Irving Oil in a big way," Arthur said in 1998. "He had the patience and the desire to do what I couldn't do. He's got the patience my father had to get into a job and stick with it, and work and work. I couldn't concentrate as well as Jack." Pat Darrah, who worked for Jack in those days, says he was the ideal boss. "If you had something in the field, he'd be there with you in the field. If there was something you needed, he made sure that you got it." Others who knew Jack say he never felt a need to compare himself to his brothers. He believed what mattered was what you did, not what you said you did. "I think he just had a different style," Darrah says. "They all were very capable, and that's been proven over the years, but they have different styles."

Different styles, different men—but they shared a single goal, a single obsession: to continue expanding the empire built by their father, to keep feeding its enormous appetite for growth and market share. In 1982, they acquired their old rival, the Rothesay Paper Company's newsprint mill. J.K. orchestrated the shipyard's successful bid to manage the construction of six frigates for the Royal Canadian Navy, a $6.2 billion contract that created a mini-boom in Saint John. Arthur oversaw an expansion of the refinery and kept sprinkling gas stations across the landscape and down the eastern seaboard of the U.S. They moved into new areas: food processing in Prince Edward Island, commercial real estate in New Brunswick. And by the early 1990s they acquired full control of two assets where they'd initially needed partners: they bought out Kimberly-Clark's 35 percent share of Irving Pulp and Paper, along with its Saint John tissue mill, and acquired SoCal's stake in the refinery and Irving Oil.

Increasingly sensitive to public opinion, they also gave more money away, ramping up their charitable giving, and spent tens of millions of dollars reducing emissions from their plants. Like their father, the brothers brushed off questions about their worth. In 1988, *Forbes* magazine estimated the Irving fortune at $8 billion, though it was impossible to know for sure, given the complex web of cross-ownership among dozens upon dozens of companies. ("He doesn't, nor does, I think, any one person have in their head all these transactions," Arthur's lawyer had protested when he was quizzed, during the divorce, about a dizzying series of share swaps involving Irving companies.) "If we've got enough for a hamburger now and again," Arthur said in 1998, "that's fine with us." On a global scale, J.K. would explain, "We see ourselves not as a big player but as a very small player.... The Maritimes are very small on a world scale. The folks we compete with on the world market, they're big." But in New Brunswick, in the Maritimes, in Canada, the Irvings *are* big.

Once it was even said that they were too big to last. Russell Hunt and Robert Campbell compared them, in their 1973 book, to a dinosaur that ravaged its surroundings simply to fuel its continued existence. But with K.C.'s tax escape to Bermuda, Hunt and Campbell predicted, "the vital spark which made the dinosaur so remarkably dynamic will be gone." Inevitably the monster would slacken, be unable to adapt, and become "increasingly quiet and senescent." But J.K., Arthur, and Jack adapted rather well. "When you look at all the things they built, the investment they've made in this province, it's just huge," Pat Darrah says. "Huge, huge, huge. You see the same vision today as you saw fifty or sixty years ago."

They adapted by adopting their father's frugality, decisiveness, and attention to detail and quality. When a mid-level Irving executive was found to be claiming the twenty-five-cent Harbour Bridge toll as a business expense, he was told to take the longer route across the toll-free Reversing Falls Bridge: those quarters added up. But Arthur also bragged that Irving Oil's gas station restaurants were popular because they used Heinz ketchup and larger napkins. And J.K. was constantly modernizing his mills with the latest technology so they could run faster and get more out of each tree. The Irving fastidiousness and obsession with customer service converged in Arthur's legendary unannounced spot checks on the cleanliness of his gas station washrooms.

They adapted, too, by remaining private and avoiding publicity—even from their own newspapers: "I talked to Irving people all the time who said, 'Sorry, we don't talk to the press,'" Michael Camp says of his *Telegraph* days. "I felt like saying, 'You know, we both have the same boss, ultimately. Surely you should be able to talk to *me*.' But no."

They adapted as well by retaining their power and influence. Richard Hatfield, New Brunswick's premier from 1970 to 1987, argued "a change had come" after Robichaud's 1967 election victory that K.C. had sought to prevent: the Irvings could no longer bully governments the way he once had. But bullying wasn't required. After winning a long court battle to tax Irving

Oil's Canaport facility, Hatfield passed a law to waive the tax, citing the company's importance to the economy. More recently, David Hawkins, a well-known consultant in the province, told author Harvey Sawler he advised people to get along with the Irvings "because it probably won't be as great an experience living here if you don't.... Any organization or operation with that many tentacles has a lot of influence, so I think people don't want to get on the wrong side of the Irvings."

And they adapted, as the three brothers loved to explain, by doing it together. Arthur described it as "equal partners, equal fun, equal responsibility, and no problems." This was another part of Irving lore: how K.C.'s boys complemented each other so perfectly. "There was only one person in the world who could have done what was done at the shipyard," Arthur told the CBC in 1998, nodding at his brother. "No one else." J.K., sitting across from him, returned the compliment: "If I'm a shipbuilder, Art's a super-salesman." J.K. picked up an old photograph of the three brothers talking with their father on a bench outside the Golden Ball, the Irving Oil headquarters on Union Street. "That's how decisions are made," he said. "Nothing more complicated than that. We don't have to have a big meeting to decide what we're going to do." With no public offerings and no shareholders, "we can deal with things on a dime," J.K. said. He glanced over at his brother. "And that's one of the advantages we have, isn't it?"

"No question about it." Arthur nodded. "We wouldn't give that one up."

It seemed like an unbreakable partnership—but even then there were tensions behind the façade of a tight-knit team.

Joan glimpsed it when her marriage to Arthur began to fray. Initially there was family solidarity: the moment she began speaking to lawyers, her special bond with K.C. was severed. "My father believes in me," Arthur explained in court, "and when anybody takes on an Irving, they are going to take on all four of us, okay?" Jack was the witness at his brother's marriage to Joan in 1957; two decades later, on the night Arthur left her for good, Jack came to their house and took his brother to his own home.

But there was another moment during the divorce, Joan says, that hinted at something quite different.

She learned of it from her lawyer, who heard it from Arthur's lawyer, Heward Stikeman, she says. K.C., during a visit to Stikeman's office in Montreal, "was doling out companies like you dole out a pack of cards," Stikeman reportedly recounted—trying, Joan believes, to reduce Arthur's holdings and his exposure to Joan's claims for money. But, as Joan heard the story, J.K. objected. "I want no part of this," he apparently said—an unfathomable breaking of family unity.

Jack's 1982 kidnapping was also a turning point, according to one family acquaintance. After the event, Jack, shaken, pulled back from his role in the triumvirate, throwing off the delicate balance among the brothers. This left a more direct rivalry between J.K. and Arthur, who were never close. Arthur, the classic middle child, was always trying to catch up, to please his father, says the acquaintance, while J.K. could be stubborn. "Unfortunately, there was always the old-buck-young-buck clash of horns" between J.K. and K.C., says Joan.

It would take years, however, for these distant rumblings to overwhelm the carefully created image of a cohesive team. In the early eighties, J.K., Arthur, and Jack were the very model of family and corporate unity—including in their defence of their newspapers.

"They're not big newspapers but they're as good as any small newspapers across Canada, and they're run by competent management," Arthur Irving said in 1981. "And [their managers] have a full say in how the paper is published. The public pretty well knows that."

Like their father, the brothers insisted they were hands-off, completely uninvolved in editorial decision-making. "I can't say [Jack] ever expressed any interest in news," says Mike Bembridge, a former managing editor and publisher of the Moncton papers. "They didn't understand the concept of news. The newspapers and the machinery and the plant—that's what made money." The Irvings weren't known to delegate, but with the newspapers they felt they had to: "We're terrified of government interference," Arthur told the Kent Commission. There was no hubris after the Irvings beat the Combines charges and Ottawa opted against regulating newspaper ownership. On the contrary, "they were haunted by Davey and Kent," according to one insider, convinced one misstep would bring the power of the state down on them. So they resolved to live up to K.C.'s assertions of non-interference and let their publishers run the papers.

Conveniently, the publishers they hired were not disposed to investigative journalism, never mind scrutiny of a company so vital to the New Brunswick economy. They shared the Irving world view that journalism ought to support economic growth, growth that happened to be generated by the newspapers' proprietors. "What we need is more industry," Tom Crowther, the publisher of the Fredericton *Daily Gleaner*, told Giles Walker for his NFB documentary. "So if you ask, 'Do we go out and attack industries,' frankly, no." Ed Larracey, another of their publishers, in Moncton, lamented in the obituary he wrote of K.C. Irving that the industrialist had been "hounded by government bureaucracy" into fleeing to Bermuda. And at the Saint John papers, Michael Camp says, publisher Ralph Costello believed "that outside the chattering classes there was this hard-working New Brunswick readership that had a level head when it came to things like the Irvings: pro-development, pro-business—the Irvings were a good force in New Brunswick." Rookie reporters like Camp who pitched stories about the companies felt they were never given the time to work on them. "It's not that you'd get a no, exactly. It was that you'd probably be working on something else. You were already busy with what they wanted you to do. And we were not a paper that had a lot of extra labour."

The publishers reflected the Irving Way in other aspects: when a group of eleven young reporters at the Fredericton *Daily Gleaner* tried to organize a union in 1977, they were fired. "Another example," says one of them, Doug Milander, "of the Irving press stomping on the little guy." According to Harry Bagley, the *Gleaner*'s advertising manager, Crowther directed his ad staff to persuade local companies to drop their ads from a new upstart weekly paper in the city. "The point here is the fanatical way that they considered any kind of competition extremely dangerous," Bagley says. Jack Irving was rarely seen at the *Gleaner*—he came in once a year to discuss major capital projects—and he kept the Fredericton and Moncton companies as distinct entities, not subsidiaries of other Irving enterprises. But this nod to autonomy meant nothing, Bagley says. "Jesus, they didn't have to exercise any editorial control," he says. "If you're a writer or a manager or an editor in the newsroom, you know that if you wanted a paycheque, you knew what treaded on their toes and you didn't write it.... They didn't have to be there or make phone calls or anything like that."

There were also few signs of Jack at his other newspaper

company, Moncton Publishing Co. Ltd. He was sent monthly financial statements and was satisfied with what he saw: "It was a bit of a cash cow," says Bembridge, the former managing editor of the *Times* and the *Transcript*. Like Bagley in Fredericton, ambitious reporters in Moncton concluded that hands-on Irving control wasn't necessary: Peter Boisseau, who arrived in 1984, a year after the two papers merged into the afternoon *Times-Transcript*, tried to adopt the "rabble-rousing style" he had learned in campus journalism, but when his stories dealt with the Irvings, he says, Bembridge edited them to tone them down, citing the need to be prudent or to protect the paper from legal challenges. "Some such nonsense would be cooked up," Boisseau says, "as opposed to 'the Irvings wouldn't like this.'"

Bembridge agrees there was self-censorship at some Irving newspapers—but not at his, he asserts, at least not on his watch. The family "had their hands in so many things that you had to be conscious of what was going on," he says, but it wasn't an issue at the *Times-Transcript* because the Irving companies were based in Saint John. The paper didn't do a lot of investigative work because the staff "didn't have much depth," he insists. Of Boisseau's complaints that his scoops were routinely watered down or spiked, Bembridge says, "Peter thought he had the goods and he did not. I sent some of the stuff to lawyers and they said, 'Sure, run it if you want your ass sued off.'"

In the summer of 1989, Boisseau says he filed an investigative piece looking at the operations of the provincial water bombers that fought forest fires. The story was of possible interest to the Irvings, given their vast forestry operations, but Boisseau says it didn't reflect badly on them. Still, he says, Bembridge heavily edited the piece. "That was his way of destroying a story that the Irvings wouldn't like. And he didn't have to have the Irvings tell him they wouldn't like that story." Boisseau says he quit over the decision. (Bembridge says he does not remember the story, and recalls Boisseau quitting over a City Hall story with no Irving connection.)

Boisseau ended up working at the CBC, but not before receiving a phone call that seemed to belie the notion of monolithic Irving control of the newspapers: he was invited to apply to the *Telegraph-Journal* in Saint John, which, under a new publisher, was venturing into investigative journalism.

"He's only 35!" Ralph Costello declared mockingly in his farewell memo to the staff, referring to his successor, Paul Willcocks. Not only was the new publisher young, he wasn't from New Brunswick, two traits that made him an unusual choice for a senior position in an Irving organization. His job interview in Toronto with Arthur and J.K., who together owned 80 percent of New Brunswick Publishing Co. Ltd., was awkward. "I don't think they knew what to make of me, or me of them," Willcocks says. He explained what he'd done as publisher of the *Red Deer Advocate* in Alberta and told them where he thought the newspaper business was going. And he asked them about the ownership issue. "If anyone ever claims we tell you what to put in the paper," Arthur answered, "he'll be a damned liar."

It was 1987, the first time in a generation that the *Telegraph-Journal* and its afternoon sister paper, the *Times-Globe,* needed a new publisher, and the media world was changing. Willcocks used a newfangled kind of computer called the Apple Macintosh. "I was young and different," Willcocks says, "and I don't think they were sure what they wanted." Elsewhere, publishers were rethinking presentation and design to compete with the rise of television. There was a push for shorter stories—more tightly written, snappier, succinct. But the Saint John papers showed no sign of adapting. "The newspapers weren't bad," he says, "but they weren't good." In Red Deer, Willcocks had felt competitive pressure from the *Edmonton Journal* and the *Calgary Herald*. In Saint John, he says, editorial employees compared themselves to the *Gleaner* and the *Times-Transcript* and perhaps the Halifax *Chronicle-Herald*. "It didn't encourage striving."

The *Telegraph*'s editors saw it differently. "We believed that we were the best," says Fred Hazel, who became editor-in-chief in 1980. "People in the legislature would go to the *Telegraph-Journal* in the morning. They considered it the *Time* magazine of New Brunswick." The *Gleaner* in Fredericton and the *Times-Transcript* in Moncton simply didn't measure up; serious political coverage was considered the *Telegraph*'s strength. Costello "saw the role of the newspaper as keeping the government honest," says Michael Camp, who points out this philosophy served another purpose. "It kept everybody's eyes on the government, made a spectacle of that, and no one felt the paper wasn't doing its job. If you're watching the politicians, you're spending less time looking critically at other things, which could include the way the Irvings were operating. [Costello] felt that the role of a newspaper was not to get in anyone's business, but to see that tax money was spent properly and everybody was accountable."

Time and resources were available to react to major stories like the 1977 Saint John jail fire, in which twenty-one inmates died. But true initiative was rare. An enterprise series on racism in Saint John was watered down before publication. There wasn't much interest in environmental stories. The *Telegraph*— despite its supposed watchdog role—was scooped on a major story by *The Saint Croix Courier*, a small, independent biweekly paper in St. Stephen, New Brunswick. It revealed illegal political contributions by two Montreal companies with contracts on the Point Lepreau nuclear generating station, which was under construction at the time and more than $500 million over budget—precisely the kind of story a flagship provincial daily newspaper ought to break. "Whether through laziness or design, New Brunswick's English dailies inflict a stultifying, recording-secretary approach to journalism on their readers," Julian Walker, an ex-*Telegraph* reporter who ran the *Courier*, had told the Kent Commission. "They cover the basic news happenings faithfully and considering the number of reporters they employ, do so reasonably well. They basically fail to bring new information before the public in an adventuresome way."

The *Telegraph-Journal* and the *Times-Globe* shared many good reporters, says Mark Tunney, who joined the Saint John newsroom in 1982, "but as much as I liked Fred Hazel, there wasn't a sense of 'let's go out and break stories.' That culture just wasn't there." Tunney and Camp don't blame Hazel, though. "Fred's job was to say yes to Ralph [Costello]," Camp says. Another reporter who worked there at the time, speaking anonymously, says senior managers who had spent their entire careers in Saint John were not inclined to upset their hometowns with aggressive journalism. Reporters "were expected to write down everything they heard and regurgitate it. No analysis, or even filtering." Those who covered City Hall and the legislature were left with little time or energy to tackle complex stories. And in an era when print journalism still ruled, the Irving monopoly meant there was no pressure to do better. "The view of the newspaper business was that you printed a newspaper, you made money, and it didn't matter a whole lot what you did with it: people would buy it."

In such a context, scrutinizing the owner's activities was inconceivable. "We were not crusading against the Irvings," Hazel says, as if that were the only alternative. The anonymous former reporter adds, "It would be a very large task in any community to cover any large industry with as many arms and legs and appendages as the Irvings ... unless they were in an adversarial relationship with the owners, which of course they weren't." Irving stories that could not be avoided were covered gingerly. On Tunney's first day at the *Times-Globe*, he found himself updating for afternoon readers the morning *Telegraph* story on police rescuing Jack Irving from his kidnapper. "At any given time, three or four guardians of my journalistic freedom hovered over me, sighing and grunting over every tentative keystroke."

When Costello retired in 1987, the tributes published in the newspapers cited his deft writing, his long tenure, his gruff-but-sentimental personality, his orchestration of the seamless move to the Crown Street building, his community activities, even his defence of the Irvings before Kent and Davey—but they did not, or could not, name a single investigative story that defined his journalistic legacy as publisher. Reporters who worked for Willcocks, whose tenure was far shorter than Costello's, easily recall such stories. "It was a bit of a Quiet Revolution, it felt like at the time," says Mark Tunney. "It was a period when there was a bit of an opening up." Willcocks is more modest—"we just did the reporting you would expect"—but his definition of reporting was strikingly broader than Costello's.

Even now, *Telegraph-Journal* and *Times-Globe* reporters from the Willcocks era speak almost in awe and reverence about a series called "Endangered Bay," by City Hall reporter Elaine Bateman. When Bateman pitched an investigation of pollution in the Bay of Fundy, Willcocks enthusiastically approved it. The resulting stories pointed out the lack of coastal zoning plans, of research on the impact of industrial pollution, and of development controls along the water. One story, "Wasting the Bay of Fundy," declared the bay "New Brunswick's toilet." A large map included data on tens of millions of gallons of industrial waste—wood fibre, resin, chemicals, paper dye, oil by-products—spewing into the bay each year from Irving companies, which it named. Another story focused on the impact of an Irving-owned paper mill on Lake Utopia in Charlotte County. "It was like cutting off the air to the nursery or dumping toxic waste in the garden," Bateman wrote. "Industry, abetted by politics, killed L'Etang Estuary, a 14-kilometre-long fjord-like inlet on the Bay of Fundy. Thousands of tons of pulp mill sludge choked it to death."

It was provocative and dramatic, an extraordinary example of enterprise journalism, and it put the newspaper's owners in a remarkably bad light. The series implicitly rebutted what Fred Hazel had explained to *The Globe and Mail* in 1969: that, to report on pollution in the bay, the newsroom would need an event, such as a protest, to which it could react. Now the newspaper was acting, not reacting, seeking out facts and publishing them. "People just ate it up," Bateman recalls. The series was republished in a special supplement, and when local schools asked for hundreds of copies to use in classes, the *Telegraph* had to do a second print run.

Willcocks heard nothing from the Irvings about the series. "I have no real idea if the stories shocked the brothers," he says. Nor did they complain about the *Telegraph*'s reporting on a study for City Hall that found the scale of the Irving holdings scared other businesses from coming to Saint John. "They never, ever said a word to me about content," Willcocks says. "People speculated that they weren't happy, but they never contacted me or gave me an indication when we met." In fact, he had a hard time scheduling meetings with J.K. and Arthur to discuss business decisions. "I went months without having contact with them or anyone from the organization." This meant delays for approval of big capital expenses, but it suited him fine editorially. "The Irvings were, in my experience, ideal owners."

The common perception is that the Irvings sent Willcocks packing in 1990—"I'm quite sure he was fired," says Mark Tunney—but Willcocks says he was poached by executives at Thomson Newspapers. "I was heartbroken when he announced he was leaving," says Elaine Bateman. "In fact I think I cried at the meeting. I felt like my world was over." Other reporters were equally deflated. "I remember thinking this was a lost opportunity and it won't come again," says one. "We will go back to the way that things were."

To replace Willcocks, J.K. and Arthur selected a known quantity, the Saint John–raised Arthur Doyle. The head of the University of New Brunswick alumni association, Doyle had built a reputation as an expert on provincial history and politics with his book *Front Benches & Back Rooms*, a romp through government scandals and corruption in the first half of the twentieth century. Doyle also grew up near the big Irving home up on Mount Pleasant Avenue, and sold newspapers as a boy on Union Street. His father, a businessman, had called K.C. Irving "my kind of man."

Doyle understood the Irvings were big news, and arranged for extensive coverage of legislative hearings in Maine into Irving Oil's expansion into the state. But newsroom employees saw his tenure as a retreat. Bateman was pitching more environmental investigations, but "there was a lack of interest in pursuing stories like that," she says. "I don't remember any pushback.

It was, 'let's direct our energies in other directions.'" Charles Enman, who joined the *Telegraph-Journal* around that time, says the new publisher had "an explicit policy of treating the Irvings with kid gloves. Doyle said that we would not be doing stories of this type again."

In the summer of 1991, a young reporter named Philip Lee walked into this dispirited atmosphere. Raised in Saint John, the son of a respected Protestant minister, educated in the classics, the quiet and intense reporter had cut his journalistic teeth at a crusading weekly newspaper in St. John's, Newfoundland, the *Sunday Express*, where he helped break the Mount Cashel sex abuse scandal. When his mentor, editor Michael Harris, left, "I decided that moment in journalism was over," Lee says. With his parents still in Saint John, and a wife and young children, he came home to a job covering City Hall for the *Evening Times-Globe*.

The newsroom Lee found was at a low point. Lee saw the grimy, battered office furniture as a metaphor: drawers in the beat-up old metal desks wouldn't open, and important stories weren't getting done, including stories about the Irvings. "Obviously they're a big story in New Brunswick, always, especially economically," Lee says, "and we just didn't cover it. I don't mean not at all—but not unless we had to." The paper was risk-averse. Another young reporter, Shaun Waters, landed a jailhouse interview with the convicted serial killer Allan Legere, whose escape from prison, murder spree, and trial captivated New Brunswickers for three years. The *Telegraph-Journal* opted not to run the story. It was too close to Christmas, Waters was told, and people would be upset. "We were just kind of grinding it out," Lee says. "It was a pretty discouraging atmosphere. There wasn't a lot of excitement about the journalism we were doing."

By early 1993, a new computerized pagination system was

running. Many of the older editors couldn't or wouldn't adjust, and by default, Lee became front-page editor of the *Times-Globe*, arriving at the newsroom at 4:30 A.M. every day to put the finishing touches on the paper so it could hit the streets before noon. "It was a totally awful job," he says. "I was barely reading the stories. We called it shovelling copy: get a headline on it, make sure there's nothing grievous in it, and whack it in there."

It was as distant from the noble calling of reporting as he could imagine, a universe away from the work he'd done on the Mount Cashel story in Newfoundland. And the worst part was there was no change on the horizon. The Paul Willcocks experiment suggested the proprietors really did leave editorial content to their publishers, but Willcocks was gone, his vision replaced by the same old passive, acquiescent journalism—tolerated by a monopoly that felt no competitive pressure to do better.

"I was thinking," Lee says, "that I probably needed to not be in journalism."

The Irving Way had prevailed, again. Or so it seemed.

5

STIRRING THE POT

▼

K.C. Irving died on Sunday, December 13, 1992, in Saint John. He had still been spending more than half the year in Bermuda, on the right side of Canadian tax legislation, but came home often to the penthouse at the top of the new J.D. Irving Ltd. building at 300 Union Street. He had come home for Christmas but took ill and died at the Saint John Regional Hospital.

Monday's *Telegraph-Journal* contained eight pages of coverage. "K.C. Irving: An Era Ends," declared the front-page headline. A long story without a byline, beginning on the front and continuing inside, contained tributes from politicians, business leaders, and others. "I've admired K.C. Irving ever since I was a kid growing up in Kent County," said former premier Louis Robichaud, now a senator. "We had our ups and downs over the years, but I never lost my admiration for his courage and determination." Another piece, also without a byline, recounted K.C. Irving's life. There were many photographs. "The pages were quite beautifully done and nicely laid out," says Philip Lee. "It was clearly something they were prepared for, the old guard.... I think perhaps Ralph Costello was involved in the approval of the final pages." Costello, though retired, was known to be advising the family. "I think maybe somebody walked the proofs up the street to the Irving building for approval," Lee says, "which I don't think would have been that out of the ordinary for a story that big about the owners."

Three days later, K.C. Irving's six grandsons—J.K.'s two sons, Arthur's two, and Jack's two—carried his casket into the Church of St. John and St. Stephen in the city centre. The chief of police had gone on local radio to ask people not to drive to the service: there was no parking available in the narrow maze of streets. Still, four hundred people were in the chapel, three hundred more watched on a closed-circuit television feed in the basement, and another thousand did the same while jammed into a school gym and auditorium across the street.

"For many decades, he has been our leader," Reverend Philip Lee, the father of the *Times-Globe* journalist, told the mourners. "Here he has put us to work; he showed us how to work, how to excel, how to accomplish what needed to be accomplished." Drawing on the last chapter of Deuteronomy, in which Moses is shown the Promised Land but dies before reaching it, Lee compared the industrialist to the Old Testament prophet: "Through more enterprises than we have the time to name, he led our people from where they were to where they are."

The laudatory coverage, like Lee's sermon, reflected the political and corporate consensus in New Brunswick that K.C. Irving was a builder, a champion of economic development, a great man. The stories touched briefly on the controversies: there were references to the Equal Opportunity battle, environmental campaigns against the stink of the pulp mill, and the Combines

Act prosecution of the newspapers. Another piece mentioned that Irving would be buried in Bermuda, without discussing why he had relocated there in the first place.

Nowhere in the pages, though, could a reader find an answer to the question that was on everyone's mind: K.C. Irving was dead—what was next for his empire?

The empire was changing. J.K., Arthur, and Jack were often seen as throwbacks to an earlier age, but in the 1980s they began modernizing the executive structures of their companies. It was unwieldy for the managers of dozens upon dozens of companies to report to at least one brother. So they hired MBAs to help organize the businesses into industry groups, then hired more MBAs to run many of them. One recruit was Valerie Millen, a Nova Scotia–born graduate of the University of Western Ontario, who arrived in 1987, just shy of her thirtieth birthday. J.K.'s son Jim, in a senior role in his father's J.D. Irving Ltd. group of companies, offered her a job, but before she left the building, J.K. asked to meet her himself. Impressed, he offered her a better-paying position, reporting directly to him.

Millen became a turnaround specialist, and a very good one. She went into several companies—Kent Lines, Universal Sales, Atlantic Towing, and Stenpro, a ship-repair subsidiary of the shipyard—and streamlined them, cutting costs and imposing benchmarks. By the time she tackled SMT, the money-losing bus company K.C. had created in the thirties, she had concluded the Irvings had a larger problem: the patriarch's vision had been to own one of everything, a logical strategy of vertical integration within a fixed area like a province. By the early nineties, however, the Irvings needed economies of scale, which dozens of small companies doing dozens of things couldn't provide. Millen told J.K. that SMT, with $10 million in annual revenue, should either expand by acquiring other bus companies outside New Brunswick or be put up for sale.

"We don't sell things," J.K. told her. "We buy things." This was his father's fundamental principle, his golden rule. "I was never trained to sell assets," J.K. explains. "I could go out and spend $10 million, buy something, whatever it was, and come back and tell my father, and he'd listen, and it was okay, whatever it was. But if I sold something—well, you didn't sell anything unless you passed it in front of my father. That's the way it was. And he wanted to know why." SMT was not for sale. "You *fix* it," he told Millen. She did, by centralizing maintenance, rationalizing bus routes, and installing an automated ticketing system. Within a year SMT eliminated a $2 million annual loss and was breaking even.

Millen's star was rising. She had gained experience across several companies, and had learned the Irving Way, arriving in the office at 7:30 A.M., and staying near the phone at home on Sunday evenings when J.K. liked to call to bat around ideas. Late in 1990, he asked her to go down to 210 Crown Street to fix New Brunswick Publishing. "We were trying to invigorate the newspapers," J.K. says. "Most businesses around from time to time need reinvigorating."

Indeed: Millen would later tell *The Globe and Mail* that she found "no management structure, no financial controls, no management information system, no organized reporting structure and no defined lines of responsibility." Circulation was plummeting. Advertising salesmen were on salaries, meaning there was no incentive to sell. Senior managers were expensing their home phone bills—a perk from the 1940s that the Irvings had forgotten about. This was the legacy of the Davey and Kent investigations into media ownership: J.K. and Arthur were so determined not to be seen running their newspaper company that they'd neglected it. "You'd go into their lumbering business, their offices and mills, and it was top-of-the-line efficient, technologically advanced, nice beautiful offices," Philip Lee says. But with the papers, "I think they really feared getting involved in a hands-on way."

CHSJ Television was also in the red, and it was split from its sister radio station and sold off, a rare exception to the family's "we don't sell" mantra. The newspapers were different, though. "There's been a lot of people around who wanted to buy the damned newspapers," J.K. says. "They've come from afar, Ontario and whatnot." Like his father, J.K. would not allow them to fall into the hands of a non–New Brunswicker, even when the *Telegraph* hit rock bottom in 1990. "That's been the damned trouble down here in the Maritimes, its lack of local ownership," he says, adopting his father's slogan as his own. "We live here and we think that things should be run for the benefit of the province, and that takes in the newspapers."

Turning around the *Telegraph* was not easy: it was read faithfully by the political and business elite, but this was not a large demographic in a small, have-not province. There were clusters of loyal subscribers around the province's hinterlands, but no natural geographic base. In the province's three main cities, people gravitated toward their three local afternoon papers, including the *Evening Times-Globe* in Saint John. The *Telegraph* "was a provincial daily based in Saint John that was not read by people in Saint John," one former employee says. This made it costly to run. While its afternoon sister paper, the *Times-Globe*, could be delivered cheaply in its compact urban market—the city of Saint John and its suburbs—the morning *Telegraph*, with its provincial mandate, was, per copy, far more expensive to distribute. "If you took the Irvings out of the equation," says the former employee, "there would be three large cities with three city-focused newspapers and there wouldn't have been a newspaper that made any real effort to cover the whole province."

K.C. had kept the *Telegraph* as a provincial daily—even if he held it at arm's length, even if it lost money—because it deterred others from starting a morning newspaper. That strategy was sustainable when the *Evening Times-Globe*'s healthy balance sheet kept New Brunswick Publishing profitable overall, but the recession at the start of the nineties changed the equation: the company as a whole was losing money. "I think that was the trigger for J.K.," says the former employee. With K.C. in the twilight of his life and Arthur no longer playing a role despite his owner-ship stake, J.K. decided to shake up the Saint John papers. "The era of having a provincial paper and not really being concerned whether it as a product was profitable, or even as profitable as the other products you owned, was passing, or had passed," says another former employee.

In 1991, Millen officially became general manager of New Brunswick Publishing, with a mandate to transform the two newspapers. She put the advertising staff on commission and installed new software to automate cold calls to potential adver-tisers. With the new pagination system in place, she told thirty composing room employees who manually pasted up pages that when their union contract expired the following year, along with its job guarantees, they would be laid off. Soon Millen—nicknamed Attila the Hen—was contending with internal sabotage. National display ads, important sources of revenue, would disappear from the composing room. More than once, Millen had to fish through Dumpsters to find them. "She would be down in the composing room at eleven thirty at night," Philip Lee recalls, "making sure the pages were getting out the door." When Arthur Doyle retired as publisher in the summer of 1992, his position was folded into Millen's, but she did not take his title. "I want employees to understand," she would explain, "that it's a business like any other."

Except it wasn't. There was another improvement J.K. Irving wanted that would be harder to measure than ad sales or circulation numbers. The proprietor seemed embarrassed by the two papers' terrible reputations and he wanted that fixed, too. He wanted the papers to be not only profitable, he told Millen, but also respected, well-regarded—*award-winning*. He wanted readers to be delighted and surprised when they opened the pages. "We want to stir the pot," he told her.

This, Millen thought, is not going to end well.

Neil Reynolds was reading *The Globe and Mail* at his home outside Kingston, Ontario, one day early in 1993, when he spied an intriguing advertisement: an unnamed newspaper company on Canada's east coast was looking for an editor. "What do you think?" he asked his wife, Donna Jacobs. Reynolds had retired as editor-in-chief of the Kingston *Whig-Standard* the previous May and had been freelancing since then. He was fifty-two years old. "It was one of those serendipitous things," Jacobs says. "We were free to move." He applied.

If Valerie Millen wanted to stir the pot and win awards, she had found the right editor, as she learned when she canvassed newspaper executives about Reynolds. During his tenure in Kingston, the *Whig*—with a circulation that never exceeded forty thousand copies in a city smaller than Saint John—won eight National Newspaper Awards, four National Magazine Awards, and two Michener Awards for public service journalism. Reynolds believed a newspaper, even a small one, could aspire to greatness by publishing big investigations and thoughtful writing. Reporters found themselves inspired by this dark, handsome, self-made intellectual with the coolness of Gary Cooper and who quoted the poetry of Matthew Arnold. Most famously, Reynolds had arranged to have three of his journalists smuggled into Afghanistan to tell the story of five Soviet prisoners of war stymied by Ottawa bureaucrats in their attempts to immigrate to Canada.

The Afghanistan caper became the stuff of legend in Canadian journalism, but was only the most dramatic in a series of bold Reynolds-led investigations on chemical food additives, the pollution of an aboriginal community by an aluminum plant, an ex-Nazi collaborator who concealed his past to immigrate to Canada, and the sexual abuse by a cathedral choirmaster of several boys in the choir. These stories fulfilled Reynolds's vision of journalists as moral custodians, "the cleaners of seashores and beaches." The story of the abuse and cover-up at the cathedral in Kingston was particularly contentious, prompting complaints that the *Whig* should not dredge up such unpleasantness. The newspaper's owner, Michael Davies, stood by his editor. "I would much rather have a tiger by the tail and be dragged through the jungle," Davies once said, "than have no tiger at all."

In a speech at a journalism convention in 1989, Reynolds argued that newspapers should never underestimate the intelligence of their readers. They could, and should, elevate the public discourse. "Newspapers are an expression, an articulation, of community," he said. "They remain serious enterprises that confront people, as individuals and citizens, with the serious personal-interest and public-interest issues of the day." This was almost heresy in 1989, when the industry was moving to shorter, brisker stories adorned with large photographs and explanatory graphics. In an age of bite-sized journalism, Reynolds defended long, deep, lushly written stories. He created a weekend literary magazine for the *Whig*, another venue for the paper's long-form journalism. "A story requires context and contradiction, cause and consequence," Reynolds told the convention. "It requires cadence and irony. It requires character and plot and dramatic resolution."

Reynolds's quiet disposition, restless spirit, and burning beliefs came naturally: he was the son of a preacher of Free Methodism, a faith that had refused the compromises required to merge into The United Church of Canada. "In our parsonage home, the Bible and the Dictionary were authorities of the highest rank," he would write. As a boy, he was introduced by a childhood friend to comic books, which were not permitted in the Reynolds house. When he spent grade 11 at a private church-run school near Toronto, the dean confiscated his copy of John Hersey's *Hiroshima*, an early example of the New Journalism. "This is the truth about books: they are subversive," Reynolds wrote. "And if they're not, they ought to be."

At first, Reynolds was a rebel of the left. "Like all sons of Methodist ministers," he would joke, "I was a communist at sixteen." He grew into a fierce libertarian, a Jeffersonian believer in self-reliance, a vegetarian enthusiast of subsistence farming. After working at the Sarnia *Observer* and the *Toronto Star* as a young man, he returned to Kingston and landed a job at the *Whig-Standard*, which he had delivered as a boy. He became editor-in-chief in 1978, and retired fourteen years later after Michael Davies sold the *Whig* to Southam Inc. To cut costs,

Southam was reshaping the paper into something more conventional than Reynolds could abide.

For Valerie Millen and J.K. Irving, the question was whether an iconoclast like Reynolds could fit in with the Irving culture at the *Telegraph-Journal* and the *Times-Globe*. In a tribute to Davies when the *Whig* was sold, Reynolds had written: "I know of not a single instance during all these years when, confronted by a journalistic challenge, he did not make the principled decision. It was an attribute that cost him a lot of money." This was not exactly the reputation the Irvings had in the industry. As a libertarian, Reynolds believed an owner was free to set the direction of his newspaper—but also that the newspaper operated best when its editor was equally free to protect the journalism from the interests and whims of the owner. "Valerie and J.K. both promised me editorial independence in very explicit terms," Reynolds would later tell the *Ryerson Review of Journalism*.

Unbeknownst to Reynolds, J.K. made the point even more strongly to Millen: he ordered her *never*, under any circumstances, to allow any member of the Irving family, including himself, to pressure her about any story before it was published in the paper. "You are not to get us in trouble with any kind of newspaper inquiry or discussion of controlling the press," he told her, still clearly preoccupied with the criticisms levelled by Davey and Kent and the possibility of regulation. And, J.K. added, if anyone in his family ever tried to influence the content of the paper, she was to prevent it, and to tell them of the secret directive he was now giving her.

Reynolds, in fact, found much to admire in the Irvings, says his widow, Donna Jacobs. "They had no affectations. They were who they were. He was so thrilled, as a country boy at heart, that he would see an Irving in a flannel shirt, that they spoke plainly."

And he admired their entrepreneurship: Reynolds believed "journalism is honourably and ethically carried out within a commercial setting," Philip Lee says. More specifically, Reynolds, as a nineteenth-century liberal, preferred individual capitalism and local entrepreneurship to the corporatism of the Southam chain and the dull conformity of its newspapers. Saint John represented "the kind of situation Neil liked," Jacobs says. "He liked to work for the person who owned the paper." Nor did the Irvings' industrial interests concern him. "He just treated it as another part of his philosophy, which was to be even-handed, provide something for everybody, try to reflect the community you're in, don't be afraid to go into issues, but go into them fairly. It just brought his beliefs more to the fore. He had no trouble negotiating that."

Reynolds was hired as editor-in-chief of the *Telegraph-Journal* and the *Evening Times-Globe* in the late spring of 1993 and spent his first weeks at 210 Crown Street watching and learning. He met with each journalist individually. When he asked Philip Lee how things were going, Lee described shovelling the barely edited copy onto the front page at 4:30 A.M. day after day. "I'm in hell," he told Reynolds. "This is not good, what's going on here, the way I'm putting out these pages."

Reynolds nodded knowingly. "What journalism does," Lee recalls him saying, "is it tends to turn itself into an assembly-line, factory-floor kind of atmosphere instead of a creative place, because that's actually easier than doing good journalism. And we're going to change that."

A month after his arrival, Reynolds addressed the editorial staff of the two papers. Reporter Charles Enman described the scene years later: "You came into this profession wanting to do something good with your lives, Reynolds told the staff—and what happened is that, yes, you got better and better at your job, but finally you found yourself coasting on technique, familiarity with the terrain, and craven willingness to accept the good enough." Journalism, Reynolds said, was more than this: a calling that was crucial to society, a way to right wrongs, "to tell stories that bore witness to the universally human, to practice one's craft with an ardour that might, on the best days, nudge over into the terrain of art."

In August of 1993 came the first hints of change in the papers. Weekday front pages of the *Telegraph-Journal* early in the month were dominated by a haphazard mix of wire stories: war in Bosnia, a propane leak in Missouri, wage restraint in the Ontario civil service. The following week, New Brunswick stories started to get more prominent play, including news that a judicial inquiry would start in October into the sexual abuse by guard Karl Toft at the provincially run Kingsclear youth reformatory. Another week went by and enterprise journalism appeared: a front-page story by Philip Lee profiled victims of the reformatory abuse and the failure by the New Brunswick government to offer them support. "Victims of Toft Cry Out for Help," blared the headline. The story was raw, human, emotional.

Lee had talked his way onto the Kingsclear story before Reynolds arrived, citing his experience covering Mount Cashel in Newfoundland. He tracked down a former superintendent who revealed he had alerted provincial officials, to no avail. The story helped prompt the inquiry, but Lee's editors at the *Times-Globe* were annoyed he was agitating to cover a Fredericton story best handled by the *Telegraph* correspondent there. Reynolds liked the sense of outrage Lee brought to the story, believing the

88

abuse of children was one of the great moral failings of society's institutions, and that journalists had a duty to hold those institutions—an Anglican cathedral in Kingston, a government-run reformatory in New Brunswick—to account. He let Lee stay on the story; among his scoops was the revelation that the Fredericton *Daily Gleaner*, at the end of an innocuous feature on the reformatory in 1971, had quoted a young resident describing "an employee" engaging in "homosexual activity" with some boys living there—a reference that had not led to any subsequent stories in the *Gleaner* or any provincial investigation.

Four days after the Kingsclear piece came the front-page exclusive on K.C. Irving's will. In five stories over three days, readers learned how the industrialist had locked his three sons, J.K., Arthur, and Jack, into a structure that prevented them from gaining control of his offshore trust unless they gave up residency in Canada. This stipulation was almost certainly designed to prevent the taxation of the trust's billions of dollars in assets. The coverage, with its analysis of the billionaire's mindset, eight months after his death, was a declaration of independence by Reynolds: "I remember Neil saying that it was important when he came to this job that everybody—*everybody*—knew that he was an independent person," says Jacobs. "He was aware that it was important for the staff to know that as well, because they need to take their cues on coverage. So he did that [coverage of the will] very deliberately, and did it soon, because his feeling was always that if you have something to sort out, do it as soon as you can and set the ground rules."

National business journalists were soon matching the scoop, turning, for once, to an Irving newspaper for news on the Irvings. More than anything the *Telegraph-Journal* had done before, the articles shed light on several Irving holding companies set up and owned by K.C. and incorporated in Bermuda, and which held shares in the various New Brunswick companies.* Now the Bermuda companies were held by a trust controlled by K.C.'s widow and two American lawyers, while their New Brunswick–based subsidiaries would continue to be operated by J.K., Arthur, and Jack. "In fact," the *Telegraph* said, "the only change may be that three trustees will fill the position that K.C. Irving himself held in his last year"—ultimate overseer and arbiter for the empire. For Saint John and New Brunswick, and the thousands of Irving jobs that fuelled their economies, everything would continue as if K.C. were still alive: "It will be business as usual," the paper declared.

The final story in the series, an analysis by Bruce Bartlett, a *Telegraph* reporter with a law degree, focused on the message K.C. was sending his heirs. Even if his sons left Canada to become trustees of the estate, each was barred from taking part in trust decisions benefitting himself or his children. Bartlett also noted there were no instructions about who the beneficiaries would be when the trust was dissolved thirty-five years later. "By so doing Irving has told his descendants they cannot sit back and wait for mega-wealth to come their way," Bartlett wrote. "Irving's will shows a determination to protect his descendants from the softness and decadence that often befalls those who grew up with the expectation of inheriting great wealth."

In a remarkable coincidence, just three days after those words were published, news broke of a court case that illustrated the kind

---

* At the end of 2013, Statistics Canada's Inter-Corporate Ownership database listed eight Irving holding companies registered in Bermuda: F.M.O. Co. Ltd.; F.M.R. Co. Ltd.; Forest Mere Investments Ltd.; F.M.P. Co. Ltd.; F.M.W. Co. Ltd.; F.M.K. Co. Ltd.; F.M.N. Co. Ltd.; and F.M.I. Co. Ltd. Two Irving shipping companies, Kent Line International Ltd., and Voyageur Shipping Ltd., are also registered there.

of circumstance K.C. Irving sought to avoid. The newsroom got a tip that a lawsuit had been filed in Fredericton by shareholders of McCain Foods, the billion-dollar frozen-food company based in Florenceville, New Brunswick. Don Richardson, the newspaper's legislature reporter, hustled down to the courthouse. He discovered that co-founder Wallace McCain and his family were suing other family members, including Wallace's brother, company co-founder Harrison McCain. The brothers, both in their sixties, were feuding over Wallace's plan to install his son Michael as the next CEO. Harrison's faction blocked Wallace by ousting him from the company—exactly the kind of fratricidal outbreak Irving must have feared when he created his offshore trust to lock in his three sons' loyalty to one another.

Before Richardson could file his story, the judge in the McCain case banned publication of the details, so all he could report the next morning was the bare fact that one McCain faction was suing another. "This is a private matter," Andrew McCain, a nephew of Harrison and Wallace, told Richardson. Reynolds was outraged: the McCains employed hundreds of people, mainly at plants in Florenceville and in nearby Grand Falls, and bought potatoes from farmers along a great stretch of the province's Saint John River Valley. And they had transformed the little company they founded in 1957 into a $3 billion global food giant, the only New Brunswick enterprise that could be discussed in the same breath as the Irvings'. Readers had a right to know what they were doing in a public courtroom. The *Telegraph* and other media organizations hired lawyers and had the ban struck down within a day.

Reynolds made the most of the victory. "MCCAIN VS. MCCAIN," announced a huge, white-on-black headline across the following morning's front page. "The story the McCain family did not want you to read is a tale of scheming, manipulation, intimidation and double-dealing," Richardson's summary of the dispute began. "It's also a story of brotherly love and jealousy, born from a relationship that runs deeper and stronger than most business partnerships." A sidebar story on the quashing of the publication ban carried the headline "McCains Can't Hide in Darkness of Secrecy." To drive the point home, Reynolds ran the complete text of Wallace's statement of claim over three inside pages, so readers could devour every word themselves.

This was an epic tale perfectly suited to Reynolds's brand of journalism—it had conflict, pathos, tension—and the *Telegraph-Journal* would ride it hard as it unfolded in the courts over the next two years. Along with K.C. Irving's will, the early, aggressive pursuit of the McCain lawsuit set the tone for the Neil Reynolds era. "That was new ground," Philip Lee says. "That was the moment when the *Telegraph-Journal* started to be noticed."

Reynolds made his next move on the first of October, fulfilling a fantasy he had long entertained but never acted on at the *Whig-Standard*: he cancelled the *Telegraph-Journal* and *Times-Globe* subscriptions to the Canadian Press, the national wire service owned by member newspapers. CP collected stories from member papers, rewrote them, and redistributed them across the country, along with articles by its own reporters. It allowed small dailies to reflect what was going on in Canada and, via its affiliation with the Associated Press, the wider world.

Reynolds loathed CP, or, more accurately, what it provided in return for the three-hundred-eighty-thousand-dollar annual fee the two Saint John papers paid. "Canadian Press has long preferred paint-by-number journalism to art-form journalism," he said in the 1989 conference speech that laid out his vision of newspapering. He denounced the conventional, formulaic writing style, the elimination of "every hint of literature" from the copy, and the dependence it fostered among small newspapers, which could more easily avoid generating their own local journalism. "CP is Canadian journalism's greatest scandal," he said, "and I do not understand our industry's indifference to it."

Now it was gone. News from the country and the world would be scraped together using other, cheaper agencies, and the total savings, five hundred thousand dollars a year after other wire services were also cancelled, paid for the hiring of more than twenty new journalists. Some of the new hires would edit a weekend magazine launched in November, the *New Brunswick Reader*; like the *Whig-Standard Magazine*, it would be, in Reynolds's words, "a quiet refuge" for people who enjoyed long-form journalism, arts coverage, book reviews, and poetry.

Other new staffers would expand the *Telegraph* bureaus in Fredericton and Moncton from one-person operations to full-strength teams of four or five reporters, so the provincial paper could investigate and break stories in the province's three main cities. "Local news and provincial news were going to be the bread and butter of the newspapers," says Carolyn Ryan, another *Whig-Standard* alumnus; Reynolds hired her as managing editor of the *Times-Globe*. Significantly, the expanded *Telegraph* bureaus would compete with the newspapers owned by J.K.'s brother Jack, the Fredericton *Daily Gleaner* and the Moncton *Times-Transcript*, sending a message, Reynolds hoped, that the Irving papers did not speak with one voice.

The new recruits included talented young reporters from across the country lured by Reynolds's reputation, New Brunswickers who finally saw the chance to aim high, and veterans who came looking for a new start. Reynolds wanted them "to patrol humanity's beaches," as he once described journalism's role, "and to do what we can to clean them up." Municipal councils with a fondness for secret meetings were skewered; the president of the Atlantic Canada Opportunities Agency, a federal job-creation agency, saw her travel expenses turned into a parable for Ottawa's centralization of power. The Saint John–based New Brunswick Museum, usually treated benignly by the newspapers, was exposed to ridicule when the vast majority of its collection of Fabergé eggs and other pieces were revealed as forgeries. "The Fakes Win," declared the headline, "117 to Six." Members of the New Brunswick Legislature, accustomed to stenographic coverage of their every utterance, complained after correspondent Don Richardson was directed to worry less about volume and more about scoops: the politicians now had to be interesting to make it into the *Telegraph-Journal*.

New Brunswick's sacred cows were gored one by one, including the most sacred of them all, the Irving family. The *Telegraph-Journal* published a series of stories on an explosion at an Irving gas station north of Fredericton that killed a man. The day before one piece was to run, managing editor Scott Anderson got a call from an Irving Oil executive. "You can't publish that story," he said. Anderson responded: "Just watch me." The *Times-Globe* reported on a plan by J.K., Arthur, and Jack Irving to pay for the restoration of the rundown Loyalist Burial Ground in Saint John, directly behind the J.D. Irving Ltd. and Irving Oil buildings on Union Street. "The Irvings had decided that this was an embarrassment for this historical treasure to be left in such a state," says Ryan. But the initiative became contentious: the brothers also wanted to install a statue of their father, K.C. Irving, a Scot, on the site, and provincial legislation said only

Loyalists could be memorialized there. The law was amended to accommodate the Irvings, but the family's critics in Saint John lobbied the city to block the statue. The brothers gave up and put the ten-foot-high bronze statue in K.C.'s hometown of Bouctouche instead—and then paid for the Saint John cemetery restoration anyway.

Despite the *Times-Globe*'s scrupulously even-handed coverage, some readers were unconvinced. "Every time the paper wrote about the Irvings," Ryan says, "people, readers and the conspiracy theorists suspected we were being told exactly what to write." But nothing was further from the truth, according to Peter Simpson, a Prince Edward Islander who took a job in 1994 editing the editorial pages. "Neil was like a bulwark between the Irvings and the newsroom," he says. Yes, they would complain from time to time—*after* something had been published. "But Neil would not buckle under." Once, Reynolds suggested Simpson make a minor edit to a column by environmentalist Janice Harvey on logging practices, not to water it down, Simpson says, but to make it clearer and more defensible if the owners complained. Simpson's edit was sloppy; it didn't make the sentence clearer. "I know the next day Neil had an earful on that from one of the Irvings." Reynolds was angry at Simpson, but with the owners, "he would stick up for his staff and for the story and for the principle."

Besides, Reynolds was giving J.K. Irving what he'd asked for: new readers for both his newspapers. In November 1993, the *Times-Globe*'s circulation was up 8 percent from a year earlier; the *Telegraph* was up more than 5 percent. *The Globe and Mail* pronounced them "an unlikely beacon of hope for the troubled Canadian newspaper industry" and "nothing short of a miracle."

And he was giving J.K. respectability. Fascinated by the Acadians, descendants of the French colonists brutally deported by the British in 1755, Reynolds decided to improve the *Telegraph*'s reporting on New Brunswick's francophones, one-third of the province's population. He devoted extensive coverage to the first Acadian World Congress, a gathering scheduled for August 1994 during which thousands of members of the Acadian diaspora returned to their ancestors' homeland for the first time. The coverage, which included reports from Louisiana and New England, ran for two weeks, then was repackaged into a special tabloid. Seventy thousand copies were distributed free to all the congress venues around southeast New Brunswick. The initiative carried extra resonance for francophones, many of whom still saw the Irving press as a bogeyman for its attacks on Premier Louis Robichaud in the 1960s. The series was also nominated for a National Newspaper Award and for the Michener Award— unprecedented recognition for the *Telegraph-Journal*.

"Neil Reynolds was one of the best persons who ever went through that place down there," J.K. reflected when he spoke to me two decades later.

"We liked him a great deal," interjected J.K.'s son Jim.

"The guy had great talent, great vision," J.K. added. "Mr. Reynolds hit the ball out of the ballpark."

In August of 1994, Neil Reynolds was fired.

6

REYNOLDS, REFINED

J.K. Irving has a morning ritual. "I have breakfast at home, and at breakfast, I have the newspaper," he tells me. "And before I get done my porridge, I could have a heart attack over what I read in the damned newspaper."

This is the chasm between the Irving family and its detractors: while the critics are certain the newspapers burnish the corporate image, the Irvings themselves suspect their journalists overcompensate for that perception by being extra hard on them. K.C. told the Davey committee that the papers "lean over backwards" to criticize, "just to keep their skirts clean." J.K.'s son Jim Irving reportedly once said, "We sign their paycheques and they piss all over us." J.K., though, claims equanimity about coverage he doesn't like. "That goes with the territory," he says. "I have never called or gone to the newspaper, upset, or 'I don't like this or that.' I understand they have a job to do, and they do their job. We've never interfered, and when my father was running the newspapers, I never recall seeing him or hearing him getting involved. He'd get upset every once in a while. But we understand our responsibility to the communities."

J.K. did, however, share his thoughts with Valerie Millen and Neil Reynolds about how they were transforming the *Telegraph-Journal* and the *Evening Times-Globe*—though always, it seems, about what had already been in the paper, not what he wanted to see in the future. He didn't like the coverage of his father's will, believing the stories misrepresented K.C.'s intentions. He felt the McCain coverage was sensational. And among J.K.'s peer group, older establishment folks, the *Times-Globe* had become too tart in its crime coverage. In a city that still operated like a small town, those readers didn't hesitate to pick up the phone and complain to J.K. directly. This wasn't Irving-related, but it bothered him. Millen promised him she would tone it down.

J.K. had a right to complain—it was *his* newspaper—but he was not always consistent. "One day it was too boring, one day it was too controversial," Millen told *Canadian Business* in 1994. Reynolds told the *Ryerson Review of Journalism* that J.K. once expressed bafflement at the choice of stories, then another time said he couldn't wait to see what the papers would do next.

Millen also heard directly from Jim Irving, J.K.'s oldest son, about what *he* did and didn't like in the newspapers. This assertiveness was not a surprise: J.K., in his mid-sixties, was ceding to his son more responsibility for the massive operations of J.D. Irving Ltd.

As a boy, Jim attended Rothesay Collegiate School, the private school outside Saint John, and Hyde School in Maine, an institution that touts "character education" but that has been criticized as a boot camp for rich kids. Perhaps his most significant education was from his grandfather, K.C., for whom Jim was a favourite grandchild. Toward the end of the NFB documentary *I Like to*

See Wheels Turn, K.C. leads Jim through one of his sprawling tree farms. "Very good growth," K.C. says, smiling as they measure and prune saplings. For Giles Walker, the film's director, the metaphor was irresistible: Jim, the heir apparent, all tawny hair and big teeth, beams as he watches his grandfather trim trees so they'll grow fast and strong.

While J.K. was said to be mellowing in the 1990s, growing more reflective and embracing philanthropy, Jim was showing K.C.'s legendary toughness: he was described as temperamental, decisive, all business. "Tense and constantly wound up, tightly wound," a source told author Harvey Sawler. In their joint interview for this book, father and son appeared to debate, several times, J.K.'s sentimental attachment to New Brunswick versus Jim's hard-nosed, bottom-line calculus. Repeating the familiar suggestion that the Irvings might be forced to relocate operations if the New Brunswick government didn't create a more favourable business climate, Jim said, "The world's moving. And we're either going to move here or we won't."

"Jim, I know that's how you look at it," J.K. cut in, "but the gosh-damn thing is, we live here, okay? The only dividend we get out of the place here besides a good night's sleep and enough to eat is the opportunity to walk around operations, meet the people who run them, and figure out how you make more of this and more of that or whatnot."

"But let's not get confused," Jim said, looking at me but rebutting his father. "We're not living in a dream world. Reality takes you over."

Valerie Millen saw this side of Jim when he complained to her about the newspapers becoming too sensational. Advertisers might flee, he said—a common worry of newspaper owners not particular to his family. In fact, Millen contended, controversy was good for business: single-copy sales of the *Telegraph*—which accounted for half its total circulation, an unusually high share in the industry—leapt 10 to 15 percent on days the front page carried titillating news and flashy headlines. Jim wasn't mollified: stirring the pot was not for him. He also complained about having the McCain legal feud, and that family empire's inner turmoil, splashed all over the front page. And he was angry about a *Times-Globe* story about Work Ready, an occupational therapy clinic opened by his wife, Lynn. The story had run on page B4, without the photograph that had been taken of Lynn with Saint John's mayor, Elsie Wayne. Millen, recalling J.K.'s instructions to avoid anything that might be seen as family interference, defended the newsroom's autonomy. Work Ready was not part of the Irving empire, but a tongue-lashing from the owner's son— even after the fact—still made her wonder about the limits of her independence.

In early 1994 came another portent. A promotional stunt to attract more readers in the Fredericton and Moncton markets collided with what appeared to be Irving family solidarity. J.K. was competitive with his brother Jack, who still owned the *Gleaner* in Fredericton and the *Times-Transcript* in Moncton. Millen arranged a one-day drop of thousands of free copies of the *Telegraph-Journal* on Fredericton doorsteps to attract subscribers in that city. When she did it again in Moncton a few weeks later, she got word to back off.

Mike Bembridge, who became publisher of the *Times-Transcript* in 1994, says he doesn't remember the free drop, nor Jack Irving complaining about it, and says he was unfazed by the *Telegraph*'s new editorial posture and its expanded Moncton reporting. "These people who believe exposés sell newspapers haven't studied circulation," he says. "It doesn't. Most people take a newspaper as a ritual, not because they're expecting something."

Still, the numbers were looking good for Millen: after the closure of unprofitable rural subscription routes, which caused a temporary dip, circulation numbers moved back up—and the new subscribers were urban dwellers in Fredericton and Moncton, more attractive to advertisers. In early 1994, ad linage at the *Telegraph* was up 0.6 percent, compared to an industry-wide decline of 6.2 percent. The numbers showed 1993 as the best year New Brunswick Publishing had ever had, and the trend suggested even better results for 1994.

Then Millen made a mistake. J.K. took flak from a Catholic organization in Saint John, the Sisters of Charity, after a sympathetic profile of abortion-rights crusader Dr. Henry Morgentaler was published in the *New Brunswick Reader* in January 1994. A letter in the *New Freeman*, a local Catholic newsletter, criticized Millen. She wrote a rebuttal to point out "misstatements and misrepresentations," violating the unwritten Irving rule against squabbling with the community in public. She was fired shortly afterward. "All I was told was that I had made a few people in the community angry with me," Millen later recounted, "and if they were angry at me, they were angry at Mr. Irving. And he couldn't have that because the Irvings had to do business in the community." One of her critics was said to be Ralph Costello, who still had J.K.'s ear. "I don't think it's possible that Mr. Irving could not have been influenced by Costello's criticisms," Reynolds would say. Millen eventually received a year's severance pay.

"Valerie Millen?" J.K. says when I ask about her departure. "She worked here for a few years, and she made a mistake putting out the newspapers at the time. She had no experience at that. But that's the way things go."

Millen's replacement as general manager was Bruce Phinney, a cheerful, outgoing, thirty-five-year-old rugby-playing accountant from Nova Scotia who had worked for Deloitte and Touche in London, England, before joining the Irvings. "My job is to keep Mr. Irving happy," he said, according to Reynolds, "and that means no complaints." Phinney denied the comment, telling *Canadian Business* his mandate was to put out "a lively paper that people enjoy reading" and—echoing the time-worn phrasing—to ensure the newsroom treated the owners "the way they would treat another story subject: fairly."

Phinney decided this required him to spend time in the newsroom, and staffers remember seeing him often. Once, he stood over the shoulder of a *Times-Globe* editor who was laying out the front page and tried, excruciatingly, to compose the headline for a story. Nearby, Reynolds held a pen to his lips, a slight tapping motion the only sign of his anger. "It was very tense," says a witness to the scene. The newsroom staff wondered whether Phinney was acting on Irving instructions, or, like publishers of old, anticipating what might displease the family. "He didn't want anything that would produce a phone call from an important person to Mr. Irving," Reynolds would tell the *Ryerson Review of Journalism*. Either way, the staff felt a chill in the air.

Phinney also commissioned an audit of circulation data, which confirmed that Millen's numbers were solid. Phinney then hired Michael Cobden, the head of journalism at the University of King's College in Halifax and a former *Whig-Standard* rival of Reynolds's, to review the editorial content. Cobden recommended more national and world news in the *Telegraph*, but otherwise declared the papers vastly improved. If Phinney wanted ammunition against the editor-in-chief, it was proving hard to come by.

In August, before leaving on vacation, Reynolds assigned a *Times-Globe* reporter to write a series on Saint John Shipbuilding, the Irving-owned shipyard then building navy frigates for the Canadian government. The stories were to examine its fraught relationship with a Quebec shipyard, MIL Davie, which had been both its rival and its subcontractor on the frigate program. The two companies had recently settled a large lawsuit over delays at the Quebec yard, a resolution reached thanks to a $323 million payment from Ottawa—a sum that caught Reynolds's attention.

On August 24, Reynolds, back from vacation, was summoned by Phinney into a conference room, where an Irving private investigator was waiting. After an hour-long discussion with Reynolds, the investigator left to meet with Phinney, who then called Reynolds into his office and fired him. Reynolds was in shock as he walked back to his office to clear out his things. When Richard Foot, a recent Reynolds recruit, arrived shortly afterward for his shift on the night desk, a distraught Scott Anderson told him of the firing. "If you have a place to go, *go*," Anderson said, "because everything's going to fall apart here."

Then Anderson's news instincts kicked in. He assigned Michael Woloschuk, another *Whig-Standard* veteran, to write a story about Reynolds's firing. Woloschuk rounded up reactions from some of the best-known names in Canadian journalism— Robert Fulford, Peter Worthington, Michael Cobden, Richard Doyle—who used words like *awful, outrageous,* and *shocking.* Phinney refused to comment on the firing, calling it "an internal personnel matter." *Telegraph* policy required stories about the newspaper to be reviewed by the general manager, so Anderson spent forty-five minutes negotiating edits with Phinney. At one point publisher and reporter had a confrontation. "You're a fat fuck," Woloschuk told Phinney. Anderson intervened to separate the two men. The story ran on page A3.

A fatalistic gloom descended on the *Telegraph-Journal* and the *Times-Globe*. Woloschuk soon quit, as did Shawna Richer, the editor of the weekend magazine, the *New Brunswick Reader*. The obvious assumption was that Reynolds was fired for his aggressive coverage of the Irvings. "Maybe I was naïve," Reynolds told me in the days after his dismissal. Phinney, he said, wanted to keep J.K. Irving happy, and "that meant keeping Saint John Shipbuilding happy, keeping Paul Zed happy," a reference to J.K.'s son-in-law, a Liberal MP. A while later, however, Reynolds told the *Ryerson Review* the private investigator had tried "to connect me to a fraud of some kind," though without revealing specifics. "I had the feeling very strongly at the time that I was supposed to believe they had something on me and I should be a good boy and not talk."

Instead, he hired a lawyer to sue for breach of contract and defamation. Reynolds soon learned the real explanation for the firing: an unnamed nemesis had falsely accused him of inflating the price of his house near Kingston, which J.K. Irving had agreed to buy as part of his employment contract. "It was a misinterpretation of information," says Donna Jacobs. Reynolds was convinced the general manager had acted alone, but regardless, the Irvings now had a problem. Even if Phinney's desire to keep the proprietors happy had no role in the firing, his comments would certainly come up during a lawsuit, reviving concerns about editorial control and conceivably rousing the regulatory ghosts in Ottawa.

J.K. invited Reynolds to his office up on Union Street. Jacobs drove in with him and watched him walk inside the building, carrying a handwritten letter to J.K. from their thirteen-year-old daughter, Jessie, "a very honest child's note," says Jacobs, in which she pleaded with the proprietor not to force her parents to move away from New Brunswick. At the end of the discussion, Reynolds would recount to Jacobs, J.K. finally told him, "I believe you."

On October 21, David Jamieson, an Irving company lawyer, arrived in the newsroom and handed a statement to editor David Spragg. Print this, Jamieson told him, and don't change a word. Under the heading "Neil Reynolds renamed editor-in-chief; assumes role of publisher," the announcement said that "as a result of several discussions between the parties, all the outstanding issues between the Company and Mr. Reynolds have been resolved." Reynolds and Phinney had made "considerable progress in improving the quality and circulation of the newspapers," the statement said, and Reynolds's return "will continue this trend." Phinney had a new title on top of general manager: executive vice-president. But Reynolds, now in the role of publisher, "will be responsible for editorial issues and policy." The maverick editor was back, and with a stronger hand than before—explicit, unambiguous control over editorial content. One night editor shook his head in disbelief. "I have never seen anyone make the Irvings eat crow," he said.

Phinney took it well, by all accounts. "I have no problem with it whatsoever," he told the Canadian Press. "We'll do a good job together." Reynolds, the victor, didn't gloat. What mattered was the work at hand. "Having been given his job back and promoted took away all the sting," says Donna Jacobs, "and gave him that sense of full steam ahead."

Soon the *Times-Globe* was breaking stories of sexual harass-
ment accusations against a local police official and of provincial
child welfare officials ignoring a case of neglect until the child
died. It also published an in-depth series on the history of
Irish migration to Saint John. Gary Dimmock, a new hire at
the *Telegraph-Journal*, exposed financial corruption on a First
Nations reserve and the use of uppers by New Brunswick long-
haul truckers driving to New England. A team of reporters
revealed a member of the provincial legislature had resigned after
being accused by his nephew of sexual abuse. When Reynolds had
to suspend Dimmock for two weeks after the Irvings saw him on
TV using profanity—news cameras caught him being roughed
up by reserve police over his corruption exposé—Reynolds paid
his salary out of his own pocket so he could keep working the
story. "I remember that period as this wonderful time of us doing
great things," Richard Foot says, "and everyone in the province
talking about us."

Amy Cameron, a reporter from Toronto, often ran into Reynolds
outside the side door by the parking lot in Saint John, where
they would both go to smoke. One day, a helicopter swung in
low and came toward them. "Come!" Reynolds said, pulling
Cameron by the arm. "We ran around the side of the building
and into the loading bay doors at the back of the building and
crouched down," she says. The chopper belonged to the Irvings—
the newspaper parking lot was the closest place to head office
where it could land—and it was surely carrying one of the three
brothers. "They certainly would raise hell if they caught anybody
smoking outside in the parking lot," Cameron says. "It was like
we were teenagers, hiding from the Irvings."

The family still loomed over everything. Richard Foot wrote a series of stories on federal subsidies to the port of Belledune, in the northern New Brunswick constituency of Doug Young, a powerful cabinet minister in the Jean Chrétien government. Foot's stories were fair and accurate, though definitely influenced by Reynolds's libertarian skepticism of government subsidies. In hindsight, however, "I can see how the Irvings would have approved of that story," he says. "Presumably their chips were with the port of Saint John. And the port of Belledune was—from an Irving perspective, but also from an economic perspective—unnecessary."

No Irving stories from the Reynolds era would be scrutinized more closely, though, than the coverage of the lengthy strike by workers at the Irving Oil refinery, which lasted from May 1994 to August 1996. It wasn't the first strike. After refinery workers unionized in 1948, they struck for a pay raise, overtime pay, a second week of vacation after five years on the job, and a reduction in their fifty-four-hour workweek. K.C. won a court injunction forbidding picketing for thirty days, in effect breaking the union and cementing his anti-labour reputation. "Some operations shouldn't have a union," K.C. once said. His defenders argued he was happy to deal with "reasonable" unions, and that he always lived up to the contracts he signed.

When the refinery workers walked out in May 1994, Irving Oil won an injunction to limit picketing and brushed off a union-led boycott of Irving gas stations. Managers kept the refinery running, even claiming increased production and sales, and later sent letters to individual union members, inviting them to cross the picket line. By October 1995, 46 of the 264 strikers had broken ranks and were back at work.

Erin Steuter, a sociologist at Mount Allison University in

Sackville, New Brunswick, would make the newspaper treatment of the strike the centrepiece of her academic critique of the Irvings. Steuter has an anti-corporate, left-wing analysis of the news and, when searching for a case study for her dissertation, settled on the strike coverage. "This seemed like a good story to tell," she says. In a 1999 academic paper Steuter concluded that Irving Oil's rough treatment of the union "was legitimized in the public eye through the Irving-owned newspaper chain." Analyzing the words used by the four Irving newspapers, *The Globe and Mail*, and others, Steuter wrote that certain phrases— "scant hope" for a contract, predictions that the strike would "drag on"—reflected a "tone of defeatism" about the union's chances. "The papers portray the strikers as foolish in their attempts to go up against the might and power of the Irving empire," she wrote. She also criticized the Irving papers for not writing about the wider context of the strike, which Steuter described as a broader assault on organized labour.

A former *Times-Globe* reporter, speaking anonymously, defends the coverage as reasonable and fair. Many Saint John residents, watching shipyard workers being laid off as the frigate program wound down, considered the refinery union inflexible, the reporter says. "We covered it as much as we wanted to cover it, but there also wasn't a lot of sympathy in the city for them." As the months passed, the dispute showed up less frequently: "There was no news there." The journalist also faults Steuter for talking about "the Irvings" as monolithic. By 1994, J.K.'s brother Arthur Irving had no role in running the newspapers. "We didn't have to answer to Irving Oil. We were never backing off Irving Oil stories. But the strike just wasn't that interesting."

Content analysis—the counting and categorization of words and phrases and their supposed ideological slant—is popular

among academic analysts of the media, though Steuter acknowledges it's not authoritative: "a really little bit of a slice and you
don't get the whole story." Indeed, she was surprised as she pored
over the 377 articles in her study. She expected Irving Oil would
"have a greater opportunity to explain their view of the situation." Instead, the union was the lead source almost twice as often
as the company, forcing her to adjust her assumptions. Given
that "it is highly unlikely that the Irvings did not have access to
the journalists, directly or indirectly, who were at the same time
Irving employees," Steuter argues the Irvings' silence is proof of
their power: they didn't *need* to speak. This assertion, however,
can't be measured quantitatively.

The New Brunswick government eventually appointed a
commission to resolve the strike. When the refinery manager did
not respond to his summons, a judge issued a warrant for him to
appear. "There was no not covering that," says the reporter, "and
it was covered as the ludicrous situation that it was—some guy
deciding he was above a subpoena." But while the union won
such procedural skirmishes, it lost the larger battle. The commissioner's final report told the workers they were beaten and should
take the best deal they could get. In August 1996, the union voted
to accept a contract that included concessions on seniority and
flexibility, and that gave the company the right to fire thirty-
seven workers, including union president Larry Washburn. Three
months later, *Telegraph-Journal* reporter Richard Foot cited the
humiliating defeat in a long, in-depth feature on the weakened
state of organized labour in New Brunswick—the kind of context
that Steuter says the coverage lacked.

Steuter writes there was a "virtually identical" anti-union bias
in the non-Irving *Globe and Mail*, but this, of course, undermines
the argument that the Irvings are the source of the problem. And

during the strike, the *Telegraph-Journal* published other items critical of the Irvings: Greenpeace called for a boycott of Irving Oil over its crude oil imports from Nigeria, where human-rights activists were executed; environmental columnist Janice Harvey lamented how discussion of J.K. Irving's philanthropic efforts to restore a coastal dune near Bouctouche focused on economic spinoffs rather than ecological merit.

Still, Steuter's work transformed her into the latest tribune for left-wing critiques of the Irvings—"I get a lot of crazy people contacting me"—and she is a frequent commentator when the company's newspapers do something controversial. And there is merit to her broader theme that the companies have become too big for New Brunswick. During an earlier strike in 1964, Irving Oil resisted a union demand that wages match those of other Canadian refineries because, the company argued, the salaries would surpass those paid to other workers in the Maritimes. In the 1994 dispute, the Maritimes were no longer Irving Oil's benchmark: the company wanted pay levels reduced to what employees earned at American refineries. The company no longer ranked itself regionally, but globally, underscoring that while the Irvings are consistent in saying they just want to be treated fairly, "fairness" can be a shifting scale.

And scale is important, as Jim Irving acknowledges when he shrugs off the academic critics like Erin Steuter. "New Brunswick's a small place," he says. "If we were sitting down in New York City, an Irving newspaper would be nothing. But this is a small pond. And people like to talk. A lot of people who talk don't have any of the facts. But it's a pastime. It's entertainment."

A much smaller refinery story during the strike—a single article, never published—left one journalist with a very different view of how Neil Reynolds handled the Irvings.

Jill Mahoney was a promising journalism student from Carleton University when she was hired as a summer intern for the *Telegraph-Journal*'s Fredericton bureau. On June 7, 1995, she was assigned a follow-up story to a June 3 piece about emissions data from the refinery. The newspaper had pushed for release of a document containing the data, which Irving Oil had been required to submit to the National Pollutant Release Inventory. The data, two years old, suggested Irving's emissions were lower in 1993 than those of other refineries. "Obviously, as a journalist, your suspicion is tweaked by that," Mahoney says, "because it's not an independent report and it was a very positive finding."

The controversy over how Irving companies were affecting air quality in Saint John was not new. In 1996, a Health Canada scientist said while Saint John wasn't the most polluted city in Canada, "it has the most acidic air we've ever measured." During the early weeks of the refinery strike, the New Brunswick government let the facility exceed normal emission levels during equipment maintenance, angering clean-air activists.

"You know," reporter Gary Dimmock told Mahoney as she started making calls, "there's a woman who recently died who was campaigning against the refinery." Cynthia Marino, a member of a Saint John group called Citizens' Coalition for Clean Air, had alleged Irving industries were making her asthma worse. She had died after an attack, just a week before Mahoney's assignment. "You might want to talk to her family," Dimmock suggested.

Mahoney called the Marino home in Saint John, hoping to reach Cynthia's husband, Bob. He wasn't home so she ended up speaking to the couple's teenage daughter, Christie. When Mahoney explained why she was calling, the girl offered her own opinion of the Irving report. "I didn't prompt her in any way," Mahoney says. "I didn't explain the report to her. She was already familiar with the content." (Dimmock, who overheard Mahoney's end of the call, corroborates her account.) According to Mahoney's notes from the interview, Christie Marino called the report "a slap in the face. I'd give it a big F." The girl made a point of not blaming Irving Oil for her mother's death, Mahoney says. "She didn't go there at all. She just said the report was really suspect because it wasn't independent."

Later that afternoon, while Mahoney was writing her story, she got a call from Scott Anderson about the interview with Cynthia Marino's daughter. "There's an issue with that and you're going to have to come here to Saint John tomorrow to talk about it," Anderson said. He refused to explain further. "We're not going to run the story. Bring your notes and come here."

Mahoney was scared. "It was my first big job." She typed up all the daughter's answers from her notes—though, crucially, not the questions she had asked. When she arrived at Crown Street, she asked Anderson, "Is this an Irving thing?"

"Oh no, no, it's not that," she remembers him saying. "We'll talk to Neil."

In Reynolds's office, she sat on a large leather couch and told them what had happened. Reynolds pointed out that Mahoney didn't have her questions transcribed, and asked her what she had said to Christie Marino. He was "quiet and kind of terrifying," Mahoney remembers. She told him she asked neutral questions, but Reynolds said he believed she had told the teenager, "You must really hate the Irvings." Mahoney said it wasn't true. Reynolds fired her.

Mahoney later heard that Bob Marino had come home to learn his daughter had spoken to a reporter and feared she had unknowingly violated a confidentiality clause in an apparent settlement he had reached with Irving Oil about his wife's death. Somewhere amid the various conversations—daughter to father, or father in his subsequent phone call to Irving Oil—Mahoney was said to have prompted the teenage girl with the suggestion that she hated the Irvings. "That's not at all how it went down," insists Gary Dimmock. "It was very clear to me" that Mahoney acted professionally: "You can see an overprotective father, whose wife had literally just died, getting it wrong and freaking out, thinking, 'Oh my God, it's the Irvings.'"

From the swirl of newsroom gossip and speculation, Mahoney says, there emerged a suggestion that after Bob Marino had called Irving Oil, "one of the Irvings was seen in the newsroom that afternoon, and had a discussion with Neil." This is uncon-firmed, and while Arthur Irving still owned 40 percent of New Brunswick Publishing, he and his family—the oil side of the empire—no longer played a role in the paper. He had not been involved in hiring Valerie Millen or Neil Reynolds. And Reynolds would swear years later that "in the four years I worked at the *Telegraph-Journal* I never had a single unwarranted interference in the operations of the paper."

Mahoney went back to her car. "I'm sure I was sobbing by that point," she says, "and the next thing is that I was running low on gas, and I had to stop to fill up on the way back to Fredericton and, of course"—she chuckles—"where do I have to stop but at an Irving gas station."

Back in Fredericton, Jackie Webster, the former *Telegraph-Journal* reporter resurrected by Reynolds as a columnist, found Mahoney a lawyer, who got her rehired for the rest of the summer.

She returned to Carleton in the fall and, thanks in part to the stir the incident created in the small world of Canadian journalism—*Frank* magazine wrote it up and called her "plucky"—she later landed a job at the *Toronto Star*. Mahoney now works for *The Globe and Mail*.

There is another possible explanation for Mahoney's firing. "Neil's big thing to me was that I shouldn't have interviewed a child," Mahoney says. She argued Christie Marino was eighteen, legally an adult, and had volunteered that she was familiar with the report. But Reynolds felt strongly about the vulnerability of children, as he'd demonstrated with the Kingston cathedral and Kingsclear stories; he may have considered the daughter off-limits. Mahoney is not persuaded: "I thought the age thing was a total red herring," she says, convinced "that Neil was grasping at things for reasons to fire me." If there was a confidential settlement between the Marinos and Irving Oil, Mahoney says, a journalist was not bound to keep it secret. "An independent-minded editor wouldn't stand for that or react the way he did," she says. "I thought he was allowing himself and the paper to be used by other forces."

Reynolds had been promised independence but "we all assumed he had a fine line to tread," Richard Foot says. Stories about the owners apparently still required extra care. "When it came to the Irvings," Dimmock says, "the rule was you just had to make sure everything was totally solid." It was a vivid reminder that the family was still very present.

And they were about to become even more present.

7

OUT OF HIS SYSTEM

In the spring of 1995, Neil Reynolds called Carolyn Ryan into his office to tell her about an unusual hiring he was making for the *Evening Times-Globe*. Jim Irving's seventeen-year-old son, Jamie, was graduating from high school in June. He was fascinated by journalism. "He would really love to be a summer student here," Reynolds told her. "The budget will be made available to us." The editor-in-chief added, Ryan remembers, that Jim Irving didn't think much of the idea, but "the family thought it would be good to let him get it out of his system."

Jamie Irving had tried the conventional Irving route the previous summer, in the woods: the kind of work his father, Jim, his grandfather J.K, and his great-grandfather K.C., adored and understood—the height of Irvingness. Jamie's job with J.D. Irving Ltd. was to walk the perimeter of each logging cut with a GPS device, generating data that allowed foresters to calculate how many trees had been cut. The primitive GPS unit was large and heavy, forcing Jamie to wear it over his shoulders like a backpack; its long antenna kept getting caught in branches. Meanwhile, bugs ate him alive. Spending his days in a newsroom looked pretty good.

Then there was Jamie's uncle, Paul Zed, an ambitious Saint John lawyer married to Judith Irving, J.K.'s second daughter. Zed was elected in 1993 as the Liberal MP for Fundy-Royal, a constituency that included a large, traditionally conservative rural area along with the well-to-do Saint John suburb of Rothesay. Politics "sort of intrigued me," Jamie said in a rare interview in 2003. And Zed's political ascent coincided with tensions between Jamie and his father. No one in Saint John will discuss the problem, but Jamie "didn't like it when his father got mad at him," says an acquaintance. Jamie once told Mark Tunney his father was "the only person that can make me piss myself." Zed, on the other hand, was a consummate politician: flashy, fun, and intoxicatingly human in the way he worked a room, a refreshing change from Jim Irving's no-nonsense style. With Uncle Paul there were no pressures, no expectations, no performance standards to live up to. "He acted like a friend to Jamie," says the acquaintance. "Zed was like the permissive father figure, the great friendly uncle who allows you to do everything because there's no consequence for him, like the relative who gives your kids sugar."

Through Zed, Jamie got to know some of the journalists working at the *Telegraph-Journal* and the *Times-Globe*. He found the newsroom romantic and exciting. "You got to gossip around a lot and it was fun," Jamie said. "I like that. And it seemed like a pretty good job." He was particularly fascinated by Neil Reynolds. "All of a sudden the papers weren't the same. They could be salacious. Reynolds was experimenting with stuff all the time.... That was the first thing I wanted to do was go work with Reynolds and those people."

This desire baffled Jamie's family. "It was like having leprosy," says someone who knew him. "His family hated having the newspapers, but had decided it was better to have them than not have them." The Irvings were said to be as perplexed by this asset as K.C. had been in 1969 when he told the Davey committee it was "pretty hard to answer" what kind of "activity" he saw the papers generating. Jamie himself acknowledged the newspapers were "a little atypical" for his family. "The media business is much more an intellectual-property business as opposed to manufacturing or something like that," he would say. "That's why it's probably perceived to be a little bit different from what they're usually doing, making lumber or paper or something."

Indeed, in 2002, Jamie would tell Geoffrey Stevens, then writing a biography of Dalton Camp, that his father, Jim, had told him, "I don't want you there. Those bastards write bad stuff about us." But—remarkably in a family that placed a premium on marching in lockstep with your forebears—Jamie Irving seemed determined to go his own way.

All of K.C. Irving's grandchildren were groomed from an early age, as their fathers had been, to assume important roles in the family empire. "As a youngster, I spent a lot of time travelling around with my father and my grandfather in the summertime, in the back of the car, the back of the airplane," Jim, Jamie's father, recalled in the 1998 CBC documentary *The Irvings: Unlocking the Mystery*. "It always seemed like we were going somewhere and it always had something to do with the woods." Jim's cousin John, Jack's son, remembered joining his dad for "quite fascinating" impromptu evening and weekend visits to Irving operations. Kenneth, Arthur's oldest son, described "the shaking-hand drill that my grandfather used to make my brother and I do before he took us through the paper mills or the refinery on the weekend. We'd have to practise looking him in the eye and shaking hands: 'How do you do?' It was important to him for us to be very polite and respectful of anyone we met along the way." Kenneth understood that he was being trained to take over Irving Oil from his father. "That would be my ultimate career goal, yes," he said.

Once K.C.'s grandchildren were ready, the path was cleared for them. After J.D. Irving Ltd. bought a Prince Edward Island frozen-food company, C.M. McLean Ltd., to expand into the potato business, the new general manager, Jack Duplessis, was demoted, replaced by Robert Irving, J.K.'s second son, eighteen years his junior. Duplessis sued for unjust dismissal and won. During the trial, J.K. testified that, in effect, it came back to family: "I needed to know everything that was going on," he told the court, "and I knew Robert would tell me."

J.K.'s eldest, Jim, also inherited the Irving eye for detail and the appetite for hard work. One of his first jobs was at the new stevedoring company Irving established to load newsprint on boats to the United States. "He was a tall, goofy-looking guy, and excitable," says Abel LeBlanc, then the president of the longshoremen's union. "He wanted to learn how we were loading the lumber and why we were doing it this way. He could see there was good productivity. That was his big concern: productivity." Doug Tyler, a former provincial cabinet minister, says Jim Irving "puts in more hours any week than any employee that works for him. You can't run an organization that big, keep it, maintain it, by putting in thirty or forty hours a week.... On the weekend, when I'm fishing, or in the winter, when I'm snowmobiling, nine times out of ten he's working."

In the nineties, Jim's generation came into its own. In his book about the Irvings, Harvey Sawler reports how a provincial government official watched J.K. defer to Jim on a land deal in Saint John. "Are you okay with that?" the father asked the son. The toughness, too, was passed down: Jim was overseeing Kent Homes, a manufacturer of prefabricated houses in K.C.'s hometown of Bouctouche, when the union went on strike in 1994. With Jim's approval, the general manager, Rino Volpé, prepared to move the company to Nova Scotia, even taking out help-wanted ads there. Volpé says the money-losing company would have been shut down long before if not for the family's sentimental attachment to K.C.'s roots. The union agreed to wage cuts, and Kent Homes stayed put, another victory for Irving brinksmanship laced with the rhetoric of hometown loyalty.

Two years later, Mary Jean Irving, J.K.'s youngest daughter, went looking for a loan from the Prince Edward Island government for the expansion of Master Packaging, a box-manufacturing company she established on the island. She had clashed with the previous Liberal government when she bought up huge tracts of the island's potato farmland, relenting only when a potential court fight risked exposing "other private aspects of the Irving family's business interests," as she put it. Despite that confrontation, the Liberals helped finance the box plant; now the new Progressive Conservative administration turned down her request for another loan. "Once I was told no, then I made my move to New Brunswick," Mary Jean recounted in 1998. The government there was happy to provide a loan for a plant in the Moncton area, and she moved two production lines—and half the jobs—from PEI. "Mary Jean has got a real business sense," J.K. would say proudly. She was eventually inducted into the Prince Edward Island Business Hall of Fame.

Kenneth, too, had to learn to be tough. He helped his father, Arthur, run the oil refinery during the two-year strike. Author Harvey Sawler quoted a source saying Kenneth "truly agonized" over it—that he was "tormented" over how the dispute affected workers and their families, but convinced Irving Oil had to stand firm "for the sake of the future of the business." A former company executive told John DeMont, "Arthur was determined that he was going to make Kenneth an Irving if it killed him. He was twice as hard on him as the other employees." The son apparently passed his father's test, moving into the top job in 2000. He later publicly thanked his father "for the corporate culture that I'm so lucky to be able to work within."

John, Jack's oldest son, was, like his father, a little different. The first Irving to earn an MBA—from Harvard—he was gregarious, fascinated by technology, and resentful that his father was frequently perceived as the junior partner to J.K. and Arthur. John often joined his father for meetings with executives at the *Gleaner* in Fredericton and the *Times-Transcript* in Moncton, where he didn't always impress. "He said he wanted the *Times-Transcript* to be the best damned newspaper in North America," publisher Mike Bembridge recalls, "without knowing what that entailed." For a time, John was a nomad in the empire. "When he came back [with his MBA] and went into Irving Oil," Joan Carlisle Irving says, "he brought some Harvard ideas, and Arthur didn't like that, so Arthur threw him out." John found his way to J.D. Irving Ltd., but was not welcome there, either: it is widely known in Saint John that Jim Irving didn't think much of his cousin John's abilities, and John was no more fond of Jim.

On the surface, however, the message was that the same harmony existed among K.C.'s grandchildren as among his three sons. "Rob, Kenneth, Arthur, and I, [and] John, we travel around together," Jim said in 1998. "Every so often we all get together, get in the plane, go visit some operations. And we'll just talk." From his cousin Kenneth, however, came a different message: autonomy. "We're all very different people," he said, "but because we all run different businesses, it doesn't pose any issue." There was no chance, the family said, of a McCain-style succession battle, because unlike McCain Foods, the Irvings were not a single company. "We're so diversified," said Robert, who ran the potato, trucking, and tissue businesses from Moncton. "Everybody has his area of responsibility and everybody's focused on trying to make that business better."

Only John—not the heir apparent to either of the signature Irving operations, forestry or oil—hinted that the future was unsettled, that there was work to be done finding roles for the various cousins. "I think it comes down to who would like to do what, how they'd like to do it, and what their skill set is," he said. "That kind of decision in the end can become somewhat self-evident. That's something we're all comfortable with."

And from Jim there was, appropriately, a tree metaphor. Asked about succession in the 1998 CBC documentary, J.K. said, "We're very fortunate because we have a very good crop coming up." Across the table, Jim chuckled: "A good crop, eh? Ha. Now we're a crop. We're going to be clear-cut in a minute here."

Jamie Irving, Jim's oldest child, represented the next generation, the eldest son of the eldest son of the eldest son, a *great*-grandchild of K.C. going to work for an Irving company. A provincial government official remembered him, at the age of fourteen, sitting in on a business meeting with his father about forestry. Now he had chosen, of all things, those gosh-damned *newspapers,* to the dismay of Jim. "He thought that wouldn't be a good idea," Jamie recalled. Jim seemed uneasy with the autonomy the papers had, with the inability to absorb them completely into Irving corporate culture. Jamie remembered his father telling him, "I don't really have much to do with the papers, and they run on their own, and they can be a bit wild and you're a young guy, and I don't think you should be down there."

There was also the question of appearance. The papers had to be *seen* as independent. "They were sensitive that having an Irving in the newsroom with an Irving byline would reinforce the impressions that they were trying to get past," Carolyn Ryan says. "They knew that this would be seen by some eyes as the family wanting to be in control of the newsroom." Jim considered it bad for the Irvings when any reporter at the *Telegraph-Journal* was tough on, say, a powerful provincial cabinet minister that other family companies had to deal with. "If it's you specifically," Jim reportedly told Jamie, "that only causes us grief."

But Jamie persisted, and Jim finally relented—and K.C. Irving's great-grandson caught the journalism bug. "The whole newsroom action was kind of exciting," Jamie recalled, describing the scramble to meet two press times a day, the *Times-Globe*'s in the morning and the *Telegraph-Journal*'s at night. "I got to watch all this stuff unfold: yelling, and excitement, and deadlines. It was fun." Soon he was writing stories, "quirky stuff," he said, "people stories," a niche that avoided the potential conflict inherent in his family's businesses. Jamie "acknowledged that it was going to be hard for him to do certain stories because of his family name," says Carolyn Ryan, "and he found better stories." That first summer, he reported on a reunion of war veterans, the life of carnies working at the Atlantic National Exhibition midway, and a farmer who grew a two-hundred-pound pumpkin for an agricultural fair. "You start to find out stories about people, and they're really interesting, or you find them interesting," he said.

Gradually, he took on more than summer fluff. Other stories that first summer under his byline were about City Hall's decision to remove an eyesore building, a cloud of forest-fire smoke blowing in over the city from Quebec, and a daring rescue of two canoeists at the Reversing Falls. "That was great," he said. "That's why I really liked the job." Jim Irving might not have realized it, but the chances of Jamie ever getting it out of his system, of wanting to run a pulp mill, were dropping fast.

Jamie's colleagues in the newsroom found him the furthest thing from the heir apparent to a billion-dollar empire. "He kind of shuffled around and didn't seem to expect the world would revolve around him," says one journalist. "I expected something different." Amy Cameron, who befriended him, says he was "quite shy and awkward and pleasant," an assessment shared by just about everyone. "He stumbled over his words," says Carolyn Ryan. "You had to figure out what he was trying to say. But he was a very good writer from the beginning. Jamie's writing was clean and clear from day one."

Jamie knew his colleagues were watching for any sign he might pull rank. He never did. He seldom spoke about his family, except jokingly, as when he described what happened when he handed his licence to the other driver in a fender-bender: "Her eyes lit up like a cash register." This let some of the other reporters relax around him—but only to a point. "I remember feeling for him, thinking that this would really suck," Cameron says. "No one's going to tell you anything. No one's going to bitch about their employer. So he had a lonely existence there. It was sort of an impossible position in some ways, but he handled it, I thought, well."

In September 1995, Jamie began his Bachelor of Arts degree in English at the University of Ottawa. This put him close to his uncle Paul Zed, who introduced him to the movers and shakers on Parliament Hill. He returned to the Saint John newsroom for two more summers. "Each year they'd give me a little bit more rope," he said. "There were some good reporters and good editors who taught me how to write, who taught me how to form a coherent sentence." After he finished his BA, he enrolled at Carleton University's journalism school. One day, Carolyn Ryan got a phone call from one of Jamie's fellow students: they were paired up to write profiles of each other, a typical reporting class assignment, and Jamie had suggested his classmate call Ryan, his former boss. "I could tell she had no idea what an Irving was," Ryan says. "What else have you found out about him?" Ryan asked. "Well, he comes from a big family, and he wants a career in journalism," the classmate said. "That's all?" Ryan asked, guessing the student would flunk the assignment if her story didn't mention who he was. "His family owns our newspaper," Ryan told the student, "and most of New Brunswick."

The conversation provided Ryan with an amusing anecdote, but it also revealed two things: Jamie Irving was shy about being an Irving—and he had not managed to get journalism out of his system.

Philip Lee was one of the journalists Jamie Irving watched closely. Lee, too, was quiet and shy, and could be awkward in conversation, but he brought a sharp intelligence and a literary ambition to his work, prompting Neil Reynolds to make him editor of the *New Brunswick Reader*. In early 1995, Reynolds was casting around for a new project, something grand and epic. "I said, 'Why don't we do something about Atlantic salmon rivers,'" remembers Lee, a dedicated angler. New Brunswick boasts two world-famous salmon rivers, the Miramichi and the Restigouche. But the number of salmon returning to spawn each year was dropping. "I wasn't interested in doing another piece about how the salmon were in trouble and the government should do more," Lee says. His research led him to a dramatically different thesis, one that captured Reynolds's imagination.

After trips to Quebec, Scotland, and Iceland, Lee wrote a series of long, beautifully crafted stories that ran on the front page for thirty-six days straight in October and November 1995 under the title "Watershed Down." They made the case for getting the government out of river regulation in favour of private, community-based management. Day after day, Lee told stories bolstering the argument, such as a profile of the non-profit, self-financing local river management groups in Quebec. The decline of the Atlantic salmon through government mismanagement became a morality tale that confirmed Reynolds's eco-libertarian views. "Hundreds of politicians and bureaucrats were amply paid to preside over the demise of the Atlantic salmon and the destruction of their rivers," Reynolds would write. Lee's prescription, local management, was positively Jeffersonian: small, organic, and driven by the moral responsibility and enlightened self-interest that come with personal freedom.

The sprawl of "Watershed Down" was the talk of the newsroom. Even Lee acknowledges it was criticized as "mind-numbing" and the volume was "maybe overkill in retrospect," but its defenders still marvel at the bravura of it. "You'd think, 'That's crazy,'" says one reporter, "but it was kind of cool that they tried it." It is Lee's most remembered work at the newspaper; people still talk to him about it. "Neil would talk about journalism being literary when people remembered it," he says, "and that was what was remarkable about that."

Some of Lee's colleagues also felt a few of the pieces dovetailed nicely with J.K. and Jim Irving's world view. One instalment, "Debunking the Myth of Clearcutting," cited a study that found the controversial tree-harvesting method did not harm nearby rivers if managed properly. "We need to fiercely protect and restore our salmon habitat," Lee wrote. "And we need to make sure that when we point fingers, they're pointed in the right direction."

The *Telegraph* certainly wasn't, to borrow Jim Irving's phrase, "pissing on" J.D. Irving Ltd. now. The company gave Lee access to its foresters and its salmon lodge on the Restigouche at Downs Gulch, but he says that played no role in how he wrote the series. Later the company helped fund the publication of "Watershed Down" in book form. "They probably somewhat agreed with the conclusions of the piece, which I pursued more for the contrarian nature of it," Lee says. "I was probably inspired by Neil to take a contrarian view that private-property ownership can be benefi-cial for conservation. I still believe that to be true."

Philip Lee wasn't the only *Telegraph-Journal* reporter traipsing around the woods with the Irvings in 1995. Richard Foot visited tree nurseries, clear-cuts, and mills for "Timber Land," a series on a core family business, the forestry industry. At the Irving paper mill in Saint John, his guide was Jim Irving himself. "He was very warm with all the employees, whether they were people in the management office or the guys operating the machines," Foot says. "He knew everything about how that place worked and who worked there."

Reynolds came up with the idea for the series after he and his two managing editors, Scott Anderson and Carolyn Ryan, were given a tour of the Irving operations. "I think they were very impressed by what they had seen," says Foot, grasping the industry's importance to the New Brunswick economy and to J.K. Irving and his family. "I think they were trying to say to the Irvings that they shared some of their values, they shared an interest in some of their core industries, and they weren't just there to 'butt heads with you guys.' So, let's explore this industry that's such a big part of their lives." This, Foot says, is an important facet of Reynolds's philosophy: his idea of civility meant not taking on the owners just for the sake of it. "Some people might assume that a fearless editor would take control of a daily newspaper and say, 'To heck with what this powerful family, with its fingers in all the pies, wants; they've hired me and I'm going to run the paper as I see fit, and I don't really care about what they do.' I don't think that's how Neil came at it. He had respect for them as owners and business people."

Forestry is always a story in New Brunswick, a province that was little more than a timber colony for the British when it was created in 1784. When Foot began his series, one in fourteen working people in the province were in the industry; in 1992, their wages, $450 million, made up 7 percent of the total provincial income. The commercial forest, including leased public land, was 90 percent of the surface area of the province. Its trees became the glossy paper of *National Geographic*, the pages of daily newspapers in Japan, the cardboard boxes of banana pickers in the Caribbean, and the phone books of Europe.

In the early days of K.C. Irving's growth, wood was plentiful. But he foresaw his mills becoming ever larger, ever more efficient, ever hungrier. He would have to grow to grow: in 1957, he started planting trees at Black Brook, in the watershed of the Restigouche River, with three thousand infant softwoods. The next year he opened a tree nursery near Juniper, at the head-waters of the Miramichi. "The whole process became a passion for him," Ralph Costello wrote in his biography. Irving roamed the long, straight rows of saplings, inspecting and pruning. He learned which species grew fastest, which were susceptible to frost, which were preferred by hungry insects—all to determine what should be planted for harvests decades later. "Many of us will not live to see today's trees grow to maturity," he said when he planted his ceremonial two-hundred-millionth sapling in 1986. "We are giving our children and our children's children the natural heritage inherited so many years ago." It was another of K.C.'s long games: as with his estate trust in Bermuda, he was ensuring that what he built would live on after he was dead. By 1995, Juniper was producing fifteen million seedlings a year.

Environmentalists objected to the plantations. Thousands of acres of monoculture destroyed the diverse natural habitat that other plants and animals relied on, they said. Clear-cutting, the industrial-scale razing of trees by giant machines, was equally destructive. But Reynolds felt that story had been done to death. In his first draft, Foot wrote, tartly, that J.D. Irving Ltd. called itself "the Tree-Planting Company" because of the four hundred million it had planted—but was silent on how many trees it cut. Reynolds removed that, but not out of fear, Foot says. "I never felt that he was afraid of the Irvings in terms of what we might say in the forestry series." Rather, "I don't think he was going to run something unnecessarily that would irritate them if it wasn't worth it. He said to me once, 'I'm prepared to take a bullet in my job, but only for a good reason.'"

What fascinated Reynolds was the economics of the industry. Within that framework, Foot asked tough questions. He profiled Lawrence McCrea, the wise old owner of a small-scale private woodlot, who accused large forestry companies, including Irving, of freeloading off New Brunswick's Crown lands. In 1982, the provincial government had reorganized its publicly owned forests into ten licences it leased to the big industrial companies, including J.D. Irving Ltd.—a subsidy in disguise, McCrea argued. "What body in Canada makes more money than the Irvings?" he asked in the front-page story. By his math, the government spent more money maintaining the Crown leases than what it collected in taxes and royalties from the companies that held those leases. "When the wood that's taken off our Crown lands doesn't pay its own way, there's something wrong," McCrea said. "It would appear to me that our public forests are almost a liability now."

In response, Foot says, he got generalities and slogans from Jim Irving. For an executive with an encyclopedic knowledge of his company's operations, "he wasn't very forthcoming" in their interview. "He didn't want to be talking to a reporter.... He didn't really go into detail. And there was this defensiveness, as if we were out to judge him unfairly."

Sometime later, after Reynolds left the *Telegraph-Journal*, Foot says Scott Anderson told him the Irvings "never understood what we wanted to do or what we were trying to do at the paper." He remembers Anderson saying, "We tried to work with them but they never *got* Neil, and they never understood that we were trying to make it a great newspaper." If Anderson was right, if there was no room in Jim Irving's all-business mindset for the idea of muckraking investigative journalism, it was no wonder he wanted his son Jamie to "get it out of his system."

By 1996, Neil Reynolds was thinking big: he wanted the *Telegraph-Journal* to be the leading newspaper not just in New Brunswick, but in all of Atlantic Canada. He had hired a journalist in Halifax to cover regional business stories, and mused about putting a correspondent in Newfoundland, where the offshore oil industry would soon transform the economy. And he hired a reporter straight out of journalism school named Steve McKinley to open a bureau in Charlottetown, Prince Edward Island. "Every day," Scott Anderson told McKinley, "we want you to file something for us on the *Irving Whale*."

The raising of the *Irving Whale* was, for Reynolds, a perfect story. Not only was it chock full of government bungling, its moral dimension lived up, almost literally, to Reynolds's metaphor that journalists should "patrol humanity's beaches and to do what we can to clean them up." And, like any good narrative, it would unfold over several weeks, building to a climax: the lifting of—or disastrous failure to lift—a wrecked ship from the ocean floor, and the extraction from its hull of thousands of litres of oil. "Neil and Scott wanted to just completely own the story," McKinley says. "They wanted it to be the definitive record of what happened."

J.K. Irving remembers well the day the *Irving Whale* sank in the Gulf of St. Lawrence, between Prince Edward Island and Quebec's Magdalen Islands. It was September 7, 1970, and he and his father were in Philadelphia on business. They stayed overnight—"it wasn't a fancy hotel," J.K. says—and were having a pre-dawn breakfast with the night watchman when the phone rang. "Is one of your names Irving?" the watchman asked. J.K. took the phone: it was the man who ran their marine division. "Mr. Irving, we've got a problem," J.K. remembers him saying. "On the other telephone here, I've got the captain of the tug, and he's got the *Whale* in tow, and he's out in the Gulf, and the *Whale* is sinking, and he wants to know what in blazes he should do."

"Head for the handiest shore," J.K. remembers telling him, "and try to beach the thing." He and his father left immediately for the airport, where the Irving company plane, a Douglas DC-3, was waiting. "We didn't stop in Saint John," J.K. says. "We flew right out to the gulf where the position was—we talked to the radio in Saint John and got the position—and we searched for the *Whale*. But the *Whale* was gone. No oil slicks. We couldn't find anything. That is what happened to the *Whale*. There's a long story after that. It was quite famous."

Famous, but not the way the Irvings would want: the boat sat on the bottom of the Gulf of St. Lawrence for a quarter century, occasionally burping up small amounts of its cargo of more than four thousand metric tonnes of Bunker C oil, which drifted to the beaches of the Magdalens, Cape Breton, and Prince Edward Island. Fishermen, whose livelihood was drawn from the waters around the ship, and who knew how hulls corrode over time, lobbied Ottawa to deal with the wreck. "If there had been a major leak, a major rupture, a major failure in the barge's ability to contain the oil, and if the wind was just so, if the wind was north-east, it could have easily driven oil onto PEI's shores," says Barry Murray, then a director of the island fishermen's association.

The federal government finally hired a salvage company to lift the boat in the summer of 1995, but just weeks before the scheduled date, J.D. Irving Ltd. revealed to federal authorities that the *Whale* had been heated by a fuel called Therminol fr-1, which was 80 percent polychlorinated biphenyls, or PCBs. Though they had been legal and in common use at the time the *Whale* sank, by 1995 the use of PCBs was increasingly restricted and regulated because of studies showing potential harm to animals.

Yet "no one involved with the recovery project had thought of the possible presence of PCBs in the heating system," a federal official said sheepishly.

The revelation added to the impetus to act: the ship would likely break up in another ten to fifteen years, releasing the remaining Bunker C oil and the 6,800 litres of PCB-laced heating fluid into the gulf. But it also complicated matters. A Quebec environmental group convinced a judge to stop the salvage operation until Ottawa conducted a new environmental assessment that took into account the added risk of the PCBs spilling into the ocean. The delay frustrated the fishermen. "We didn't think it was going to make much difference," Murray says. "It was a ticking bomb, so if you blow yourself up dismantling the bomb, is that worse than letting the bomb blow up?" But the raising of the *Whale* was pushed back to 1996.

As McKinley headed to Charlottetown to establish the *Telegraph* bureau that summer, he told Anderson his main concern about covering the *Whale*. "You're going to ask me to write stories about the guys who own the paper all the time," he remembers saying. "They're not always going to like that." Anderson agreed, but told McKinley, "You can write whatever you want and as long as you get it right, I won't let them touch you. But if you get it wrong, I'm probably going to have to fire you." In the end, McKinley "never heard a peep" from the Irvings, though when he later relocated to Saint John, he was told they had complained to Anderson several times.

The lifting of the *Whale* would be difficult and expensive: salvagers needed forty-eight hours of clear, calm weather so they could place slings under the ship and raise it to the surface. Then they would have to move a submersible barge under it to complete the lift and carry the wreck to shore. A Halifax consultant had tried to convince Ottawa to pump the cargo out first, citing "the inherent risk of massive and uncontrollable oil release" if the hull broke during the lift. This was a powerful argument: the Gulf of St. Lawrence, a federal study noted, was home to almost forty endangered, threatened, or vulnerable species, as well as being "a highly regarded tourist area noted for its unique beauty and mystery." The closure of the commercial snow crab fishery alone would cost almost a thousand jobs and millions of dollars in lost economic activity. But an American consultant, Willard Searle, a former chief salvage officer for the U.S. Navy, said the barge was structurally sound. "The ship must be raised immediately and all efforts should be spent towards not disturbing the cargo or the heating fluid," he wrote in a report for Ottawa in early 1996. "The effort should be directed towards preserving what you've got and getting it the hell out of there. And quickly."

During Ottawa's environmental assessment consultations in the winter of 1995–96, one question had come up again and again in meetings with provincial officials and organizations around the gulf: what were the Irvings contributing to clean up their mess? Four of their companies were involved: the tug pulling the *Whale* was owned by Universal Sales, but chartered to Atlantic Towing; J.D. Irving Ltd. owned the *Whale* and Irving Oil the cargo. Even so, their legal obligation was not clear. When the *Whale* sank, Canada's offshore legal jurisdiction was only twelve miles, meaning the barge went down in what were then international waters. Nor was it certain whether a shipping-spill insurance fund should pay, given the fund didn't exist in 1970. "Our lawyers are looking at remedies we might have against Irving," a federal official said.

Atlantic Towing offered to provide backup emergency response equipment at the site, and to tow the barge to its shipyard in Halifax, remove the Bunker C, and clean the wreck, the company said in a letter, "in the best interests of the environment in general"—hoping, it added, that in return Ottawa would let the Irvings keep the barge. Officials estimated the Irving offer was worth about $2 million of the $16 million the salvage was then estimated to cost, not enough to dissuade the federal environment minister, Sheila Copps, from rattling her regulatory sabre. In late 1995, Copps had asked the RCMP to investigate whether the Irvings had broken any laws by waiting twenty-five years to mention the PCBs, even though other federal officials acknowledged knowing of their presence as early as 1992.

The *Whale* salvage was becoming a public relations battle. "The government of the day was pursuing a political agenda," a judge later wrote, because, in the wake of the *Exxon Valdez* disaster, "the principle of 'polluter pays' was in vogue." As the weather window for the lift approached, Ottawa arranged for the Coast Guard to carry journalists out to the site in helicopters so they could photograph the salvage vessels getting into position. "They were overzealous as far as we were concerned," Jim Irving says. "That's a nice way to say it."

The day the salvage finally took place, "it happened way faster than it was supposed to," Steve McKinley says. The crews planned to inspect the hull mid-lift, but everything was going so smoothly they pressed ahead. When the ship reached the surface, one of the salvagers jumped aboard, then radioed back, "This is the *Irving Whale* calling." This became the *Telegraph-Journal*'s front-page headline the next day, superimposed on a striking photo McKinley snapped of the rusty hulk sitting on the surface of the Gulf of St. Lawrence. "Seeing the thing above the water was the most exciting thing I'd done as a reporter," he says. Reynolds had the dramatic resolution of his narrative—but, McKinley points out, "it was an ending, but not *the* ending."

The *Whale* lived on, cleaned and refurbished by the Irvings and put back into service carrying wood chips for J.D. Irving Ltd., first as ATL 2701, then as the *Atlantic Sea Lion.* "You know, gosh-damn it, after we got it up, Jim, you changed the name on it," J.K. says during their interview for this book. Jim, all business, replies: "We didn't need to keep perpetuating that [name] every time." J.K. shakes his head. "I disagreed with you on that." Finally Jim laughs. "I know," he says. "Okay. Give it a rest. Geez. The *Whale.*"

The story lived on, too, long after Steve McKinley left Charlottetown and after Neil Reynolds left the *Telegraph-Journal.* The federal government sued the Irving companies for $42 million in costs in 1998. Two years later, the *Telegraph* reported, they settled the case with the Irvings agreeing to pay $5 million. "This is home to us," Jim Irving says now, falling back on the familiar trope. "If something goes wrong, we'll do our darnedest to fix it, [with] everything we've got, all our energy and resources." He nods at his father: "Right away, you jump in the plane and you go look for the *Whale.* Bang, Sunday morning, no fooling around. That's how we go about it, because this is home. We don't want a mess in our backyard."

There was one more chapter to the story. Jim's paean aside, the Irvings didn't actually have to pay Ottawa that $5 million settlement. They filed a claim with their insurers for it. The insurers refused the claim, arguing, in part, that the settlement was not a legal requirement but merely another tactic in Irving's public-relations battle with Ottawa. In 2012, Federal Court justice Sean Harrington ruled for the Irvings. "Although favourable publicity may have been achieved," he wrote, "Irving was putting paid to its liability, no more, no less." Forty-two years after the sinking of the *Irving Whale*, the insurers paid the bill. The *Telegraph-Journal*, which had covered the salvage so breathlessly fourteen years earlier, did not report on Harrington's ruling.

Jim Irving chuckles now about the wall-to-wall coverage in 1996. "I thought there must be precious little to do," he says, "if that's all they've got to do, is write about a sunken boat." What may have been a more candid assessment of the affair—and the attendant publicity—came in the months after the lift, when J.K. Irving had a rare meeting with the *Telegraph* editors who had been touring the forestry operations. One asked him what he learned from the *Irving Whale* saga. "I learned," he answered, "to never put your name on something that's going to sink."

On May 21, 1996, Neil Reynolds sent a memo to the staff of the *Telegraph-Journal* and the *Evening Times-Globe* to tell them the papers had won the Canadian Journalism Foundation's inaugural Excellence in Journalism Award for overall editorial content. "I hope that you share this sense of achievement with me," Reynolds wrote. "In this award, we all share." At the award ceremony at Rideau Hall in Ottawa, Reynolds "gave this nice little talk," says Philip Lee, "about how he felt we were knights who had been out fighting battles and had been called in for commendations from the king. It was a lovely image. And he praised J.K. Irving and said he felt he was a perfect owner."

It was Reynolds's last triumph at the Irving newspapers. Conrad Black's Hollinger Inc. had taken control of Southam News and recruited him to shake up the *Ottawa Citizen*. "I did some scouting around," Black says, "and it didn't take long for Neil Reynolds's name to come up." At his going-away party in

October 1996, the newsroom staff presented Reynolds with a spoof front page featuring his journalistic obsessions: "Salmon Blah Blah," "Forestry Blah Blah," "Animals Blah Blah," "Acadians Blah Blah," said the headlines.

A week later, the *Telegraph-Journal* carried an essay by its departing editor. The foreword for the book version of Philip Lee's salmon series, it doubled as Reynolds's New Brunswick valedictory. Returning to his favourite themes, he cited Lee's series as the epitome of a newspaper's higher calling as "a daily journal of moral conduct." Anticipating the skepticism of some readers— "do newspaper writers not exist merely to fill the space between the ads?"—he responded: "Newspapers remain—beyond all dispute—the primary forum for the written word. Newspapers remain the literature of the people." On a nearby page, the lead editorial was a glowing tribute to Reynolds, containing a hopeful prediction: "In New Brunswick, the business of journalism will no doubt continue evolving without him, just as it has always done. But the art of journalism as it is practiced here will for a long time be coloured by his legacy."

No one could say for sure, though, whether Reynolds had made any lasting change to how the Irvings saw their newspapers. In 2009, he would describe them as "essentially ideal proprietors," but Richard Foot would often ponder Scott Anderson telling him how they never "got" Reynolds. "From their point of view," Foot says, "the family never understood the investigative journalism, putting the paper on the map, making it a great paper."

For one Irving, however, Reynolds remained a touchstone. Young Jamie freelanced for the *Citizen* while studying in Ottawa, and Reynolds later wrote him a reference letter to the admissions staff of the School of Journalism at Columbia University in New York City. "It was very genuine," says Reynolds's widow, Donna

Jacobs. "It was basically, 'Here's a person who's young and who's going to be in a position to take over a newspaper empire,' if you want to put it that way —a large number of papers, 'and it would be a good thing if you would accept him.'"

Reynolds understood the importance of that moment in 1995 when he agreed to hire Jamie Irving as a summer reporter. It wasn't just the introduction of an Irving byline to the news pages: it was a turning point for all the family's newspapers. Amy Cameron says many of the reporters who got to know Jamie in the newsroom that summer sensed "that he would ultimately be their boss one day."

That would inevitably revive the question of the Irving monopoly, but with a new twist. Jamie had limited himself to stories about two-hundred-pound pumpkins that first summer. Now he was on a path toward making decisions about stories considerably more consequential than that—stories about his own family and the future of its multi-billion-dollar empire.

8

STOP THE PRESSES

▼

Something was wrong. It was a Sunday afternoon in the late spring of 1997, and Scott Honeyman, the new editor-in-chief of the *Telegraph-Journal* and the *Evening Times-Globe,* answered his front door to find his boss, the publisher of the papers, Jamie Milne, standing there. The two men saw each other every weekday at the office; an unannounced weekend visit was a sure sign of trouble. Milne, a large, kind-faced man, looked uncomfortable. "There's going to be a letter on page one of tomorrow's paper that you may not like very much," he said.

Honeyman guessed what the problem was. The previous day, in its Saturday lead editorial, the *Telegraph-Journal* had endorsed the Progressive Conservative Party of Canada in the federal election coming on Monday. "The Tories Are the Best Bet for a Prosperous, United Canada," the headline said. Though the PCs were not that different from the governing Liberals in policy, the editorial argued, after four years of the Reform Party and the Bloc Québécois dominating the opposition in Ottawa, "Canada urgently needs a second party with genuine national stature and a base of policy and experience that gives it the capacity to govern." Only the Tories led by Jean Charest could provide that in 1997, the editorial argued.

Anyone paying attention would have seen the endorsement coming. Leading up to Saturday, "we did the full striptease," Honeyman says, running daily editorials eliminating the other parties—Reform, the NDP, the governing Liberals—as unworthy of support. "Certainly by the day before, it would have been very clear where we were going, and nobody said anything." Honeyman had also mentioned the pending PC endorsement to Milne. "I assumed if he had been interested, he would have transmitted it to the Irvings."

Now the Irvings had transmitted something back: extreme displeasure. The letter to the editor on the front page the following day, election day, was from J.K. Irving himself. "It is not simply a matter of not sharing the newspaper's opinion," he wrote. "In this case I disagree completely with the editorial course set by the newspaper."

Honeyman had held senior positions at the *Ottawa Citizen* and *The Vancouver Sun*, and when he applied for Neil Reynolds's job, he was familiar with the criticisms of the Irving papers that had been levied by the Davey committee and the Kent Commission. But, he was told during the interview, "they had taken it seriously, and were trying to stand back from the operation of the papers." Milne, who had replaced Bruce Phinney, hired Honeyman; the new editor met J.K. a week after he'd started the job. "He basically confirmed what [Milne] had said: when you're dealing with matters of the family, all we can ask is that you be fair. And I thought that was a pretty good marching order."

The bigger preoccupation for the new editor was the apprehensive staff. With a commanding bearing and blazing red hair and beard, Honeyman looked like a sea captain of old—but he wasn't Neil Reynolds. "Scott was always being compared to this ghost," says Lisa Hrabluk, one of the first reporters Honeyman hired. For Amy Cameron, "that sense of adventure and excitement and anything goes was no longer there." Others were more forgiving: Richard Foot says while Honeyman lacked Reynolds's flair, "he was harshly judged and unfairly judged." Honeyman understood the dynamic. "There was certainly a lot of suspicion that I was going to change somehow," he says. One fear was he would bring back Canadian Press, an expense that would require cutting reporters. He quickly ruled it out. Honeyman understood, says Steve McKinley, "that people knew what they were doing and how they were working, [so] he let people do what they were good at.... and the paper kind of chugged along quite nicely."

Taking J.K.'s assurance to heart, Honeyman set out to cover the family and its businesses as if they were any other company. "There were certainly stories that you knew were going to annoy the family, and I never heard from them about any of those," he says. Jim Irving dropped by once after a story about logging, and, "without directly addressing what we had done, tried to explain to me the rationale of the forestry division." There was no pressure, though. "He presented it to me as a chance to understand the forestry division. There was no kind of threat, or 'Here's how you were wrong.'" So Honeyman wasn't preoccupied with what they might think when he sat down with the editorial-page staff to discuss the federal election endorsement.

The Irvings usually don't talk about who they vote for. "Ordinarily, politically, we stay quiet," J.K. says. His father, K.C., had been a Liberal until he abandoned the provincial party over the Equal Opportunity Program, though J.K. and Jim liked Liberal premier Frank McKenna's pro-business style and were considered supporters of the party. They could hardly ignore politics: government policy in myriad areas—taxation, shipbuilding, Crown logging leases, environmental reviews, gasoline prices— affected Irving interests. Saint John officials had been lobbying Jean Chrétien's Liberal government in Ottawa to help Saint John Shipbuilding compete with low-cost overseas competitors after it finished the navy frigate contract. In the 1997 campaign, the family had another stake: J.K.'s son-in-law Paul Zed was seeking re-election as a Liberal MP.

J.K.'s letter to the editor mentioned none of this. Instead, he argued the PC endorsement was unrealistic. The prospect of the Tories going from just two seats in the House of Commons to winning power, he pointed out correctly, was "impossible now." The more likely outcome of a PC surge would be an unstable minority government in Ottawa, which—less than two years after Quebecers voted narrowly to reject independence— "could play into the hands of those who would tear the country apart." Chrétien's Liberals had brought Canada's economy back from the brink of disaster, J.K. wrote, and it was not the time to change course. "I believe the newspaper's editorial opinions in the current election are both wrong and short-sighted," he concluded. "I disassociate myself with them completely."

In the interview for this book, J.K. brought up the letter before I could ask about it, during a discussion of editorial independence. "I put one thing in the paper once and I signed it," he offered. "That was the only time. We had a lot at stake. We were that close to—I shouldn't. I shouldn't go there, I guess." When I asked him a bit later to talk about the episode, however, he said, "The frigate program, we were coming that close"—he held his thumb and index finger a half-inch apart—"to closing a deal on a batch of vessels." Then he hesitated again. "I shouldn't go there." Jim spoke up, suggesting the matter not be discussed on the record.

As Saint Johners picked up their papers Monday morning, the day they would vote, they saw the letter at the bottom of the front page, under the headline "Irving Says Telegraph-Journal Is Wrong." It caused a sensation. "There was a buzz," says Mark Leger, one of the editorial-page editors. "How can there not be, when the owner has a front-page letter criticizing the editorial board?" Some saw an attempt to rescue Paul Zed's campaign; Zed was in trouble in his partly rural riding for hedging on gun control. (Zed lost.) Erin Steuter, the Mount Allison University professor, saw it as confirmation that the Irvings controlled their newspapers. "The person who signed the paycheques had made his views clear," she says. "That had to have a chilling effect." Some *Telegraph* journalists found the letter embarrassing and dispiriting, but others took it as evidence that the Irvings did not vet editorials before they were published. "It was indisputable proof of the independence of the newsroom," says editorial writer Peter Simpson. Honeyman calls the post-endorsement letter "the right way to do it." There was a long history of newspaper owners expressing their views on the editorial page, and he saw the letter as merely a variation on that.

For Mark Leger, who was immersed in Irving talk while growing up in Saint John, the letter was "a real signal event.... I remember finding it invigorating, thinking, what a great example of how a paper can function independently. And nothing changed. We all went about our jobs. I remember growing up here, with that shadow, thinking things like this couldn't happen.

To see it actually happen was pretty invigorating for somebody like me."

Still, Honeyman felt a shift in the air. "That whole episode half-convinced me that I was not the right guy for them," he says. "I think I made them uncomfortable from the start, because my editorial judgment was coloured a lot by having worked on big papers." There were stories on crime and the courts, non-Irving stuff, which were sensational and intrusive, and which Honeyman wonders in retrospect whether he should have published. "Some of the shit we disturbed we shouldn't have, or we should have done it in a different way." In the fall of 1997, Honeyman was told he would now be editor-in-chief only of the local afternoon *Evening Times-Globe*, and that Philip Lee would become editor-in-chief of the provincial *Telegraph-Journal*.

That wasn't the only surprise: the two papers, working out of the same newsroom, were now expected to compete with each other rather than cooperate—a baffling move. "It was a bit contentious," says one *Times-Globe* reporter, describing a new mood of suspicion and rivalry among colleagues who could no longer share notes and copy. "We would hoard our information and try to scoop each other.... You were holding your notebook close to your chest." If you needed a photograph the other paper had, Lee says, "you couldn't get it. It was kind of crazy." The relationship had been fraught already: it was believed the *Telegraph-Journal*, despite its editorial success under Reynolds, was back in the red, subsidized once again by the *Times-Globe*. Yet "the money, the talent, the resources were being poured into the *Telegraph* because they saw it as having the most potential," says Carolyn Ryan. Now, intra-newsroom competition exacerbated the tension. Honeyman says there was "quite a rift" between him and Philip Lee.

Reynolds loyalists at the *Telegraph*, meanwhile, were happy Lee was back. "He had worked closely with Neil," says Mark Leger, "and was seen by people there as someone who embodied his sense of what journalism was and where the paper should go." Lee recruited Mark Tunney, then at the CBC, to return and take charge of the *New Brunswick Reader*; he also encouraged journalists to pitch investigative and in-depth projects. But bringing back the Reynolds magic would not be easy. Conrad Black's *National Post* was hiring the best reporters and editors across Canada, triggering a migration of talent that trickled down to small-market papers. "There was a huge exodus, including good young people," Lee says. "That was tough."

Lee was also preoccupied with something else. Not long after becoming editor of the *Telegraph-Journal*, he had learned that, starting in March 1998, it and the *Times-Globe* would no longer be printed on the hulking old press in the basement, a machine installed when 210 Crown Street opened in 1963. The press would be shut down, the men who ran it laid off, and the two Saint John newspapers would be printed ninety minutes away in Moncton— at the *Times-Transcript*. That meant Lee had to adjust the design of the *Telegraph-Journal* to fit the narrower page size in Moncton. "We had a matter of weeks before we were going onto the press, and nothing had been done to prepare us for that," Lee says.

Pulling it off in time was such a complex task that few grasped the larger significance: in 1971, K.C. Irving, on the defensive from both a parliamentary inquiry and a Combines Act prosecution, had erected the wall between his sons' newspaper companies. Jack owned the Moncton and Fredericton papers; J.K. and Arthur owned Saint John. They were distinct, autonomous operations, set up to persuade policy-makers and the public that there was no Irving monopoly.

That wall had stood for almost three decades and now it was coming down.

Mike Bembridge had always wondered about that printing press in Moncton. When Bembridge was the managing editor of the *Times-Transcript* in the mid-eighties, J.K.'s brother Jack Irving and his son John had decided to replace the previous one. "We went up and down the eastern seaboard looking at presses," Bembridge says. "They were fixated on colour. They wanted a lot of colour in the newspaper." Part of it, he figured, was Irvings being Irvings: at the end of every year, Jack would call to ask if anything in the building needed upgrading. Pouring revenue back into the operation kept the black ink—and the tax bill—to a minimum.

But this was different. The price of the giant machine, a Goss Urbanite, was $9 million. The new wing that Jack built onto the landmark white *Times-Transcript* building to house it cost another $12 million. The interest payments alone would be $900,000—"Horrendous," Bembridge says. Jack told him it was "the cost of doing business." What Bembridge couldn't fathom was why they wanted *that* press, with extra speed and capacity exceeding what the *Times-Transcript* would ever need. "That press was capable of blanketing the entire province with newspapers and then some," he says. "It was overkill to the nth degree for our needs, but these are reasons the empire doesn't share with anyone."

A decade later, Jack's costly new Moncton press was sitting idle most of the day. There are differing accounts of who first raised the idea of sharing it: in one version, J.K. mentioned to Jack during a brotherly chat that the *Telegraph* and *Times-Globe* press in Saint John was due to be replaced and Jack suggested he print in Moncton. Another version is that Jack was seeking to pay off the Moncton press more quickly, and when *The Globe and Mail* turned down a bid to print its Atlantic edition there, he turned to his brother J.K.'s two Saint John papers as a source of revenue, proposing a printing contract only, with no editorial cooperation.

A third iteration is that Jamie Milne, the publisher of the Saint John papers, was pushing for greater integration and saw printing as merely a first step. The Irvings had erected silos to defer to Davey and Kent, but "he convinced them that was dumb, and that it was hurting their business," says a company insider. The logical location for the expensive new press, he told them, would have been Sussex, a town in the middle of the Moncton–Saint John–Fredericton triangle, but because the brothers refused to cooperate, it sat now in Moncton. Despite the distance, Milne said, printing the *Telegraph* there still made sense. J.K. and his son Jim saw the logic. Tired of marginal or money-losing papers, they struck a deal with Jack and John.

The new reality saved money, but was enormously complicated for the *Telegraph*'s Saint John newsroom. The *Times-Transcript* had become a morning paper, and was printed late at night, roughly at the same time as the *Telegraph-Journal*. Only one of them could have the later, more advantageous press time, which allowed more last-minute news. "I came in with the idea, and it was probably foolish, that the *Telegraph-Journal* was the preeminent New Brunswick paper and should be treated as such by the company," Philip Lee says. "And it wasn't." The *Telegraph* would print first, requiring earlier deadlines that prevented the inclusion of late-breaking news and scores from nighttime sports games. "It was their press, and they were having quite a lot of economic success over there, so they had the better press time in my view," Lee says. In the first test of the new fraternal relationship, J.K.'s newspaper lost—not for the last time.

The last press run on Crown Street was March 9, 1998. For Saint John as a whole, the implications went beyond the lost pressmen jobs. The city had long seen itself as the economic heart of the province, the capital of New Brunswick entrepreneurship, but during the nineties, Moncton—flashy, modern, bilingual— emerged as a provincial success story. Now even Saint John's *newspapers* were coming from there. "You would call someone to interview them," says one *Times-Globe* reporter, "and they would say, 'Where are you, in Moncton?' They thought the whole paper had moved to Moncton."

The resulting angst and ill will were far from what Philip Lee had hoped for when he became editor-in-chief. "I was trying to continue the vision that Neil had for the paper," he says. "It was probably in retrospect a hard thing to do, and not the thing for the times we were in. I may have been trying to hold on to something or re-create something. As an older person now, I realize that these moments that occur in journalism are just that: moments."

A new moment had arrived, and with it a new Irving.

John Irving, Jack's son, had started appearing at 210 Crown Street. "He made a real bad impression," Mark Tunney says. "There was a water cooler [in the newsroom] and he said, 'There's already a water cooler out front. Take that out of here right away. I want that out of here.' Everybody was pissed off." Another reporter recalls John being preoccupied with the landscaping outside: "The building didn't look nice." And he and Scott Honeyman once had "a quite protracted discussion about whether people in the newsrooms should wear uniforms," Honeyman says, "because people in the gas stations did, and it raised their morale and made them feel like a team." To Honeyman, John appeared to consider the newspapers "just another business that didn't have any special kind of mission."

Some Irving-watchers in Saint John believe John, with his Harvard MBA, is the smartest Irving of all, but there were problems between him and his cousin Jim. Mark Tunney was told that, after John left Irving Oil to work at J.D. Irving Ltd., Jim "just said, 'I don't want him around anymore. I don't want this guy.'" But John's father, Jack, reminded his brothers, J.K. and Arthur, that he and his family were one-third of the empire: a place had to be found for John. "And as a result [J.K. and Jim] said, 'Okay, why don't you try to run the news-papers?'" The family was warming to the idea that the papers should cooperate more, and the Saturday *Times-Transcript* in Moncton—a Jack-and-John product—had the highest circulation of all the Irving papers; the flagship *Telegraph-Journal* and *Times-Globe* might benefit from the Jack-and-John approach.

They had recruited Jonathan Franklin, a South African who had worked for Thomson Newspapers in British Columbia, to be their publisher in Moncton. Franklin had faced down a four-week strike at a group of Thomson dailies in Kelowna, Vernon, and Penticton, a dispute brought on in part by the centraliza-tion of printing—a potentially relevant testing ground. Mike Bembridge says he erased the *Times-Transcript*'s losses, including the debt from the new press, by the time he retired as publisher in 1996; Franklin says the newspaper was still losing a million dollars a year when he arrived.

Franklin in turn hired Al Hogan, who had been his managing editor in Kelowna, to turn the bland *Times-Transcript* into a flashy, bright chronicle that put Moncton squarely at the centre of everything—a relentlessly local product. "That was what people were interested in reading," Franklin says. "My focus at the time was to turn the paper into a Moncton paper." Hogan's style was local boosterism. Over the years, he launched numerous editorial crusades: against a new toll highway; for a casino to be built in Moncton; and for the province to locate a new diagnostic lab there. The stories were pro-Moncton, supporting the conventional wisdom of the city. "It's easy to say you're for more health services in your area," says Daniel McHardie, a former *Times-Transcript* reporter.

Philip Lee looked on with distaste. "Their kind of paper wasn't my kind of paper: short and snappy stories, a graphic-heavy paper," he says. "I wanted a paper that didn't look like them." Lee toned down the front page of the *Telegraph-Journal*, opting for a more traditional design. The papers were rolling off the same presses, but they had never been more different in tone and content—and it was the *Times-Transcript* raking in the profits.

Lee and Hogan found themselves together one wintry weekend at a hotel in the seaside resort town of St. Andrew's, New Brunswick, where John Irving had decided all the Irving editors should meet and hash out how to cooperate even more. Lee had been asked to develop a proposal to turn the *Telegraph* into a truly provincial paper, with a circulation of a hundred thousand that would attract more lucrative advertising. Now he found himself on the defensive, with Franklin and Hogan pushing to have the *Times-Transcript* supplant the *Telegraph* as the leading provincial newspaper. "Al Hogan was the darling," says Mark Tunney. "They already knew him and they were okay with his vision. There was a sense that, 'The *Telegraph* thinks it's the flagship paper? No. We want you to listen to Al about how to run a newspaper.'"

Lee felt under siege. Scott Honeyman, his *Times-Globe* rival with whom he still awkwardly shared a newsroom at 210 Crown Street, poached the *Telegraph-Journal*'s Fredericton bureau chief and political columnist, Don Richardson, to write a political column for the *Times-Globe*—and for the *Times-Transcript* and the *Daily Gleaner*. The three city papers would share his salary, lighten his workload, and triple his audience. More defections followed: Gary Dimmock, a *Telegraph* investigative reporter, wanted out after his six-year relationship with a newsroom colleague came to an end; he leapt at Hogan's promise that he could write investigative features for the Saturday *Times-Transcript*. "It was clear they were going up against the *Telegraph*," Dimmock says. A few weeks later, Dimmock's Fredericton bureau colleague and friend, David Stonehouse, was lured to Moncton as well. "This was predatory," says one journalist. But none of the Irvings seemed bothered that one of their papers was cannibalizing another. (The Moncton paper's investigative fervour proved short-lived, and Dimmock and Stonehouse soon moved on.)

Despite the barrage, the *Telegraph-Journal* still scored some notable coups, winning its first National Newspaper Award for its September 1998 coverage of a young aboriginal leader who fled to Florida and was then extradited to face murder charges. "There was a lot of good stuff," Lee says. "We were doing pretty solid, original kind of work." Attempting to seize back the initiative, Lee drafted a long memo to Jamie Milne, whose strategy was to make the *Telegraph* a must-read *second* newspaper for many of those who subscribed to the three local city papers. Lee believed those who could afford two newspapers were more likely to sign up for the new *National Post*, or *The Globe and Mail*, which had given itself a makeover in response to new competition from the *Post*. And in the meantime, the Irving press, far from being a monolith, was becoming the complete opposite: a chaotic, dysfunctional confederation of warring fiefdoms. "There was a lot of turmoil within the company, a lot of uncertainty about exactly what the vision was," Lee says.

Lee proposed something that had been unthinkable a couple of years earlier: the sharing of editorial content among the Irving newspapers. "We had reporters all over the province covering the same stuff," he says. Eliminating the overlap would free up reporters to do more in-depth features and investigations, he reasoned. "We were, in this crazy kind of way, competing within our own company in a way that was harmful to the business: all being out at the same time in the morning, and me trying to sell in Moncton against the *Times-Transcript*. It seemed kind of crazy at the time." There needed to be a reckoning.

Scott Honeyman, too, was apprehensive. He had broken new ground by poaching the *Telegraph-Journal*'s marquee political columnist for the *Evening Times-Globe*, but he also saw the downside of the evolution: the Irvings were becoming increasingly hands-on in their drive to have the papers make a profit. "I certainly felt it was the end of that free and easy period for the newsrooms," he says. "The control got ever more centralized after I left."

Honeyman retired at the end of 1998. He confesses he still didn't understand the Irvings any better than when he arrived. "It was interesting to try to figure out where the line was that you could tread. You look at it from the family point of view and it has to be like something biting you in the ass every day. What you own is biting your ass every day. That must be a difficult thing. I think the senior Irvings were willing to put up with it but John and that next generation maybe were not. The older guys certainly took the Kent Commission more seriously than the younger guys do."

Little did Honeyman realize that on that point—on that most fundamental of questions for the Irving newspapers—the family was not of one mind. Here, too, there would have to be a reckoning.

9

SPICY, BUT NOT HOT

A͏t the end of December 1998, the Irvings incorporated a new company, Brunswick News Inc., to own all four newspapers. The structure that had been created in 1971 to convey autonomy and forestall government intervention ceased to exist: New Brunswick Publishing, in which J.K. and Arthur each held 40 percent, and Summit Publishing, which Jack had recently formed to publish the Moncton and Fredericton papers, were folded into Brunswick News. The three Irving brothers had equal shares, and thus collectively owned all the newspapers. "It was all about efficiency," Jim Irving says. "It was just common sense and good business. We needed to streamline the business.... It was trying to get synergies. It was basic stuff."

Basic common sense—but still a move the Irvings had not dared contemplate before. By 1998, however, the prospect of state intervention in the newspaper industry was remote. Nationally, consolidation was accelerating: it was far greater than when Davey and Kent treated it as a national crisis. Yet Ottawa was doing nothing. "The government clearly did not view this as an area where they were concerned," says one insider. Meanwhile, critics on the left, focused on Conrad Black's gobbling up of market share, paid little attention to the Irvings bringing their papers back under a single company. Compared to Black, a family-owned chain of four small daily papers seemed relatively benign—less the conglomerate nightmare once denounced and prosecuted and more a quaint example of local, independent ownership.

Even so, the Irvings were conscious of appearances. John, who grew up watching his father, Jack, delegate control of editorial matters to the publishers in Moncton and Fredericton, considered it important that the same ethos remain in place. With a single newspaper company, it was more important than ever that no Irving family member have a say, or be seen to have a say, in day-to-day editorial matters. While John was nominally president of Brunswick News, he believed the publishers, all non–family members, should retain the last word on content.

And they did, says Jonathan Franklin. "I never had any direction" on Irving coverage from them, he says. "I never had any questions about why stories ran. It was extraordinary." Franklin concedes, however, that the papers didn't take on major investigative projects about the Irvings either; he calls the notion unrealistic. "It would be crazy to expect owners to have a press, tabloid-style, going after them," he says, citing the same false dilemma as publishers of old: either passive reporting or outright attacks, with no room in the middle for better, Neil Reynolds–style coverage. Fortunately, Franklin says, the Irvings were good corporate citizens who didn't require muckraking scrutiny. "If they were gangsters, there might have been a different scenario. I would have had to ask myself the question."

And the newspapers, particularly the *Telegraph-Journal* and the *Times-Globe*, did continue to cover Irving stories: layoffs at Irving-owned Thorne's Hardware; a court ruling on aboriginal logging rights that alarmed the forestry industry; a dispute between J.D. Irving Ltd. and a Nova Scotia monastery about noisy tree-cutting operations.

But one Irving story had dominated all others in 1998: a collision of business and politics—the *Telegraph-Journal*'s bread and butter—in which J.K. Irving's son Jim and Arthur's son Kenneth joined forces against New Brunswick's *other* billion-dollar family.

It was a hot story—maybe too hot.

Harrison McCain was one of the first people the *Telegraph-Journal* called for a comment on the day K.C. Irving died in 1992. Irving "influenced everyone's life that he came in contact with," McCain said. "He had a very, very powerful personality, and I think he influenced all of us." This was particularly true of the McCains: Harrison worked for K.C. in the fifties, managing his gas station chain in three provinces. His brother Wallace ran the Irving-owned Thorne's Hardware chain from Saint John. Wallace's wife, Margaret, was a close friend of Arthur Irving's wife, Joan Carlisle. When the McCain boys returned to their hometown of Florenceville in 1957 to launch their frozen-french-fry company, they took the Irving Way with them: ambition, discipline, decisiveness, and attention to detail.

As McCain Foods grew rapidly over the next two decades, the two companies stayed out of each other's way, avoiding direct competition. They also approached expansion differently: the Irvings created dozens and dozens of vertically integrated companies, some of which moved into neighbouring provinces, but all of which were tied to the twin hearts of the operations, the Saint John oil refinery and New Brunswick's vast forest land. The McCains, while expanding into a few complementary areas such as trucking and equipment manufacturing, focused on their one core business, frozen food, and spread it across the globe, putting down processing plants wherever potatoes grew. Eventually their American and European operations dwarfed their Canadian facilities, a contrast to K.C. Irving's dominant, ubiquitous presence in New Brunswick.

Then, in 1980, J.D. Irving Ltd. moved onto McCain's turf when it bought the C.M. McLean potato company in Prince Edward Island. If there had been a non-aggression pact between the two empires, that ended it—though some said the McCains had fired the first shot by dropping Irving Oil as their fuel supplier a few years earlier. Regardless, Irving was soon marketing its own frozen fries under the Cavendish Farms brand.

When the island government went shopping for private-sector investment in 1989, dangling generous subsidies, they approached McCain first, but he didn't bite—until the Irvings did. Then McCain became belatedly interested, and lobbied against the taxpayer-funded package promised to the Irvings. After several rounds of nasty accusations, both companies ended up with new plants on the island, and a new level of bad blood between them. Harrison McCain was outraged again when Cavendish decided to build another taxpayer-subsidized plant in Grand Falls, New Brunswick, near a McCain plant. Pointing to the proposed Cavendish location overlooking the international border with Maine, McCain stoked American fears of cheap Canadian potatoes flooding the U.S. market; when Maine politicians made noises about asking Washington for punitive tariffs, Robert Irving cancelled the Grand Falls plant.

And now, as Harrison McCain saw it, the Irvings were at it again—and this time, Kenneth and Jim were working together. No one doubted they would win, but McCain decided to take them on regardless.

A new energy source, natural gas from beneath the ocean off Nova Scotia, was coming to New Brunswick, and Kenneth, now the CEO of Irving Oil, wanted some of it. A consortium called Maritimes & Northeast Pipeline was building a 1,100-kilometre line to send the gas into New England; the pipeline's route through New Brunswick would allow some of the gas to be sold to homes and businesses there. Kenneth saw it as a lucrative opportunity, a chance to transform Irving Oil from a conventional oil company into something bigger. "It's a strategic question about being able to get into other energy products that our competitors have been able to participate in," he said. He signed a partnership with Westcoast Power Inc., a Vancouver pipeline company, to bid for the licence to build branch lines to New Brunswick customers. At the same time, the two firms planned to buy from the provincial energy utility an oil-fired power station in Saint John, convert it to burn natural gas, and sell the electricity into the United States through New Brunswick's transmission-line link to neighbouring Maine. Irving Oil already had a 30 percent market share of the retail gas market down the eastern seaboard, but natural gas would let Kenneth become an even bigger regional player.

Few questioned that the New Brunswick government would award Kenneth the licence: the Irvings usually got what they wanted. But there was another bidder, a partnership between Enbridge Gas and twenty-nine New Brunswick investors— including Harrison McCain. Fredericton businessman Bud Bird put together the consortium, and it wasn't easy. "The influence of Irving Oil is so strong in New Brunswick that a great many business people in the province simply did not want to be seen to be in competition with them," Bird recalled. For Enbridge, he said, only an all-star list of prominent New Brunswickers "would be a sufficiently strong political influence to neutralize Irving's home-grown advantage." As the one entrepreneur in the province in the same league as the Irvings, Harrison McCain gave the bid instant credibility.

In September 1998, a special committee of the legislature began hearings into who should get the natural gas licence. Kenneth Irving appeared on the same day as his cousin Jim, and Harrison McCain was apoplectic when he learned what they had to say.

Jim Irving was supporting his cousin Kenneth's bid—though Jim's company, J.D. Irving Ltd., did not itself plan to buy its natural gas from Irving Oil. Jim asked the province to create an exemption in the rules so large industries like his could bypass the local franchisee, whoever it was, and plug directly into the main Maritimes and Northeast pipeline. They could thus avoid the distribution fee the franchisee would charge its customers. In fact, Jim told the committee, he already had a tentative agreement with Maritimes and Northeast to buy a billion dollars' worth of natural gas for both the J.D. Irving Ltd. paper mill in Saint John and a gas-fired generating station he would build to supply electricity to his other mills—but, he said, the deal would happen only if he got direct access to the pipeline. If forced to be part of the distribution-fee regime, he said, "we will not participate." At the same time, Kenneth himself, though seeking the franchise to sell retail natural gas to others, wanted the same no-fee direct access to gas to power the Irving Oil refinery—an exemption from the very distribution fee he proposed to charge smaller customers.

This, McCain concluded, was so hypocritical, so monopolistic—so *Irving*. He wasn't alone in thinking so, but Harrison McCain was no anti-capitalist crank. There was a solid business case for turning down Jim and Kenneth: if big industry could bypass the distribution-fee system, it might destroy Enbridge's business case in New Brunswick. If it couldn't sell huge volumes of gas to heavy industry and collect the fee, Enbridge might not recoup the cost of building its branch lines. That would deprive it of the capital to further expand the network and would force the company to levy even higher fees on smaller customers—a vicious circle that could make natural gas unaffordable.

Harrison McCain was furious about the Irving cousins' push for special treatment, and his fury turned the September hearings into an irresistible tycoon-versus-tycoon story. He appeared before the committee two weeks after the Irvings. Wearing a blue pinstriped suit with his Order of Canada pin on the lapel, he ripped into his fellow billionaires, reviving the accusation that they were monopolists.

"We want a pipeline for the people, for all the people of New Brunswick," he told the committee. "With a people's pipeline, there would be savings for the man on the street." But, he warned, those savings would vanish if the Irvings won the right to buy gas direct from the main line, and the right to burn it to generate electricity, and the exclusive right to distribute it to customers—while already dominating the petroleum industry in the province. "It is simply too much," McCain said. "They are great guys, but it is too much, and it is a conflict of interest." He scoffed at Jim Irving's suggestion that his mills deserved a break because they would be heavy users of the gas. McCain Foods' headquarters in Florenceville was the phone company's second- or third-largest customer in New Brunswick, he said, but "I don't see them sending us any rebate."

The *Telegraph-Journal* was covering the gas battle closely, and now the only man in New Brunswick who could go toe-to-toe with the Irvings was taking the fight to them. Lee decided to play it big. "We covered it the only way that it could be covered," he says. "This was covered in a straight way. It never crossed my mind that we would do it any other way." The day after Harrison McCain's appearance, the front page was dominated by a photo of McCain peering over his glasses at the members of the committee. The headline, bold and simple, quoted his testimony: "The People's Pipeline."

That front page is still striking today, not only because it shows Lee's willingness to give prominence to an attack on the newspaper's owners, but also because Harrison McCain's warning was prophetic. In 1999, the Enbridge team won the franchise; Irving Oil was disqualified for refusing to disclose all the information the government required, a case of the family's penchant for secrecy catching up with it. But Jim Irving got what he wanted: for a nominal fee, J.D. Irving Ltd.'s mills were given direct access to the pipeline outside Enbridge's distribution-fee system. Bud Bird called it "a major public policy error" that deprived Enbridge of the revenue from that large volume: 80 percent of the natural gas consumed in New Brunswick goes to six large industrial users with direct access, three of them Irving mills. It meant Enbridge would carry an enormous debt on its network of New Brunswick pipes. As McCain foresaw, the debt helped drive the distribution fee ever higher, making natural gas a less appealing option for other potential customers.

One of the loudest complainers about the fee was Jim Irving. He built a gypsum plant in Saint John, Atlantic Wallboard Ltd., in 2007. It was ineligible for the direct access he won for his mills in 1999, and so wound up paying the same inflated distribution rate as other Enbridge customers. "This is a tragedy, what's going on here," he would say in 2011. "The Enbridge Gas monopoly is not working for New Brunswickers."

An Enbridge official would call Jim Irving's comments "puzzling," because while other factors, including Enbridge's own decisions, had helped to push rates up, Jim Irving had also played a role in the increases: by winning the distribution-fee exemptions for his mills, he had aided in starving Enbridge of the revenue it needed to pay its debt—contributing, arguably, to the very rate increases he was complaining about.

Harrison McCain had died in 2004, and was no longer around to say he'd told them so.

Even before Harrison McCain's broadside, Jim Irving was paying close attention to the pipeline coverage in the *Telegraph-Journal*. Lisa Hrabluk remembers being sent to 300 Union Street on a Friday in early September 1998 to interview Jim and a couple of J.D. Irving Ltd. executives. A story by a colleague in that day's paper, she says, "did not strike the right chord." The story quoted Bud Bird calling Jim's presentation to the committee an "ultimatum," but did not give Irving the chance to respond. So, for two hours on a Friday afternoon, Hrabluk listened to three men explain the company's position. "Jim sat beside me and said, 'Did you understand that point?' or, 'Do you understand what they just said?'" But he never told her what to write, she says. The next day's headline: "Natural-Gas 'Ultimatum' Just 'Facts,' says Irving." Two weeks later came the McCain front page.

That winter, Philip Lee was summoned up to Union Street for his own meeting with Jim, where he was told he would no longer be in charge of the newspaper. Officially, the stated reason was "unsatisfactory results," but, Lee says, "I remember him saying he liked a paper that was spicy, but not hot. The nature of the conversation was that he did business in the province every day, and when the paper was making the people he saw uncomfortable, it made him uncomfortable, and he didn't like that." Lee responded that sometimes journalism has to make us uncomfortable. The meeting "wasn't unpleasant," he says. "He told me several times that I was a fine young man with a promising future in the company and they wanted to keep me at the newspaper, but they wanted to bring someone in above me who would give them a level of comfort that I didn't offer them."

J.K. and Jim had complained that they were getting grief from the provincial Liberal government about *Telegraph-Journal* columnist Dalton Camp, the iconic Tory political strategist who lived near Fredericton. The paper had been publishing his nationally syndicated *Toronto Star* column, but Lee persuaded Camp to write an extra column once a week, exclusively for the *Telegraph*, on New Brunswick politics. Camp's frequent barbs aimed at Premier Camille Thériault, who took over after Frank McKenna's retirement, were provoking alarm among Liberals, who were preparing for an election. According to Geoffrey Stevens's biography of Camp, the Irvings received an angry call from a minister in Thériault's cabinet—the same cabinet that would award the natural gas distribution licence and decide on direct access.

At the same time, Lee was having problems in his personal life that spilled over into the newsroom and became the subject of gossip around Saint John and among Fredericton's political class. The Irvings are known to dislike messy personal situations in their workplaces, but "I never heard from anybody about those things," Lee says. "I don't think they were motivated by that."

Mark Tunney, the editor of the *Reader*, says Jamie Irving later told him the coverage of the energy hearings was "the last straw" for his father. "Sometimes you have to deal with Jim Irving's temper," Tunney says.

Lee was told he could stay as editor but would report to a new "senior editor," Howie Trainor, a former *Telegraph-Journal* managing editor who had been in charge of the McKenna government's public relations operation for most of the nineties. "I said to the owners that I thought that was a mistake, optically, to have the person who was running the government news wire come in as the head of editorial in an election year," Lee says. Rather than report to Trainor, he negotiated a deal in March 1999 to become a senior writer for the *Telegraph*.

Reporter Lisa Hrabluk saw Trainor's hiring as symptomatic of the Irvings' ambivalence about their newspapers, their inability to accommodate journalism in their corporate mindset. "It has never been and will never be their priority or their vanity project, like the *National Post* was for Conrad Black or *The Wall Street Journal* is for Rupert Murdoch. So they don't watch it enough, and they're not immersed in the culture enough, and they don't hang out with that crowd." The result, Hrabluk says, is that when something goes wrong "to the point where Jim Irving or J.K. Irving notices," they have no instinct for what to do. "The short-term solution is to go with what they already know"—which, in early 1999, was safe, familiar Howie Trainor, a throwback to the pre–Neil Reynolds days.

Another known quantity arrived at Brunswick News around the same time: Rino Volpé, who had become vice-president of the company shortly before Lee's departure. Volpé grew up on a chicken farm in French-speaking northwest New Brunswick and had the rough-hewn quality of a man who didn't put up with nonsense. He was the Irving boss who broke the strike at Kent Homes. "When the chickens are squawking and running 'round all crazy, you know what you do?" he once said. "You grab the craziest one and snap the neck." Volpé reorganized Brunswick News, declaring individual papers no longer needed their own publishers. Jonathan Franklin would now oversee both the *Times-Transcript* in Moncton and the *Telegraph-Journal* in Saint John, while Victor Mlodecki, a veteran of the Thomson chain, was hired as publisher of the *Evening Times-Globe* in Saint John and *The Daily Gleaner* in Fredericton. The company, Volpé explains, was "a non-performing asset" that had to be fixed. The journalistic mission was irrelevant. "To me, it was just another company. We had a target. I told everyone in the company, 'This is the performance we want.'" It was time to snap some necks at Brunswick News.

Volpé was disruptive in another way. "When I arrived," he says, "I asked to report to Jim Irving." John Irving was the president of Brunswick News, but Volpé insisted on reporting to his cousin Jim. "I knew him, and they accepted that," Volpé says. This made things awkward at quarterly meetings, where Volpé, Franklin, Mlodecki, Jim, and John would go over the numbers and plan ahead. John was nominally the boss, Volpé says, but "it was Jim who took care of things. I answered to him." This could only exacerbate the existing tension between Jim and John. "There was friction between them," says Franklin. In the new era of Brunswick News, it wasn't just publishers and editors who had to work together: Irving family unity itself was at stake.

Howie Trainor was an interim fix at the *Telegraph-Journal*. Late in 1999, Jonathan Franklin hired as managing editor Peter Haggert, who had worked at a Thomson newspaper in Thunder Bay. Haggert would help oversee the next step in the integration of the newspapers into Brunswick News: a coordinated carving up of the New Brunswick market in which the papers had once competed. The Irving monopoly was going to start acting like one.

For the first time, the four papers would be considered a single editorial product, each targeting a different segment of the audience. The three city newspapers would be local and generally lighter; some of their essential stories would be shared with the *Telegraph*. This copy sharing would free up *Telegraph* reporters to do in-depth work to attract readers lured to the new *National Post* and the improved *Globe and Mail*. It was the reckoning Philip Lee had recommended before his removal, effectively a ceasefire imposed on the *Times-Transcript* to halt its attacks on the bloodied *Telegraph*, one reporter says. Continued competition within Brunswick News "would have run the TJ into the ground, so that was stopped," he says. "Someone at some point said, 'We're going to lose the TJ brand if we don't step in.'"

But the reckoning was still not complete. Neil Reynolds had built up the *Telegraph*'s Moncton bureau in part to prove there wasn't a single Irving editorial voice. Now its five journalists were moved from their own office across town into the *Times-Transcript* newsroom. "There was suddenly a very, very deep understanding that there was no more competition," says Amy Cameron, one of the relocated reporters. In February 2000, Haggert dissolved the bureau, buying out three of the five employees, two of whom refused transfers to remote communities in northern New Brunswick.* The idea of a *Telegraph* that

---

* As Moncton bureau chief at the time, I was offered a choice between demotion to a reporting position at a lower salary or a buyout. I chose the latter.

would compete for *The Globe and Mail*'s New Brunswick readership gave way to a community newspaper for the entire province, with a network of correspondents covering small-town municipal news and events.

Around the same time, seven of the *Telegraph*'s best-known op-ed columnists—most of them recruited by Reynolds— were dropped after they refused to sign new contracts allowing Brunswick News to resell their work. Two of them, Dalton Camp and Jackie Webster, had been acting as mentors to Jim Irving's son Jamie, and often met him for drinks whenever he visited Fredericton. Jamie by now was watching developments at the papers, first from Ottawa and then from New York, where he attended Columbia University. Camp, an alumnus, had written a reference for him to the admissions department. Camp was "impressed by the fact that someone who could do basically whatever he wanted to do was genuinely interested in journalism," says Camp's son Michael. Webster says Jamie was already planning to undo the changes Franklin was bringing to the *Telegraph*. "He'd say, 'What I want to do is take over that paper and have you and Dalton as columnists, and make it into the best newspaper in New Brunswick,' and so on," Webster says. "He saw no reason why it couldn't be the best newspaper in eastern Canada."

In Saint John, some newsroom staff began to think of the twenty-three-year-old Irving heir as a potential saviour. They remembered his admiration of Reynolds and were also aware that "he hated Jonathan Franklin," according to one journalist. Jamie "had a real loyalty to the *Telegraph-Journal* and *Times-Globe*, and he thought they'd been shafted by Franklin." He reportedly told acquaintances, "When I run these things, he's gone."

And so the Irvings' battered and bruised flagship *Telegraph-Journal* found itself in a Catch-22. The two most effective defences for the newspapers, whenever critics spoke of the monopoly, had been that they were distinct, autonomous companies, and that no Irving family member ever had a hand in their day-to-day management.

The creation of Brunswick News, a single, centrally controlled editorial product, had demolished the first of those defences, making the second defence all the more important. Indeed, John Irving felt the only way to avoid accusations of interference was to run Brunswick News the way his father had run the Fredericton and Moncton newspapers—with independent managers at arm's length from the family.

But as the *Telegraph-Journal* reporters saw their paper's one-time greatness diluted into the corporate fold, they became convinced the only person who could save its reputation, its *independence*, was Jamie Irving himself—precisely the kind of family control that John Irving believed would be fatal to the newspapers' credibility.

Two visions of the Irving press—two incompatible visions— were on a collision course.

10

ROWING IN THE SAME DIRECTION

▼

In his final essay in the *Telegraph-Journal* in 1996, Neil Reynolds lamented that some print journalists had become "embarrassed by the idiosyncratic Industrial Age character of their business"—ink on paper—and "more obsessed with the electronic delivery of data-bank information than with the writing of memorable stories." Even then, Reynolds grasped that the internet, still new, was a threat to the print journalism he revered. The best defence, he argued, was a good offence: thoughtful, well-written, engaging stories.

The *Telegraph-Journal* had tentatively experimented with the internet, working with the provincial telephone utility to create a primitive website to host campaign stories during the 1995 New Brunswick election campaign. By 1997, the paper had a new site that gave readers access to earlier stories providing background to the day's news. Reporters were dazzled by the potential of the Web; few pondered what free online access might mean for subscribers' willingness to spend money on a printed newspaper.

Rino Volpé pondered it, though. One of his first moves when he became vice-president of Brunswick News in early 1999 was to close the website. "No one could tell me what the business model was," he says. "People were logging on, reading what was in the paper, and they didn't have to buy the paper. There was no advertising revenue—nothing. It wasn't a hard decision." Nor was it difficult to persuade the Irvings, who Volpé says rarely try new things. Better to let others stick their necks out, then learn from their mistakes. "That's how they operate: let's examine it, and once we figure how out it works, we'll decide whether we want to get into it."

For the Irvings, printed pages—great rolls of newsprint manufactured at their Saint John mill, rolling off that new Moncton press at high speed, covered with advertising—were still king. And with the newspapers now fully integrated as Brunswick News, there was no reason the new entity could not be an efficient, money-making machine.

Paradoxically, their first move was to close the *Evening Times-Globe*, Saint John's local afternoon paper. In September 2001, the employees were told the newspaper would cease to exist and they would become part of a new Saint John edition of the *Telegraph-Journal*. The *Telegraph*'s circulation was seventeen thousand at the time, the *Times-Globe*'s twenty-six thousand. "They were running different pages and different ads," says Jonathan Franklin. Putting them together gave the advertising staff a single, large paper to sell.

For the *Times-Globe* staff, it was a bitter calculus. "It was like the city was losing its paper, losing its voice, losing its stories," says one reporter. Lisa Hrabluk says it was the latest example of "a lack of appreciation for the heart and soul of those papers and how the people who work there feel about them." But for monopoly owners, the closure had plenty of benefits and few risks, says Carolyn Ryan, who was the *Times-Globe*'s editor-in-chief when the news came. "There was no other game in town in terms of Saint John subscribers who wanted local news, so what could they do if they wanted a newspaper?"

The same logic fuelled speculation that the Irvings would eventually merge all the papers into a single provincial daily. Even Philip Lee had reluctantly endorsed the idea at the height of Al Hogan's attacks on the *Telegraph*. But the owners wouldn't consider it. "The figures show you you'll do so much better," J.K. Irving acknowledges, "but that's not the point. The newspapers are New Brunswick's newspapers, and our obligation is to run those newspapers in the best way possible for the benefit of all New Brunswickers." This was J.K.'s old-fashioned sentimentality, but also his intuitive understanding of the province's peculiar localisms—which aligned perfectly with Victor Mlodecki's cold math. "It is a concept that we have looked at," Mlodecki said in 2005 when asked about the idea of a single daily.* "If you take the province of New Brunswick, with our 750,000 population, we are about three-quarters as big as Calgary." But, he said, New Brunswickers don't think of the entire province as their hometown. Saint John, Moncton, and Fredericton see themselves as distinct communities. "The appeal of newspapers today is primarily in local news coverage," Mlodecki said. "Readers are not that interested in finding out what is going on in a city that is an hour and a half away."

In fact, the executives of Brunswick News decided that, with the exception of the *Times-Globe*, the future lay not with fewer

---

* Victor Mlodecki declined to be interviewed for this book. His comments are from his appearance in 2005 before a Senate committee investigating media ownership.

newspapers, but with *more* of them. In 2002, the company looked at buying several other Maritime papers, Volpé says. Canwest was selling many of the smaller papers it had acquired from Conrad Black's Hollinger, including the Halifax *Daily News* and dailies in Sydney, Truro, Amherst, and Charlottetown. "They would be good customers for the newsprint plant," says one observer, invoking the Irving vertical integration model. "You could be sure you'd have newsprint customers." But Canwest ended up selling them to the Transcontinental chain. Conrad Black, who watched the transaction of his former assets with interest, says the ever-frugal Irvings weren't willing to pay a decent price. "They didn't slosh the money around," he says. "They had an aversion to paying what something was worth."

Volpé, Jonathan Franklin, and Victor Mlodecki also met in Halifax with the Dennis family, owners of the Halifax *Chronicle-Herald*, the dominant daily newspaper in Nova Scotia. The Irvings had made several bids for the *Herald* over the years— "They are constantly hovering," says a key player in Halifax—and were convinced now that stand-alone dailies could not survive in a consolidating media world. But the Dennises held firm. "They were very polite and everything, but I don't think they were particularly interested," Franklin says.

And so Brunswick News moved on to another part of the newspaper industry where the ground was shifting: weekly newspapers.

In Miramichi, a gritty city roughly an hour north of Moncton, David Cadogan, the owner of the local paper, the *Miramichi Leader*, realized it was time to get out. The *Leader* was a solid, twice-weekly community paper; Cadogan loved the work but was getting old, and his children were not interested in taking over. "Even if they had been, I would not have wanted to saddle them with the new realities of the marketplace," he recounted. So when John Irving, who always considered Miramichi part of the *Times-Transcript*'s market, came to see him, Cadogan realized this might be his only chance: there were few other potential buyers. "I did feel somewhat forced to deal," he said, but "we have all seen local department stores, clothing stores, drugstores and restaurants driven out of business by national and international chains. Why should it be any different for newspapers?" The agreement, announced in January 2002, saw Brunswick News acquire a minority stake in Cadogan's company, which also published the *Kings County Record*, a weekly in Sussex. It included a clause that either party could buy out the other's interest when they decided to sell— the template K.C. Irving and Michael Wardell had used in 1957. "It's not likely I would buy them out," Cadogan said at the time. "It's more likely they would buy me out."

Later that year, Brunswick News acquired four more weeklies in western New Brunswick, all owned by Woodstock businessman David Henley: *The Woodstock Bugle*, *The Victoria Star* in Perth-Andover, the Grand Falls *Cataracte*, and the *Northside News*, a weekly in Fredericton. Like Cadogan, Henley, too, was getting old, and his children were likewise not interested in taking over. And, he would explain, "some pressures were brought to bear as we got closer to making that decision."

In 2005, Henley told a Senate committee studying media ownership that his weekly in Fredericton had trouble selling advertising to businesses already placing ads with *The Daily Gleaner*. "Irving felt that we were really operating in their territory," he said. "That was sacred ground as far as they were concerned and they really did not want us to be there." One sales rep told him she had almost sold a full-page ad to a major chain retailer—until the *Gleaner* cut its price for a full page from fifteen thousand dollars to four hundred.

Meanwhile, in Woodstock, a small town an hour north-west of Fredericton, a former employee of Henley's had started a local "shopper," a publication devoted solely to advertising. It foundered and was sold; the new owner also ran into trouble with his creditors, including Brunswick News, which printed the shopper on the *Gleaner*'s press in Fredericton. Brunswick News quickly acquired the operation, "and things then changed," Henley recounted. It started offering free classified ads, under-cutting the *Bugle*, and sold display ads at far below its listed prices. This drove down the value of his company at precisely the time Henley wanted to put it on the market. "Obviously, the price would have reflected the decreased revenue," he said. He considered complaining to the Competition Bureau, but his lawyers advised against it, citing the cost of taking on "a company that could afford legal rates that we could not."

Victor Mlodecki explained the episode differently: shoppers are cheaper to produce than newspapers, and their ad rates reflect that, he said. "Prices change from week to week, and for different elements of the newspapers, different prices are charged." Mlodecki said he contacted Henley to buy the weeklies in 2000 and "he was eager to sell them, but it did take another two years to negotiate a price." Henley said he had sought other buyers, including Transcontinental, but "there was absolutely no interest." He guessed they saw no point in trying to break into an Irving-dominated market. So he sold to Brunswick News, which promptly closed the *Northside News* and merged the *Bugle* with another weekly it acquired, the Hartland *Observer*.

The Cadogan sale, in isolation, raised eyebrows; the Henley purchase—and the subsequent acquisition of two more

English-language weeklies, in Campbellton and Bathurst—made it clear the Irvings had a master plan. By purchasing weeklies that had a lock on smaller, local markets, they were turning their chain of daily newspapers in the three cities into a truly provincial operation that would dominate print journalism in English New Brunswick.

As it turned out, the Irvings were thinking even beyond that.

Francophones are one-third of New Brunswick's population, and were the majority in K.C. Irving's hometown of Bouctouche; his mills and gas stations knew no linguistic boundaries, and his first tree plantations were in the province's French-speaking northwest. Yet for decades he and his sons gave no consideration to the French-language newspaper market.

Then, in 1996, after the *Telegraph-Journal*'s blanket coverage of the Acadian World Congress, some francophones had suggested to Neil Reynolds that he introduce French-language content into the *New Brunswick Reader*. Instead, André Veniot, who had coordinated the congress project, was called to Saint John one day and asked by Reynolds and J.K. Irving to launch a new weekly, *Le Journal*, full of in-depth features and arts writing, published in French.

Le Journal was not designed to target a market niche, Veniot says, but as a labour of love. "This was a Neil Reynolds creation that J.K. Irving bought into." J.K. has remained the most attached of the Irving brothers to the Kent County shore where his father grew up; he still has a summer place there and helped pay for the creation of the Bouctouche Dune ecotourism site. Veniot says the idea of publishing a newspaper for Acadians appealed to him.

Sentiment—even J.K. Irving's—only went so far, it turned out.

175

The paper was a tough sell. A significant share of francophones in southeastern New Brunswick, around Moncton, are comfortable in English, read the *Times-Transcript*, and weren't interested in a new paper. Veniot says *Le Journal*'s advertising sales staff, based in Saint John, didn't know the market. And, Veniot says, the "literacy challenges" of many francophones were an obstacle: *Le Journal* was too highbrow. "I made an incorrect assumption. I thought most people could read that. Unfortunately most people couldn't. It had to be rethought." When a small weekly in Kent County, *Le Papier*, went bankrupt in February 1998, Brunswick News bought it, shut it down, and moved its staff to *Le Journal* to overhaul the product, now under Jonathan Franklin's supervision. Veniot was sent back to the *Telegraph-Journal* as a reporter. "I remember talking to Mr. Irving," he says, "and he said I had done the best I could under the circumstances."

This moment, as much as any other, may have signalled the passing of the newspapers to a new generation with new sensibilities. J.K.'s impulse to publish a French paper for the Acadians of his hometown gave way to his son Jim's focus on the bottom line. Jonathan Franklin relished the opportunity to go after francophone readers. "I was very enthusiastic about that because it was a market segment we were not serving," he says. "That was the big thinking behind everything in the group. Let's go after revenue." To that end, long features and highbrow culture were banished. The focus of the redesigned weekly, renamed *L'Étoile*, would be light community news from around Moncton and southeast New Brunswick.

L'Étoile went it alone for almost five years, posing no apparent threat to *L'Acadie Nouvelle*, the independently owned French-language daily newspaper. But in January 2003, not long after the acquisition of Cadogan's and Henley's weeklies, *Le Madawaska*, the weekly serving the mostly francophone northwest, ran into financial trouble and was sold to the Irvings. Brunswick News also launched a free weekly on the northeast shore of New Brunswick, *Hebdo Chaleur*, giving the company French weeklies in all three francophone population centres in the province. Now prominent francophones began sounding the alarm that *L'Acadie Nouvelle* was threatened. Rino Volpé says, however, that he was ordered by the Irvings not to move too aggressively into *L'Acadie Nouvelle*'s base in the northeasternmost corner of the province. That would "stir things up" and invite too much of a backlash, he says, something the Irvings still feared. "You don't have to take *all* of someone's market."

Acadian concerns about an Irving incursion were two-fold: some were wary of such a powerful industrial family controlling their newspapers; others objected on principle to a non-francophone owner. "The independence of the print media, which was a source of pride for the Acadian community, has been seriously undermined," Marie-Linda Lord, a journalism professor at the Université de Moncton, would argue. "Irving's vast business empire should never be far from our thoughts. Irving does not just monopolize the press." When Brunswick News created a $1 million endowment in the department where Lord taught, she denounced it as an Irving threat to academic independence and boycotted the announcement. "She was really anti-Irving," says Veniot, who defends the family's move into the French market. *Le Madawaska* would have disappeared, he argues, if the Irvings had not bought it. "There's a lot of things you can say about the Irvings—they were forced to do some things, they consolidated some newspapers—but they saved some newspapers."

Still, the pressure was real. *L'Acadie Nouvelle*'s editors fretted that Irving's French weeklies were fragmenting the market, covering little bits of community news they couldn't match, while selling little bits of advertising to local businesses that saw more value in a very local publication. Brunswick News was marrying local content—"what is happening down the block," as Mlodecki put it—to its ability "to realize cost savings by virtue of our scale."

The scale was decidedly non-local, centralized, and efficient. To reduce costs, Volpé consolidated all of Brunswick News's non-journalism functions—circulation, human resources, accounting, and, of course, printing—at the *Times-Transcript* building in Moncton. The Irving papers were one big company now, the farthest thing from distinct operations. "This gives the giant corporation an unparalleled venue to promote its own interests as well as insulate itself from inquiries and criticism," Erin Steuter would write. Even once-loyal defenders questioned the consolidation: Jim Morrison, a veteran *Gleaner* and *Telegraph-Journal* editor who calls the Davey and Kent investigations "a bunch of horseshit," nonetheless told me, "I don't think they should be in the weeklies.... I think they lose something when they're all printed in Moncton. It hasn't been proofread. Too many mistakes." Bob Rupert, who worked as a consultant for Brunswick News, says even Tom Crowther, the former *Gleaner* publisher and ultimate company man, was critical. "This Brunswick News idea stinks," Rupert quotes him saying. "Those papers should be competing with each other. They should be independent. This is a money decision. It's not based on good newspapers."

Victor Mlodecki brushed off the critics. Brunswick News would provide quality newspapers, he said. "It is regulated by the hard laws of the marketplace and is in a battle for long-term survival as information sources continue to proliferate and young readers are attracted to electronic information sources." Nor could the company be called a monopoly, he argued in 2005: "The barriers of entry into the newspaper business are next to nothing. Anybody can start a newspaper. All they need is a computer." And to the concerns of Erin Steuter and Marie-Linda Lord, he responded, "The guiding principle in the story on an Irving business would be, what do our readers want to know, not what the Irvings want to be said."

The Irvings' motive for expanding Brunswick News, Jonathan Franklin says, was "to make money. Papers were very profitable still in those days. They're basically businessmen, you know. I never had the impression it was to control the information. It was, 'Hey, it's a great business, it's making a pisspot of money and that's wonderful.' We made a lot of money." The Irvings wanted to dominate the market—but not the market for news, Franklin explains. The news, he says, was merely a vehicle for a potential source of revenue growth: advertising flyers.

Canada Post had dominated the flyer business, using its size and its federal funding to offer discounts that undercut competitors, until 1996, when Ottawa ordered the Crown corporation to withdraw from non-core functions. This opened the field for any private business capable of carrying flyers to people's doors— and no business was better positioned to do that than daily print journalism. "The newspapers are nice," Victor Mlodecki would declare, "but it is the distribution systems that are important to me. That is the future of the business in many respects, you know." Underscoring Mlodecki's argument is the Brunswick News decision not to bid for the *Sackville Tribune-Post*, a weekly within the Moncton *Times-Transcript*'s circulation area. "The Sackville paper has little interest to me because we already have a distribution system in that community," he explained.

Rino Volpé laughs about the hand-wringing over the journalism. He used market surveys to needle newsroom managers, asking them to guess what readers wanted most. "They said sports, editorials, obituaries. I told them they were all wrong: it was the flyers." Mlodecki explained in 2005 how, a few years earlier, "I would receive several calls a month from customers saying, 'Do not put those flyers in my newspaper. I do not want them. I just throw them out.'" By 2005, he said, the calls had stopped. "People like to sit down on Saturday morning with their twenty or twenty-five colour catalogues of things that they can buy that week." Franklin says more and more advertisers preferred flyers to ad space inside newspapers. Seeing the potential for "a huge source of revenue," Jack Irving and his son John had dispatched Franklin to Florida to buy high-speed inserting equipment to bundle flyers with newspapers. "Jack and John said, 'This is a good industry, let's see how far we can go.'"

They were aggressive, as in all things. Gilles Haché, the publisher of a small newspaper in southeast New Brunswick, described how Brunswick News, after buying the paid-subscription *Le Madawaska*, also launched a free, flyer-bundled weekly, *La République,* to drive an existing flyer distributor out of the market. "That is what they do. They create competition and then slowly squeeze the lifeblood from their competitors.... They are putting us under constant pressure." Volpé confirms that "yes, when we go into a market, we compete." Under his direction, the circulation department in Moncton built a computerized mapping system with every road and home across New Brunswick, a template for even bigger possibilities. "We were thinking that maybe down the road, we might be able to deliver other things," Volpé says, smiling mischievously. "I thought maybe someday we could deliver the mail."

Volpé is visibly proud of what he built at Brunswick News. "People said it was the Irvings. It wasn't the Irvings. It was me." Critics like Erin Steuter can believe what they want about controlling the news: "There was no Irving scheme," he says. "We came up with the scheme. The reason wasn't complicated. It was for the distribution of flyers."

Having gained market share, the Irvings were determined to protect it. In 2000, Mark Leger quit the *Telegraph-Journal* and, with two business partners, launched a free alternative weekly for urban Saint John called *here*. "*Here* was young; it was liberal; and, most importantly, it was independent," wrote Megan Wennberg, a journalism student who chronicled its rise and fall. Besides the typical arts stories and listings, it also included smart local coverage aimed at engaging young people in civic affairs. One Saint John businesswoman who catered to young people told me in 2003, "People call *here* 'the paper.' No one calls the *Telegraph* 'the paper.'"

Brunswick News tolerated *here* until April 2004, when it expanded to Moncton—"a strategic error," Leger admitted later. They had poked the bear. Within five weeks, Brunswick News launched a free, youth-oriented weekly called *Metro Marquee* that offered discounted, or even free, advertising—which the Irvings could afford. "We looked at their ad rates the first week [they] came out," Leger told Wennberg, "and said, 'We can't do it. We can't print the paper for that.'" Jonathan Franklin says he remembers little of *here*, but "I would have supported going very aggressively after any little market segment that we did not have." *Here* offered a valuable one: young readers who might "graduate" to other Brunswick News publications.

Leger and his partners looked for new investors, but "nobody was going to buy into that paper knowing the Irvings were trying to take it down," Leger said. Defeated, they contacted Brunswick News and offered to sell. "Brunswick News has promised to carry on *here*'s tradition of offering a fresh perspective on local issues," said the press release announcing the sale. But the content was eventually watered down. Leger, who stayed on under Irving ownership for a few months, told Wennberg the new owners wanted to break down, "in a way I'd never witnessed before," the traditional wall that blocked advertisers from influencing editorial content. A sex column was killed, even though Leger argued it would send the wrong signal to young readers. "You can't own the mainstream and the alternative," Leger said. But Brunswick News could: those labels were just two demographic segments, fair game by the rules of the market.

The swallowing of *here* bookended a remarkable period for the Irving press. In just six years, two companies publishing four English daily newspapers had become a single enterprise overseeing three dailies, six English weeklies, six French weeklies, and an alternative weekly. If the reorganized, repurposed company was not as editorially ambitious as the *Telegraph* under Neil Reynolds, it was a lean, ruthlessly competitive and profitable machine. In 2004, Jonathan Franklin says, Brunswick News made $12 million in profit for the Irvings. "It was clear they had changed their minds about newspapers," says a former employee. "They liked newspapers now, because they were making money."

The internet age was dawning, but between J.K.'s nostalgia for ownership and Jim's singular focus on what worked, the Irvings weren't through with newspapers. "We were enthusiastic about the papers," Jim says. Turning to his father, he adds: "You were enthusiastic. You said, 'Boys, we gotta run it, keep 'er going, and do a good job.'"

"I'll tell you something else," J.K. says. "I have a grandson, Jamie, down at the newspapers." J.K.'s family pride and his well-known affection for his oldest grandson are evident as he describes Jamie's summer work for Neil Reynolds and his studies at Carleton and Columbia. "So we had somebody in the outfit who was coming along, who appreciated journalism and the newspapers.... That influenced me to a certain extent."

"Yeah, but basically, we had a business, right?" Jim says, gently dismissing his father's emotional motives. "That was Jamie's *interest*," he says of his son, "which was fine."

"But with me," J.K. says, "you asked me a question: what was making my mind tick." And it was the chance to see his grandson at the helm. "Okay?" he says. "For better or for worse."

The 2002 deal with David Cadogan that gave Brunswick News a minority stake in the *Miramichi Leader* and the *Kings County Record* in Sussex contained an unusual hiring clause: Jamie Irving would become publisher of the *Record* so he could learn the business. "I did not pay him anything," Cadogan would say. "He was given to me."

At twenty-four, Jamie became the first member of the Irving family listed on the masthead of one of its newspapers. Yet he was no different from his forebears, he claimed. "Everyone thinks they're just business guys, and they are, but ... my grandfather [is] very passionate about the woods," Jamie said. "The business interests usually spun out of their own personal interests. At least in my family, it's always, 'If you love it, and you want to live it, and you can make a buck at it, then it's okay to chase it.'"

Jamie knew what he loved. "I believe that he does truly want to put out good newspapers," Cadogan said in 2005. The Brunswick News brain trust suggested he turn the *Record* into a shopper, a free paper packed with advertising but light on editorial content, the kind of high-return product that made Victor Mlodecki happy. But for Jamie, there was no excitement in that, none of the heady intersection of politics and journalism he had learned from his uncle Paul Zed. Listening to the accountants during a meeting one day at 210 Crown Street, Jamie noticed the premier of New Brunswick was in the boardroom next door for a *Telegraph-Journal* editorial board meeting. The accountants were trying to curb his desire for more staff and more pages at the *Record*. "This could get expensive," they told him. As Jamie recounted later, he told them, "I want the premier to come and do *my* editorial board meetings, too. I want a *newspaper*."*

Jamie still relished being in the thick of politics. In 2000, Zed made a failed attempt at a comeback in federal politics, running in Saint John. Jamie helped his campaign. When reporters tried to keep Zed talking at his headquarters on election night, Jamie "thrust himself between the media and his uncle, saying the interview was over," the *Times-Globe* had reported. Jamie later worked at Hawk Communications, a public relations firm with ties to the Liberals that J.K. had bought for his daughter Judith, Zed's wife, to run. At Columbia, Jamie was captivated by professors who had worked at *The New York Times* and *Time* magazine, but also by guest speakers like Rupert Murdoch and Tina Brown,

---

* Jamie Irving declined my request for an interview. His comments here and throughout the book are drawn from his 2003 interview with Kim Kierans of the University of King's College School of Journalism.

media giants whose reputations were built on their power and influence over politicians.

In an interview for a CBC documentary in early 2003, one of the few times he has spoken publicly about why he loves journalism, Jamie said that "ultimately it's about reaching people ... and pushing on those issues that impact those people. I don't mean pushing like ram-rodding the agenda, but bringing the issues to light, creating a good dialogue, making people understand them, informing them. That part is very gratifying: when you take an issue, think about it, put your two cents in, and then you get to spread it around through a newspaper, have some people say it's wrong because of this, or that's a good idea, and you flesh the ideas out and something happens because of it."

Jamie hired reporters and had the *Record* redesigned with a front-page look inspired by the *International Herald Tribune*. "I didn't want it to be too parochial. I wanted it to be a community paper, but I wanted it to have a little bit of a bigger vision for the region." He missed seeing his own byline in the paper, he confessed, but this was balanced by the ability to shape the product overall. "Any idea that you had as a reporter or an editor that you thought would be brilliant if only you had the authority to make it happen—you now have the authority to play with stuff, and ideas, and copy things that you like."

Jamie struggled at first with advertising and human resources, and Rino Volpé worried he would be preoccupied with the Sussex newsroom, but circulation at the *Record* was up 15 percent in his first year on the job. The paper "had been bleeding money," says an insider, "and Jamie came in and turned it around, and then it started making a lot of money." Jim Irving and Rino Volpé soon rewarded him with responsibility for all the Brunswick News weeklies. "We're trying to give them each their own individual little flair, and let them reflect their community," Jamie said. The Irving critics were "trying to make it sound like a Walmart thing, where everyone's going to have to wear blue Nikes now because Walmart got a deal on them. But journalism's a different business than that. The business model is very much dependent on local news for local readers and local advertisers." If the critics "understood the business," he said, "they'd know it was not going to be one world, one voice."

The world the critics worried about was an Irving World, a concern Jamie dismissed using the same argument as other Irving publishers: "The news is the news." Keeping a lid on controversy might work for a year or two, he said. "You might be able to cover up a spill or something that happened, but it would never last forever. People would talk." His family was committed to New Brunswick for the long term, "so they've always had the best intentions," he said, echoing the platitudes uttered by his forebears over the decades. "As long as they're treated fairly and equally, the same as anybody else would be, and they get both sides of the story in the paper, they're not going to discourage you from anything."

Even before Jamie uttered those assurances, their underlying logic had been tested. At Thanksgiving 2002, an Irving-owned sawmill in Sussex, Bayshore Lumber, shut down, laying off more than twenty employees. "That's just market conditions," Jamie told Kierans, blending a defence of the shutdown and of the *Record*'s coverage into a single argument. "You had to have the story. It's a big employer in the community, the mill. You can't hide the news. The whole town would know if we didn't put it in. But it wasn't a big black eye for the sawmill either. It was just a straight story that had to be in the paper—because of global market conditions, softwood lumber tariffs, things like that are affecting Sussex quite directly, and we were reporting that." But it was not as straightforward for John Steeves, a veteran reporter who covered the story for the *Record*. No one from J.D. Irving Ltd. would comment, he would recount in 2005, but then he remembered Jamie was spending the weekend with his family. "I asked him to get confirmation. We had double-sourced the story, but it is always nice to get the other side. The confirmation came back with an order to hold the story for a week."

More broadly, Jamie's conversation with Kim Kierans contained hints that he did not fully embrace the approach of his mentor Neil Reynolds, who believed democracy was best served by a noisy, vigorous clash of ideas. Jamie felt a newspaper should smooth out those clashes by "just trying to get everybody to row in the same direction, so that we can move forward.... You try to build consensus." It sounded less like Reynolds's vision and more like Al Hogan's rally-the-community approach in Moncton—or even his father's, grandfather's, and great-grandfather's pleas to keep the wheels turning: a newspaper in Atlantic Canada, Jamie said, should make people "feel good about living here, make them feel these communities can grow. The newspaper can be a great cheerleader. That's what I love about the newspapers, ultimately. It's all the good stuff that a politician should be without any of the baggage of being a politician. It's bringing people together."

In his hirings, Jamie often reached back to the period he felt Jonathan Franklin had dismantled: the golden age of the *Telegraph-Journal*. He put Michael Woloschuk, who broke the story of the counterfeit Fabergé eggs, in charge of the Woodstock *Bugle-Observer*; Mike Tenszen, a former Toronto newsman who had covered Miramichi for the *Telegraph*, was hired as editor of the *Record*. Neither man lasted very long. Jackie Webster, who was a friend of both Woloschuk and Jamie, says they had "a falling out. They disagreed almost from the start.... I don't know what happened between them but they didn't part on very good terms."*

Another recruit was Bob Rupert, a retired journalism professor Jamie knew from Carleton University. A year or two after Jamie left Carleton without finishing his degree, they crossed paths at the wedding of a classmate. Rupert mentioned he had bought a summer place in Miramichi. In early 2003, Jamie asked him to spend some time at the *Miramichi Leader* as an in-house editorial consultant. Rupert was soon made editor-in-chief and instilled a new investigative ethos. The paper went after city councillors who had voted to subsidize a local company, Atcon, in its building of a new plywood factory, despite potential conflicts of interest. "We socked it right to them," Rupert says. "They'd never seen anything like that in the Miramichi paper." The *Leader* was selling more copies, and ad sales took off. Jamie was "delighted," Rupert says, but he sensed discomfort with the approach higher up the chain of command at Brunswick News.

There were more signs of trouble when Jamie asked Rupert to help fix *The Daily Gleaner* in Fredericton. "There was no buzz" in the paper, Rupert says. "It was totally predictable." The day before Rupert was to start, the new publisher of the *Gleaner*, Eric Lawson, called to tell him not to show up. Rupert sensed a power struggle: at meetings he attended, Rino Volpé seemed to support Jamie's editorial ambitions, but Victor Mlodecki was cool to them—and "Mlodecki really seemed to have more

---

* Michael Woloschuk did not respond to my requests for an interview. In September 2013, he returned to the *Telegraph-Journal* as a contributing editor.

clout than Rino." With Jamie's support, Rupert set up shop at the *Gleaner* anyway and worked there for six months, but "everything that we were trying to do there … we never seemed to be able to get it done." Volpé wanted to give Rupert four extra news pages he had requested, but Lawson vetoed it. "Mlodecki was backing [Lawson] and I think Jamie's father had a lot of time for Mlodecki, because Mlodecki was making him a lot of money," Rupert says. "All of his decisions were based on bottom line. He had no interest in the editorial product."

When Volpé left the job of vice-president in 2004 after the death of his son in an accident, Mlodecki took the position, tilting the balance of power away from Jamie's editorial vision. "That's when Jamie's role as an Irving seemed not to matter," Rupert says. "I think his father wasn't taking a huge interest in the papers either. He had other things that he was more interested in." After a few months at *The Bugle-Observer*, Rupert moved on to Bathurst, where Jamie asked him to set up a management team for the French weekly *Hebdo Chaleur*. But he clashed with Mlodecki, and after he wrote a *Gleaner* column criticizing Walmart for firing employees in Montreal who had tried to unionize, Jamie called to tell him his contract was cancelled.

"I still didn't dislike Jamie and I still don't dislike Jamie," Rupert says. "I should, I guess, but I don't. He's an okay guy." The problem was that "the newspapers were not his father's main concern.… I hope as he gets older and more experienced, he can do a good job with those papers, because I believe he wants to publish good papers."

In their 2003 interview, Kim Kierans asked Jamie Irving if he saw himself running all the Irving newspapers someday. "I don't know what they've got planned for me," he answered. "I just work away." In the *Telegraph-Journal* newsroom in Saint John, "there was some speculation that he was being groomed," says one reporter, "but it seemed kind of crazy. He was so young and new to the industry, I don't think that a lot of people believed that it was going to happen. And would his father trust him to run the province's newspaper?" Lisa Hrabluk, who had left the newspaper to work on a project for the University of New Brunswick, says Jamie's stated reverence for the Reynolds years made him "the golden child" in the eyes of the newsroom.

Jamie's future was always a "touchy" subject, Rino Volpé says, which he left Jamie and his father to sort out themselves. But Jamie had a powerful supporter in his corner: his grandfather, with whom he shared a special bond. J.K. had long before ceded daily decision-making to Jim, but his opinions still weighed on the big questions—and Jamie's future with the newspapers was one such big question. In November 2004, the announcement was made: Jamie Irving would become publisher of the New Brunswick *Telegraph-Journal*.

The decision left J.K.'s brother Jack and Jack's son John out in the cold. They still believed the newspapers—even as part of a single company—would be more credible, and would attract less controversy, if they were not managed directly by members of the Irving family. "John didn't want Jamie in the paper," says one observer, "but J.K. made it happen."

Jamie saw the question differently, defending his family's new, more direct involvement in the media business. "I think for years the newspapers were a little bit rudderless," he said. "There's a lot of rhetoric around about the owners having too much influence, and it was never true. Quite frankly, I think the surest way to kill a good newspaper is to take the owners out of it." If the employees "sense that the owners don't want to have anything to do with them, or are not allowed to have anything to do with them," it affects morale, he said. "I'm biased, obviously, but I do think it's important that the owners get involved in the papers. And I think the best thing that's happened in the last few years is that they've got involved again."

Now that involvement would be there for all to see. Jamie's name would appear in print not as a lowly summer reporter's byline, not on the masthead of the *Kings County Record* out in little Sussex—but as publisher of the *Telegraph-Journal*, the flagship paper, the one that saw itself as an essential guide to the overlapping worlds of politics and business. *The Daily Gleaner*, the Moncton *Times-Transcript* and the weeklies would soon become almost peripheral to the debate over Irving ownership: that debate would now focus on the *Telegraph* and the Irving who was running it—exactly the scenario Jack and John had wanted to avoid.

Jamie's promotion to publisher of the *Telegraph-Journal* was a more important turning point than anyone understood at the time. It was contributing to a growing fissure in the Irving family, one that would not remain a secret much longer.

11

BLUEBERRY MUFFINS

On his first day as publisher of the *Telegraph-Journal*, Jamie Irving called the editorial staff into a meeting in the cafeteria off the newsroom. "He gave quite a passionate speech," one reporter recalls. "He said we'd always been the poor sister or the poor cousin to all the other Irving companies, but those days were over. I remember him saying that what matters is grey matter, and we were all wondering what he meant until he pointed at his head. We were going to do great things." The publisher's attitude, the reporter says, was "rah-rah, let's-go-team, tackle-the-world."

Jamie quickly sent Peter Haggert to run *The Daily Gleaner* in Fredericton. Haggert had recruited some well-liked deputy editors, "but because of the culture in the newsroom at that time, they weren't willing to take any risks," says one reporter. "So, it was a hard time when you had a really good story. It could be frustrating." Jamie replaced Haggert with Mark Tunney, who returned for his third tour of duty with the *Telegraph*. "Mark was well known among the veterans and respected for his journalistic smarts," says one.

Tunney took the job because, to him, Jamie seemed more like his grandfather J.K. than his father, Jim. "Where Jim sees controversy as being bad for business," Tunney later wrote, "J.K. likes a more exciting paper, one that is combative and occasionally titillating, one unafraid to go on crusades or tilt at windmills." And of the new publisher himself—bulky, blond, young, and ambitious—Tunney said, in retrospect, that "it was easy to find hope in his practised disdain towards his family's Protestant work ethic and catholic business interests, its devotion to abstinence; his interest in producing news rather than newsprint; the way he distanced himself from his family without ever giving anything up."

Jamie's personal style, though, was off-putting. "He's very socially awkward," says one former editor. "He had a kind of slouched kind of walk—not what you'd call a confident walk. He doesn't hold his head up high or anything like that." Another reporter calls him "one of the most awkward people I've ever come across…. He can't say good morning, he can't chit-chat, he can't look you in the eye." His aspirations were clear—he told the staff he wanted the *Telegraph-Journal* to be *The Globe and Mail* or *The Wall Street Journal* of New Brunswick—but he didn't inspire. "He'd sit in his chair and he'd slouch down like the kid in class who didn't want to be there…. He'd be leaning back and fidgeting with his hands while he was talking."

Sometimes Jamie would quote from a scene in the Martin Scorsese film *Casino* in which Sam Rothstein, the Robert De Niro character who oversees a Las Vegas casino for the mob, complains that some of the kitchen's muffins have too many blueberries while others have too few. He orders the chef to be consistent, and brushes off his protests that it will take too much time: "I don't care. Put an equal amount in each muffin." This analogy baffled the reporters. "He's trying to articulate that he wants this high-quality, consistent product, and everybody in the room is just looking at him," says David Shipley, a rookie reporter. "They're not following him." John Mazerolle, another reporter, said Jamie clearly misunderstood De Niro's character. "That guy was crazy," Mazerolle said. "*That* was the point of that scene."

Two weeks after Tunney took over as editor-in-chief, Irving Oil was suddenly in the midst of its biggest corporate controversy since the refinery strike of the mid-nineties. Saint John was quickly and bitterly polarized by a tax concession right out of the 1950s world of K.C. Irving—a story that would put the *Telegraph-Journal*'s young new publisher to the test.

Kenneth Irving, K.C.'s grandson and namesake, and the first cousin of Jamie's father, had not let his natural gas loss to Enbridge deter him: he was still on a quest to transform Irving Oil from a fuel refiner and retailer into a regional energy company. Oil, of course, remained the core product in the short term: Kenneth and his father, Arthur, had invested a billion dollars in upgrading the refinery, helped by the provincial Department of the Environment, which, according to documents made public by the NDP, blocked demands by public health officials for a full environmental impact assessment. The upgrade allowed the refinery to produce a new low-sulphur gasoline to stay ahead of looming American regulations, essential if Irving Oil was to retain its growing market share in the U.S. Northeast. By 2005, the refinery was producing two hundred and fifty thousand barrels of oil a day, its output accounting for more than half the dollar value of all New Brunswick exports. Canaport, the massive floating dock that stretched out into the deep waters of the Bay of Fundy, was welcoming supertankers carrying three hundred and fifty thousand tonnes of crude.

But Kenneth's eye was fixed on the growing American appetite for greener energy products. He moved Irving Oil's marketing department to Portsmouth, New Hampshire, so he could focus on what he called "our front yard"—the area running from the Maritimes down the eastern seaboard to New York City, a market of 50 million people looking for "reliable, environmentally efficient energy." Bayside Power, the gas-fired generating station Irving co-owned with Westcoast, was up and running, with electricity it hoped to sell to New England. The next step would be a $750 million terminal at the Canaport site to bring in liquefied natural gas, or LNG, from ships and regassify it so Irving could send it by pipeline to customers, including in the United States.

Saint John residents woke up on Tuesday, March 17, 2005, to discover their city councillors had voted the previous evening to give Irving Oil a staggering tax concession: Canaport LNG's property-tax bill would be capped for twenty-five years at five hundred thousand dollars—far below the millions Irving would pay otherwise. "We have no interest in building an LNG terminal anywhere but here," Kenneth would explain, echoing the professions of hometown loyalty of his father and grandfather—which, as was often the case, carried a costly asterisk. "The one outstanding issue was the property tax rate," Kenneth said. "We had to make sure the competitive landscape was also attractive."

The mayor, Norm McFarlane, had secretly negotiated with Kenneth for months, revealing the deal to councillors as a *fait accompli* at the last minute. They had to vote on it that very night, the mayor explained, because Irving Oil's partner, the Spanish LNG company Repsol, would pull out if there was no approval by midnight. Several councillors were taken aback. The ultimatum gave them no time to study the details. Yet it passed, seven to four—after the mayor assured them they could trust Kenneth Irving. "I asked him very clearly, and looked into his eyes, and said, 'Kenneth, you look into my eyes and tell me, if this does not happen, will this facility not be here?'" McFarlane explained. "And he very clearly said, 'Yes, it is true.'" McFarlane would be mocked repeatedly for this leap of faith.

The tax concession flew in the face of Premier Louis Robichaud's Equal Opportunity Program, which, to prevent bidding wars, had banned municipalities from offering property-tax incentives. Indeed, the New Brunswick government would have to amend its statutes to legalize Mayor McFarlane's deal with Kenneth Irving. But few were surprised: governments had been helping the Irvings at public expense for years, and this latest example, while particularly egregious—the city was estimated to be forsaking as much as $112 million in revenue over a quarter century—was hardly a departure.

The jaded, cynical ratepayers of Saint John must have raised their eyebrows, then, when they opened their copies of the *Telegraph-Journal* the following Saturday and read an editorial condemning the council's vote. Under a headline that proclaimed the tax break "must be revisited," the editorial criticized both the terms of the deal—the twenty-five-year cap "seems extreme"—and "the flawed process by which it was reached," particularly the "inadequate and inaccurate" information councillors had received and the insistence that they vote before the midnight deadline. Considering how much time Irving Oil and Repsol likely spent on the proposal, the editorial said, councillors should have called their bluff and demanded more time.

Jamie "read and signed off on" the tough editorial, Tunney would recall. The publisher told his editor-in-chief the mayor "got snookered." The paper rapped Irving Oil again when a company press release condemned a group of concerned citizens who disrupted a subsequent council meeting to demand the decision be reversed. The tax concession "opened old and deep wounds in the city," it said, criticizing Irving Oil's "aggressive and defensive" public relations strategy and its "facetious," "unpro-fessional" press release that amounted to "bully tactics." The newspaper went on to urge council to rescind its decision.

This was something new, unseen even in the Neil Reynolds years: an Irving newspaper savaging an Irving company. "I must admit I was a bit shocked," said Glen Tait, one of the four councillors who voted against the deal. The LNG controversy "was covered for and against—and it was equal," he told *The Globe and Mail*. Michael Camp, the former reporter who became a journalism professor, said the paper's posture "may not mean that we have a free press in New Brunswick, but it's a lot more nuanced than some big man behind a curtain somewhere who directs all the activity." Even Erin Steuter, the Mount Allison professor and Irving critic, called the treatment "a bright spot … I thought that was appropriate coverage in a lot of ways."

Mark Tunney was proud of the coverage, though he would label a follow-up story, an exclusive interview with Kenneth Irving by Reynolds-era veteran Marty Klinkenberg, "a total puff piece." Klinkenberg's tone was deferential as Kenneth defended the company, but Tunney called that "a result of editorial neglect, not control." In fact, Tunney wrote, "there's not much love lost" between Jamie and "his svelte and sophisticated cousin Kenneth."

This raises the possibility of another explanation for the aggressive LNG coverage: a growing chasm between the J.K. and Arthur branches of the family. The stories, Camp says, proved "that Jamie has some sense of righteousness, but also that the Irvings' interests are somewhat divided." Lisa Hrabluk, who returned to the *Telegraph* as a columnist not long after the controversy, says she never measured the paper's independence by its Irving Oil coverage because "I knew that you could shit all over Irving Oil in a way that you couldn't" with J.D. Irving Ltd. "There was always a difference." J.K. was reportedly furious that Kenneth—and by extension his own brother, Kenneth's father, Arthur—had undone the good will that J.K.'s side of the family had built up in the city through its philanthropy. "You gotta pay some kind of reasonable taxes," Jim Irving says during our interview, though he shies away from discussing the LNG coverage in detail. "I can't even remember now what the fracas was down at the newspaper."

By 2013, Canaport LNG's assessed value was $300 million, the most valuable property in New Brunswick by far—yet its tax bill remained capped at $500,000, a fraction of what universities, hospitals, shopping malls, and potash mines, all worth far less, were paying. The lost revenue was particularly galling as Saint John grappled with a shortfall in its employee pension plan of more than $100 million. In 2005, however, the controversy represented an opportunity for Jamie Irving, just as his great-grandfather's will had for Neil Reynolds. "I think he wanted to set himself apart," says Lisa Hrabluk. "He wanted to appear independent."

If Jamie Irving was trying to prove something in 2005, the Senate of Canada barely noticed. A month after the LNG story exploded, the Standing Senate Committee on Transportation and Communications arrived in New Brunswick for two days of hearings, part of a national tour to study media ownership. Philip Lee, now a journalism professor, mentioned the tough LNG coverage, but the senators did not seem interested. Rod Allen, a veteran reporter for the *Times-Transcript* who covered the sessions, wrote that the hearings took place "against a backdrop of largely negative and somewhat shopworn allegations" about the Irving newspapers.

Erin Steuter and Marie-Linda Lord presented their familiar critiques of Brunswick News. Steuter suggested recent editorials in the *Telegraph-Journal*, *Times-Transcript*, and *The Daily Gleaner* praising the appointment of former premier Frank McKenna as Canada's ambassador to the United States were proof of Irving groupthink. She was politely rebutted by the committee chair, Senator Joan Fraser, a former journalist, who said it was more likely a case of applauding hometown success. "It is an almost natural, instinctive reaction, and I would not have thought of that as evidence of Irving control, necessarily," Fraser said.

Despite Fraser's rejoinder, she and several other senators asked detailed questions about the Irving monopoly. The only senator on the committee representing New Brunswick, Marilyn Trenholme Counsell, showed less curiosity. "I am certainly not an advocate for anyone's business interests," she said, "but could it ever be said that in New Brunswick we are lucky to have a family that will keep all these papers going?" Trenholme Counsell did not mention that her daughter, Lorna, had dated Jamie Irving while they both lived in Ottawa.

The hearings did not lead to changes in Canadian laws governing media ownership, but they were revealing: Irving-watchers in New Brunswick heard David Cadogan and David

Henley give their accounts of selling their weekly papers to Brunswick News, and Victor Mlodecki explain why flyer distribution quickened his pulse.

And it was there Mlodecki mentioned a significant milestone: earlier in the year J.D. Irving Ltd. had stopped producing newsprint. The company had spent half a billion dollars converting its Saint John paper mill so it could produce higher-grade products. This removed Brunswick News from the vertically integrated forestry chain the Irvings had built over the decades. The newspaper company was no longer a customer for Irving newsprint, but a business the family owned and ran on its merits, for its own money-making potential.

Other changes were afoot. Mlodecki sketched for the senators the history and structure of Brunswick News Inc. The common shares in the company were held by Otter Brook Holdings, he said, and Otter Brook's common shares "are wholly owned and controlled" by the three brothers, "James K. Irving, Arthur L. Irving and John E. Irving." His testimony, though, would soon be out of date.

There is a twinkle in J.K.'s eye when I ask him about the company. "Do you know where Otter Brook is?" he says. Jim jumps in: "We'll have to show you Otter Brook. Not many journalists up there. More blackflies." It's east of Juniper, somewhere out in the vast woodlands J.K. adores, not far from the tree nursery his father founded more than a half century earlier. "Google it," he suggests.

Otter Brook Holdings was incorporated in 1997, and Brunswick News was created as a subsidiary. Brunswick News in turn became the owner of the old CHSJ radio company,

Acadia Broadcasting, which had been owned by New Brunswick Publishing. But in May 2005, the pieces of the puzzle moved again. Acadia Broadcasting was transferred from Brunswick News to Jack Irving, who became its sole owner; around the same time, his son John left Brunswick News to run Acadia.

Then on June 28, 2005, Otter Brook's corporate registration was amended to remove the names of five directors: Jack and his son John, and Arthur and his two sons, Kenneth and Arthur Jr. The only remaining directors were J.K. Irving and his two sons, Jim and Robert. Otter Brook Holdings—and thus Brunswick News and all its newspapers—was no longer controlled by K.C. Irving's three sons. It now belonged solely to J.K.

"Art wanted out of the newspapers," J.K. explains. "Jack and I were going to buy Art out, and then Jack decided, for reasons, that he didn't want to stay in. So I bought both of them out." When I asked why, he continued: "I suppose when Art read those newspapers in the morning, he got upset, really upset," J.K. says, adding, "*I* can live with it."

At that point Jim cuts in. "You get to a point in life when you look at things and you want to do things, and change things or do different things," he says. But J.K. appears to lament one of the changes more than the other. "Art wanted out, and that's fine," he says. "And Jack should have stayed in with me, but he decided he should get out."

Jonathan Franklin suggests Jack may have pulled out because of his long-standing belief that no one from the family should directly control the newspapers. "I think there was a rift," Franklin says. "They had been quite canny over the years in having non-Irving names as their managers." Jamie's appointment as publisher of the *Telegraph-Journal* broke from that practice; Jim Irving acknowledges it raised eyebrows in the province. "You've got the Irving name and so on, his family, that's a bit controversial."

If Franklin is right, this change in ownership was another reckoning—the inevitable outcome of the Irvings' rethinking of their newspapers that began in 1998 when they decided to take a firmer hand. But Jack's departure may also have been a symptom of larger tensions building within the empire. Mark Tunney says not long after he took over as editor in March 2005, "I was told all these negotiations were going on to separate the families, and the newspapers were part of that. The parts were starting to move."

In September 2006, Jamie Irving hosted a splashy "sneak preview" of a redesigned *Telegraph-Journal* at Saint John's Imperial Theatre. There was a healthy dose of nostalgia, with Fred Hazel, the former editor-in-chief, sitting up front among the VIPs as teenagers dressed as newsies dashed down the aisles, hawking copies of the paper. But the emphasis was on modernity: the city's political and business elite watched a well-choreographed rollout of the bright new look by Montreal design consultant Lucie Lacava. "This is not your ancestors' paper," Lacava said as she showed off a giant replica of the front page. "It reminds me of a big-time newspaper," gushed Mayor Norm McFarlane, so recently gored on the editorial page over the LNG deal. "It puts Jamie Irving's stamp on the newspaper as its publisher, and I'm glad for that."

The launch was typical of Jamie, who was eschewing tradi-tional Irving privacy in favour of being a very public publisher. Overcoming his shyness, he began introducing the premier at the annual state of the province address, a Fredericton ritual co-sponsored by the newspaper. He joined the boards of the Saint John Airport Authority, the St. Joseph's Hospital Foundation, and Fredericton's Beaverbrook Art Gallery. "Jamie wants to be respected for his good taste," Mark Tunney wrote. Later, Jamie created a partnership with the provincial government to start a literacy foundation. Four years earlier he had called running a newspaper "all the good stuff that a politician should be without any of the baggage of being a politician." Now he was living up to that ambition, helping shape the direction of the city and the province.

Paradoxically, the *Telegraph-Journal* he published was— despite its bright design—dull. Jamie "had a hard time with anything that was human interest," says former reporter David Shipley. Experts, think-tank reports, studies, economic forecasts were the order of the day. "It all had to be related to public policy," one reporter remembers. "If I could interview Donald Savoie"—a Université de Moncton professor and an authority on the mechanics of government policy—"that would be on the front page." Lacava's design template called for a large, six-column, all-cap headline every day that implied excitement, but in practice—"TAKING STOCK," screamed one; "CONFLICTING VIEWS," announced another—they often heralded lifeless stories about a consultant's recommendations or conflicting policy proposals. "How does that square up with the average person?" Shipley asks. The main photograph was often of an economist or an expert. "The big joke was that if you wanted to get on the front page, you wore a suit and tie, you crossed your arms and you looked stern," one reporter remembers.

When a reporter pitched a light piece that real people would talk about—a price increase at Tim Hortons—it was rejected as not important enough to the *Telegraph*'s target audience. But policy wonks are not a large demographic in a small province. Jamie would explain to Tunney that his father, Jim, "liked it when the front page was dominated by business and political stories with good take-away information," but the aversion to brighter, populist stories struck many reporters as suicidal. "Early in my tenure as editor, Jamie told me he wanted the paper to be a *Wall Street Journal* for New Brunswick, a business-driven political newspaper," Mark Tunney said. "With that strategy, I told him, he could capture the billionaire market but most of them already had free subscriptions."

Jamie, though, was gaining confidence—Brunswick News made $24 million in 2005—and was less willing to heed Tunney's advice. "The daily story meetings were being held in Jamie's office, so there's no doubt he had a very big influence," says one former editor. "All stories from all sections were being pitched to him and he had the final say. There were times when Mark tried to guide him in the right direction, and would sometimes be overruled." When Tunney expressed unease with "economic boosterism" creeping into the newspaper, Jamie pointed out Moncton had a "positive newspaper," as if Al Hogan's upbeat approach to journalism at the *Times-Transcript* had spawned the city's success, and would do the same for Saint John if adopted by the *Telegraph*. "I don't want to make myself into some big rebel or anything, but I didn't like the way things were going," Tunney says.

Jamie was enjoying his ability to shape the agenda, to invite political leaders to editorial boards where they had to respond to his priorities. "He liked to sit there and say 'What about this?'" Tunney says. "I found he was enjoying that a bit too much, the power that went with that." Inevitably, the journalism collided with Irving interests. Lisa Hrabluk, who had returned to the paper, remembers being at an editorial board meeting about forestry policy, "and I expressed the view that we needed to walk carefully on this because Jamie was in the newsroom," she says. With the publisher listening, "I said you have to be careful because there's a perception of a newspaper that now has an Irving as the publisher having such a strong viewpoint on forestry." A couple of hours later, Hrabluk says, Tunney was sent to tell her she was no longer welcome at editorial board meetings. "So I had been back a matter of weeks and my career was done."

In April 2006, Jamie demoted Mark Tunney, making him editor of the feature-heavy Saturday paper—"a sign that I was on my way out," he says—and putting David Stonehouse, a returning Neil Reynolds veteran, in charge of daily provincial and business news. Stonehouse was a thoughtful, intelligent journalist, but as an editor shared Jamie's appetite for policy-heavy think-pieces—and accepted the publisher's role in editorial content. "I can't think of any times they had any battles," says reporter Daniel McHardie. Any story touching on the Irvings, says another newsroom employee, went through Stonehouse. "Dave was using these guiding principles: Business is good. Jamie likes business. The Irvings are a big business," says a former editor. "So, we'll do everything we can to promote business."

In little more than a year, the *Telegraph-Journal* had transformed from LNG pit bull to economic cheerleader. Jamie's vision of the paper increasingly echoed his father's: "Covering our businesses should be no different than anybody else's business," Jim Irving tells me. "If it's newsworthy, publish it." But in the next breath, he makes it clear he doesn't favour Neil Reynolds–style investigative reporting, nor anything too contentious, as if the price of Jamie's installation as publisher was making the newspaper an enterprise Jim could understand. "Our view of business in general in the province, we tell the folks at the paper, is, 'We're about New Brunswick. We're for New Brunswick,'" he says. "We're not in it to raise hell with everything that goes by. We don't think that's very constructive. There's lots of people out there who talk, and criticize all kinds of businesses and things. It's about how we make the place better."

This is completely defensible by the rules of capitalism—growth is always good, the theory goes—but for the owner of a newspaper, "we're not in it to raise hell" is a narrow journalistic mandate and a repudiation of virtuous muckraking. John Mazerolle, a City Hall reporter at the time, called the *Telegraph* "an advocacy paper for business," reminiscent of what Tom Crowther, the publisher of *The Daily Gleaner*, had described decades earlier: "What we need is more industry, so if you ask, 'Do we go out and attack industries,' frankly, no." The difference now was that a member of the Irving family was making that call.

Two Irvings, in fact: however reluctant Jim had once been to see his son in journalism, and however much Jamie once feared his father—whatever the rift had been between them—they were united now. Jamie was giving his father the newspaper he wanted, a *Telegraph-Journal* that was a voice for progress and for growth, defined in Irving terms.

In mid-2006, Mark Tunney returned from a vacation to a chilling greeting from Jamie Irving. "I enjoyed being able to do anything I wanted," he remembers the publisher telling him about his absence. "I didn't have you arguing with me and telling me why I can't do it." Not long afterward, he fired Tunney.

Jamie Irving's rally-the-troops speech on his first day felt like a distant memory. Tunney's removal was only one of many discouraging signs. The promised increase in newsroom resources to pay for better journalism failed to materialize. "It was a lot of talk and no action," says one reporter. "You just never saw the follow-through," says another.

Staff morale was important, of course, but the real measure of Jamie Irving would be on the front page of his newspaper. Over the course of a year, three major stories about his family would make the LNG coverage seem like a distant memory as well.

The first Irving story was another announcement by Kenneth Irving in October 2006, an announcement so breathtaking the company had delayed it to avoid influencing the New Brunswick election in September: the construction of a second refinery, a $7 billion project to double the company's processing capacity. It would create five thousand jobs during construction, and one thousand permanent jobs, increasing the province's exports by 50 percent—news actually worthy of a banner, all-caps *Telegraph-Journal* headline: "OUR BLACK GOLD."

Lisa Hrabluk saw that headline as confirmation that Jamie was now on board as a full-fledged supporter of Irving solidarity. "It's either he truly does believe in it, and he instructs the paper because it's his right as the publisher to say 'Hey, we're going to get behind this'—or it was too important a project for the family for it not to happen. But that's where it changes, I'd say: that headline."

Around Saint John the hype was dizzying. "When you talked to businessmen and politicians, you could almost see the dollar signs in their eyes," says David Shipley, who covered the announcement for the *Telegraph-Journal* business pages. "All of a sudden Saint John looked like an industrial renaissance. The good old days were back." The provincial government helped fund a study on how the city could manage the rapid growth. Shawn Graham, elected premier just two weeks before the announcement, described the job impact as "a planeload of New Brunswickers coming home every week from out west." Another *Telegraph* headline echoed that: "COME EAST, YOUNG MAN." A third triumphantly labeled Saint John "CALGARY EAST."

The coverage was "over the top," David Shipley says. The *Telegraph* had lost a lot of veteran reporters, he says, and young, inexperienced journalists like him were easily wowed. And despite Irving Oil's caution that feasibility and environmental studies still had to be done, "I don't think anyone doubted that that family could do a second refinery if that's what its intention was," Shipley says. "This was a guy who built a gas station in Bouctouche and built it into this massive company. A New Brunswicker did this. There was an aura that when these guys set their mind to something, they're going to achieve it." That enthusiasm triggered a small real estate bubble in Saint John and led Graham's government to green-light a costly new highway interchange to accommodate anticipated refinery traffic. "The TJ has some responsibility for part of that," Shipley says, "and, by extension, my exuberance as a reporter." Still, "never once did I ever get an overt talk like, 'You've got to play a story this way,'" he says. "You know you work for an Irving newspaper but that's not necessarily their fault, per se." On the other hand, "you didn't want to have a career-ending move. In the back of your mind, that was at play."

The second Irving story inspired less exuberance in Irvingland, and less in the *Telegraph-Journal*: it never made the front page, even though it was a gripping yarn that had tongues wagging across New Brunswick. It began on September 19, 2007, when Ken Langdon decided to take on the newspaper monopoly.

Brunswick News hired Langdon to be publisher of *The Woodstock Bugle* shortly after the company bought the paper in 2003. Langdon merged the *Bugle* with the paper in nearby Hartland to create *The Bugle-Observer*, streamlining the operation and converting a $118,000 loss in 2003 to a $560,000 profit three years later. But, he would testify, Victor Mlodecki—in 2007 the vice-president of Brunswick News—was not satisfied: he accused Langdon of missing budget forecasts and "running the *Bugle-Observer* into the ground." Langdon blamed Mlodecki's frugality. "They were not willing to pay drivers what they were worth," he said. "People became frustrated with the delivery and would ultimately cancel their subscriptions." Sensing his days were numbered in the summer of 2007, Langdon emailed internal documents to his home computer—in case, he said, he needed to sue for wrongful dismissal.

When Langdon called Jamie Irving to resign, he was offered a year's salary as severance if he would sign a three-year non-compete clause. Langdon refused. Brunswick News lawyers prepared a breach of trust lawsuit over his plans to launch his own paper serving Woodstock and the rest of Carleton County. In a hearing in Saint John, without Langdon's knowledge, they asked Judge Peter Glennie of the Court of Queen's Bench for an emergency injunction. By emailing corporate secrets to his home—income statements, budgets, sales data, business plans—Langdon had, in Mlodecki's words, given himself "a complete guide to the entire operation of the *Bugle*." Not only would Langdon's newspaper, *The Carleton Free Press*, "compete unfairly" in *The Bugle-Observer*'s market, Mlodecki said, it was "in a position to replicate the entire business of the *Bugle* on a virtually immediate basis."

Glennie granted Brunswick News its request for a rare Anton

Piller order, which allowed the company to send private investigators and KPMG accountants, with warrants, into Langdon's home to recover the documents. First devised by a British judge, Hugh Laddie, in the 1970s to let a plaintiff use the element of surprise to prevent the destruction of evidence, it was later described by Laddie himself as "a Frankenstein's monster" that had been used far beyond his original intent.

Langdon learned of the search when it was already under way. He hurried from his rented office in downtown Woodstock to his home, discovering that "the searchers had started to search through my wife's lingerie ... I assured them they would find no records there." They seized hard drives, pay stubs, employment contracts, eight CDs belonging to his wife, and video games belonging to his son. In a folder in a computer's virtual trash bin, they found information on flyer carriers and routes. Brunswick News pointed to these documents when they asked Glennie, in a full public hearing, for an injunction blocking Langdon from using information he'd taken from the *Bugle-Observer*; the company later amended its request to ask that Langdon be stopped from launching the *Free Press* altogether for one year. When Glennie admonished Brunswick News for "ratcheting up the remedy"—an Anton Piller order can be used only to preserve evidence, not add to a plaintiff's case—the company reverted to its original request.

The attack on Langdon fed existing perceptions of the Irvings, and was widely seen as an attempt to snuff out a potential competitor. "They have taken whatever steps they deem necessary in order to ensure they achieve their desired result," Langdon's lawyer, Eugene Mockler, argued. Even more damaging, Langdon's letter of resignation, filed in court, accused Mlodecki of telling Brunswick News publishers he would spend $1 million to undercut a competing flyer distributor in the Bathurst market and drive it out of business. Langdon also said Brunswick News tried to force a competing flyer distributor in Edmundston to sell out to them. "The object of BNI is to capture the total flyer market in New Brunswick," Langdon said.

After ignoring the case for several days, Brunswick News started reporting the hearing. Strangely, while it took place in a Saint John courtroom, no one from the *Telegraph-Journal* was assigned to it. Instead, Rod Allen, a *Times-Transcript* reporter, travelled from Moncton, Mlodecki's base of operations, to file reports for all the Brunswick News newspapers. Allen, who snidely referred to criticism of the Irvings at the 2005 Senate hearings as "shopworn," played this one straight: his reporting was even-handed toward Langdon and his lawyer, Eugene Mockler, and he identified Brunswick News as an Irving company.

Glennie rejected the injunction request. Langdon was free to compete, he ruled, as long as he didn't use the information he took from the *Bugle-Observer*. Brunswick News, the judge said, "cannot claim a monopoly over its advertisers and customers." Deliciously, he quoted Mlodecki's own comments at the 2005 Senate committee hearing that the media are "regulated by the hard laws of the marketplace." Langdon told reporters he was "excited to forge ahead with the new paper," but in the Irving newspapers there were no exuberant headlines, no cheerleading for a new company creating new jobs in New Brunswick, and none of Allen's stories made it onto the front page.

The first issue of *The Carleton Free Press* appeared the same week. Bob Rupert, the retired Carleton professor who had worked for Jamie, heard about the case and called to congratulate Langdon, whom he'd met while working on the Brunswick News weeklies; Langdon hired him to run the *Free Press*. "I really,

really wanted that paper to go," Rupert said. By December, he was the editor-in-chief, injecting investigative zeal into the small editorial staff. The paper began to gain circulation and advertising. Sensing it had been bested in the court of public opinion, Brunswick News dropped its broader lawsuit for breach of trust.

But the battle wasn't over. *The Bugle-Observer* slashed its advertising and subscription rates, sometimes by more than half—to undercut the *Free Press*, Rupert insists. "They were blowing money right out the window there, and we knew why," he says. "They wanted their monopoly back." Langdon and Rupert filed a complaint with the federal Competition Bureau, documenting deeply discounted offers to *Bugle-Observer* advertisers, but it went nowhere. "The reason for that legislation is to protect consumers," Rupert says. "Woodstock now had two newspapers instead of one, so the consumers were doing fine." Brunswick News denied the accusation. "We are offering a volume discount for buying longer-term packages, which is normal business," the company's manager of weeklies, Kelly Madden, would argue.

The *Free Press* could not match the discounts, and the global recession dealt the final blow. The paper published its last edition on October 28, 2008, a year after it launched. While *The Daily Gleaner* ran a Canadian Press item on the paper's demise, the *Telegraph-Journal* did not report on it. Though it had been unable to ignore the spectacle of the hearing before Justice Glennie a year earlier, the Irvings' flagship newspaper of politics and business was silent on the final chapter in a political-business story that had captured the imagination of New Brunswickers.

The third Irving story—the biggest of them all—came to light not in New Brunswick, but near the top of the TD Tower in downtown Toronto. On Tuesday, November 20, 2007, Gordon Pitts, a business reporter for *The Globe and Mail*, rode an elevator to the fifty-fourth floor, to the private dining room, where a wall of windows offered a spectacular view of the CN Tower and Lake Ontario. The occasion was a luncheon to announce the latest inductees into the Canadian Business Hall of Fame, including the three Irving brothers, J.K., Arthur, and Jack. Pitts, who wrote a book about Atlantic Canada tycoons, *The Codfathers*, was hoping to land a good story. "What a chance to talk to the Irvings," Pitts recalls. "You rarely get that in Toronto."

There would be no joint interview. Arthur and Jack stayed away, leaving only J.K. to attend along with his sons, Jim and Robert. "That was another signal to me," Pitts says. He sat down with J.K. on a sofa in a reception area, and "somewhere in the middle of it," Pitts says, "I asked—I can't remember the exact question, but—'Any thoughts of breaking it all up?' And he shocked me: he said, 'We're undergoing that process.'" Just like that, Pitts had a major scoop.

Hints that something important was happening within the empire had appeared earlier in 2007, when Harvey Sawler's book, *Twenty-First-Century Irvings*, was published. A largely positive portrait of the family that took their statements at face value and argued their biggest problem was ineffectual public relations, the book nonetheless observed delicately that the Irvings were "not necessarily engaged in an orderly process of succession." There was talk in Saint John about a growing divide, Sawler reported, exacerbated by diverging fortunes: Irving Oil was soaring while J.D. Irving Ltd. struggled. Kenneth's LNG deal, and the resulting blow to the family's reputation, still rankled with the forestry Irvings. And Sawler pointed to a dinner held in 2006 to honour the contributions of Jean Irving, J.K.'s wife, to the Salvation

Army: twelve hundred people attended, but not a single member of Arthur's family.

"This is nothing to fret about," Sawler wrote. "It is natural and happens to most families." Except, as Pitts recognized that November day in Toronto, the Irvings were not most families.

Pitts hurried back to *The Globe and Mail* newsroom. He had heard rumours, "but I had no idea they were actually in the throes of doing a total re-org," he says. Pitts and several *Report on Business* colleagues hit the phones and worked their sources, and within a couple of hours, they put together the story that appeared on the front page of *The Globe and Mail* the next day: "Irving Brothers Look to Break Up Empire," the headline said.

The *Telegraph-Journal* also had a reporter at the top of the TD Tower that day. Marty Klinkenberg, the likeable feature writer, had been dispatched to Toronto to cover the Hall of Fame announcement. Klinkenberg filed a conventionally positive story, with a nice description of the luncheon menu, a bit of corporate name-dropping, and quotations from J.K. paying tribute to his father. There was no sign that Klinkenberg had any idea about the split, nor that J.K. had thought to ensure his own paper could match the scoop he had obligingly given Pitts.

The *Globe* story was brimming with juicy details: J.K.'s son Jim and Arthur's son Kenneth, it said, were at odds over the strategic direction of their respective divisions, and increasingly fed up about how the complex, overlapping ownership structure required them to consult each other. Jack and his son John, meanwhile, "grew tired of being also-rans" and resented Jim's "blustery" dominance. Adding to the hard feelings was a reversal of fortune: in the early nineties, when Irving Oil was short on cash to finish its refinery expansion, J.D. Irving Ltd. had provided funds; now, with J.D. Irving Ltd. strapped for cash, Kenneth, citing the cost of the new refinery, had begged off when Jim asked for help. These tensions had, in turn, "driven a wedge" between J.K. and his two brothers. And so they had decided to restructure everything, disentangling the various holding companies to create clear lines of ownership: J.K. and his family would have more direct control over forestry while Arthur and Jack, along with Arthur's son Kenneth, would have clear command of the energy business.

This would likely require breaking up the trust K.C. had established in Bermuda through his will—the trust designed to last thirty-five years and keep the empire intact by discouraging family members from stepping out of line. "It is understood that an international team of tax, corporate and restructuring lawyers and financial specialists are currently working on a plan to carve up the company," the piece said.

The story hit New Brunswick like a bomb. It was the talk of the province's political and business power brokers, especially in Saint John. Everyone had a theory about the feud that now threatened an empire estimated to be worth $8 billion. Joan Carlisle Irving traces the dispute back to her divorce from Arthur, and J.K.'s refusal to shuffle ownership of companies to help his brother; others suggest that J.K. and Jim were cool to Kenneth's refinery ambitions, and that Jim had made a play to control Irving Oil, arguing Kenneth wasn't up to the job: "Arthur pushed back," says one Saint John business person.

Another theory is that Jim, by dismissing John's abilities when he worked for J.D. Irving Ltd., had unwisely turned his cousin and potential ally into a rival. John's father, Jack, represented the tie-breaking vote in the three-brother triumvirate. In a follow-up story, Pitts reported that John's "grievances, and his particular enmity toward first cousin Jim, are so strong ... that he is driving the division between the camps." Others in Saint John believe Jamie's appointment as publisher of the *Telegraph-Journal* exacerbated the clash between Jim and John.

Only a handful of New Brunswickers knew the truth, of course, and one of them was that very same publisher. In story meetings, Jamie had been "kind of open about the fact that there were frictions in the family," one editor remembers. The *Globe* story captivated the newsroom as it did the rest of the province. "Obviously everybody had to read it," says one staffer. "It was the only thing everybody was reading all day." Now Jamie was in the awkward position of knowing his own future might hinge on how the Bermuda trust would be dissolved and paid out—while at the same time having to decide how to cover the process in his newspaper. It was an undeniably huge story of singular importance to his target readership. Political and business leaders in New Brunswick, after all, needed to know what was going on with the Irvings.

The next day, a small story appeared on the front of the *Telegraph*'s business section: "It should surprise no one," the article explained, that the Irvings had started succession planning. The headline, quoting a written statement by J.D. Irving Ltd.'s vice-president of communications, Mary Keith, was succinct and definitive: "'It's Business as Usual,' Irving Says."

It was the first and last reference to the split that would ever run in the *Telegraph-Journal*. In sharp contrast to Neil Reynolds's three days of news and analysis on K.C.'s will, the story of the Irving divide vanished after one mention, never to reappear. "It was fairly obvious we weren't going to be big on that," says David Shipley, the business reporter. Those who wanted to understand the Irving breakup would have to rely on *The Globe and Mail* and whatever gossip they could pick up around Saint John. It was a reminder of how the Irving ownership continued to complicate the newspaper's reputation, as it had for decades—except now no one could claim that family members weren't involved in editorial decisions.

That single, brief story in the *Telegraph* was noteworthy in another way: its key phrase—"business as usual"—was the same line that had appeared in the paper on August 24, 1993, when the McCain brothers denied that their feud would have any impact on their empire.

And it was just as wrong in 2007.

12

MORE TREES ARE THE ANSWER

▼

Two weeks into the 2006 New Brunswick election campaign, Progressive Conservative strategists resigned themselves to the idea that they weren't going to get any breaks from the *Telegraph-Journal*. On the front page of the Saturday edition on the Labour Day weekend was a large photograph of Jacqueline Robichaud, the widow of the late former premier Louis Robichaud. Her hands cupped the youthful face of the Liberal opposition leader, Shawn Graham, at an event the previous night. "Mrs. Robichaud passes the torch," said the caption. Jacqueline Robichaud had been Robichaud's second wife, and hadn't known him when he enacted his famous reforms in the sixties; arguably, the torch wasn't hers to pass. Regardless, for New Brunswickers who idolized the late premier, the image of her laying on of hands was powerful.

Two days later came another front page damaging to the PC re-election effort. The Monday *Telegraph* featured an interview with a Progressive Conservative candidate in Saint John,

Peter Hyslop, calling on his own leader—Premier Bernard Lord, seeking a third mandate—to apologize to New Brunswickers for a botched fuel-purchase contract by the provincial power utility that looked like it would cost taxpayers hundreds of millions of dollars.

The story took an oddly circuitous route to the *Telegraph*'s front page. Written by Daniel McHardie, then a Moncton *Times-Transcript* reporter, it was buried on page A9 of the Moncton paper the previous Friday. The papers were sharing stories frequently by this time, but McHardie's piece wasn't picked up elsewhere. After he filed a follow-up story on Sunday with Lord's reaction, however, the *Telegraph* blasted it—and the original interview story with Hyslop—across Monday's front page. "That really changed the narrative of the campaign," McHardie recalls. The Liberals revived the issue and soon were rising in the polls. A few days later, Graham celebrated his surge by hopping on a horse—and that triumphant image, too, ran prominently on the *Telegraph*'s front page.

These three editorial decisions prove nothing. Each is easily defended: the two photographs were irresistible, and Hyslop's comments were undeniably newsworthy. The Tories, however, saw a pattern. After all, thirty-eight-year-old Shawn Graham was not just any Liberal. His father, Alan Graham, the minister of natural resources in Frank McKenna's government, had eliminated a law that forced J.D. Irving Ltd. and other companies to buy wood first from small private woodlot owners—a costlier proposition than buying from their own subsidized Crown land leases. Shawn was his father's political assistant at the time. "I was very sensitized to the importance of this company, more on the wood side than the oil side," says the younger Graham, who grew up not far from K.C. Irving's hometown of Bouctouche. "The

Irvings have always had a very strong and influential role in the economy of Kent County."

Graham seemed like the kind of premier the Irvings would want to deal with, and it looked to the Tories like the *Telegraph-Journal* understood that. Even one of Graham's closest advisors, Doug Tyler—another former Liberal minister of natural resources—says "any fair-minded person" would admit the *Telegraph* had a favourite in the 2006 campaign. "If you read their editorials it wouldn't take you long to understand that they were not too happy with the current government and were looking for change," he says. "You'd have to be blind not to understand that." But Tyler and Graham both argue persuasively that the Moncton *Times-Transcript* was pro-Tory in 2006, and in two previous elections. There can't be Irving control, Tyler argues, if two of their papers favour different parties. "I just don't understand how any owner could try to figure all that out," he says. In 2006, however, only one paper was directly controlled by a member of the family. Jamie's role has "made it more challenging for them," Tyler admits. "It's difficult for people to understand that there can be that separation."

Tyler grew up in a rural area where the biggest employer is a large Irving sawmill, so the fascination with the family is nothing new to him. "Where I come from, every day, that's what people talk about: the Irvings, all the time. Their mill, how they're doing this, what's going on here. They're not a publicly traded company. They don't have quarterly meetings. No one knows how much money they make or don't make. It's a great topic." But complaints of partisan bias are inherently subjective, he says. "No one gets too concerned," Tyler notes astutely, "if the Irving papers are taking a position they agree with." Tyler says he infuriated J.K. and Jim in the late nineties when, as minister of natural resources, he allocated some Crown wood to First Nations communities after they won a treaty-rights case—and then he was criticized in a *Telegraph-Journal* editorial for not giving more to aboriginal people. He also points to the paper's recent support for reform of the federal Employment Insurance program, even though it potentially complicates J.D. Irving Ltd.'s ability to hire seasonal forestry workers.

Graham's Liberals won the 2006 election with a three-seat majority despite a slightly lower popular vote than the Tories; the narrow win made the *Telegraph*'s perceived bias all the more infuriating to the PCs. Jeannot Volpé, the interim PC leader after Lord retired, was among the most bitter, and in the spring of 2008, he lashed out at the Irving newspapers in a manner rarely seen among mainstream politicians. *The Carleton Free Press*, still alive then but bleeding money, had filed its complaint against Brunswick News with the federal Competition Bureau. Volpé introduced a resolution in the legislature to ask the Senate committee on communications to return to New Brunswick for another look at the Irvings, who were now "getting directly involved with the paper," he said.

The debate on Volpé's motion was far from the legislature's best moment, with members digressing into self-promotion or lamenting media behaviour that had nothing to do with ownership. A veteran Liberal from Saint John, Roly MacIntyre, defending the Irvings, seemed to confirm Volpé's thesis when he asked Tory members, "Have you ever heard the saying, 'Do not beat up on somebody who buys ink by the barrel?' It's still valid." Bob Rupert, who came from Woodstock with Ken Langdon to watch, says the quality of the debate was "in the basement." The Tory member for Woodstock, David Alward, was one of the few to get to the point—what he called "unfair business practices....

The Irving newspaper empire is using its clout to put *The Carleton Free Press* out of business."

The Liberals, however, used their majority to amend Volpé's motion, removing the call for new Senate scrutiny and inserting a line "to affirm the independence of the press from undue governmental and commercial influence." The watered-down motion passed, and nothing came of it. In the wake of the debate, Daniel McHardie, who had moved from the *Times-Transcript* to the *Telegraph-Journal*, proposed the paper publish an in-depth exploration of the Irving media issue. Like other staffers who had made similar pitches over the years, he was rebuffed.

In office, the Graham Liberals established "a very close relationship" with Jim Irving, according to one insider. Tyler, who became a key advisor in Graham's office in 2009, says he spoke to Jim Irving "certainly a few times every month"—a frequency he calls appropriate for a major employer competing in the world market. "Government at any level has to always consider how policies might affect thousands and thousands and thousands of jobs," he says.

Layered on top of that reality was the Irvings' ownership of the newspapers. "You couldn't have a conversation with an Irving," says one senior official, "without wondering if something was going to appear in a newspaper, or lead to a line of questioning." In this symbiotic relationship, each took cues from the other: Liberal communications staffers found the *Telegraph* receptive to leaks of looming announcements—and willing to abide by the condition they not contact government opponents and critics in time to include their reactions in the initial story. "So we'd get it early," says a reporter, "but the story was totally one-sided." Graham's advisors, meanwhile, flattered Jamie's desire to be a political insider, calling him often to "bend his ear about something," one reporter says. A former cabinet minister says Graham's people "were constantly trying to see if you could appease Jamie Irving." Ministers with policies to promote were sent to Saint John to lunch with the publisher or speak to the editorial board. "When you're asked to go down and meet with a kid who at twenty-seven is publisher of all these newspapers," says the ex-minister, "I found it not only appalling but kind of surreal."

The *Telegraph*'s perceived importance was encoded in Liberal DNA. When Frank McKenna was premier from 1987 to 1997, the paper was "hugely important" to the government's elaborate public relations efforts, says one insider. "It was pervasive. There was always an anticipation: how can we craft the headline the next day?" Many of the architects of that strategy, including McKenna's director of communications, Maurice Robichaud, now worked for Graham. In the intervening years, however, newspapers—already waning in the nineties—had seen circulation plummet. "It's a very closed community, those who actually read the newspapers and care what those headlines are," says the insider. Yet Graham's spin doctors felt they could influence public opinion through Jamie and the *Telegraph*. Even within Brunswick News, the *Times-Transcript* in Moncton and *The Daily Gleaner* in Fredericton had more circulation, yet the media strategy in Graham's office "started and ended" with the *Telegraph*, a source says.

Graham's Liberals didn't always get a free ride from Jamie's *Telegraph-Journal*: on reforms to health care governance and community college training, the editorial page was critical. But the government's overall orientation—relentless, upbeat touting of large projects like the new Irving refinery that would jump-start economic growth—aligned nicely with J.K.'s view that provincial policy should be "to keep the wheels turning," with Jim's philosophy that journalism should be about "how we make the place better," with Jamie's vision that a newspaper should get everyone "rowing in the same direction."

The apotheosis of this alignment hit newsstands on August 4, 2008, the New Brunswick Day holiday: a thick Saturday edition of the paper devoted to celebrating the province. The Graham government's often-mocked and weirdly existentialist marketing slogan, "BE IN THIS PLACE," was the giant front-page headline. The paper was packed with stories, columns, and essays extolling all that was positive about New Brunswick, with only the briefest, token acknowledgment of problems. The new editor-in-chief, Shawna Richer, wrote that the paper wanted "to put the government's campaign to the test. Do the concepts hold up under scrutiny?"

The answer was an overwhelming yes: headlines rang with uplifting phrases such as "HOPE RESTORED," "LET'S BUILD ON THE STRENGTH OF BEING SMALL," and "BOOM TIMES"—Jamie Irving's "cheerleader" philosophy writ large. Shawn Graham, not surprisingly, defends it: New Brunswick's population decline had stopped, school test scores were improving, and purchasing power was rising, he says. "Yes, the paper was touting that, but I think it was also promoting what New Brunswickers themselves were starting to feel," he says. "That optimism was there."

Jim Irving measures a government by one policy above all others: how it accommodates the forest industry. "New Brunswick has to compete in the global marketplace," he says, "and the forest product business in many ways is a global business. So we just encourage the province to make sure they understand what it takes to have a globally competitive company operate from New Brunswick, because public policy drives a lot of our input costs."

By input costs, Jim means the price of doing business: taxes, power rates, and wood supply. J.D. Irving Ltd.'s wood supply doesn't grow only on the vast tracts of land it owns outright: much of it comes from the publicly owned Crown lands it and other forest companies lease from the province—a system nominally answerable to citizens, but with a regulatory framework designed for the pulp industry. Trees in New Brunswick take forty years to mature, so companies file twenty-five-year management plans for their leases while the government establishes five-year logging limits. The idea is to let industry cut what it needs now while conserving enough to guarantee a supply of trees for decades into the future. The trick is balancing the cycle for both short-term and long-term goals; Irving's constant drive to build bigger, faster, more efficient mills to process ever more wood complicates the equation. The solution, the company argues, is to allow more and more tree-growing plantations on public land.

For governments, the political temptation is obvious. Without intensive, industrial harvesting, an Irving forester told the *Telegraph-Journal*'s Richard Foot in 1996, "we wouldn't have the number and the size of the mills that we have, and the number of employees." It also helps Irving obtain the capital for more mill expansion: banks are reluctant to lend to forestry companies that don't have a guaranteed long-term wood supply. So newer, bigger mills require more trees, which capitalize newer, bigger mills: a circular logic that keeps wheels turning.

In 2001, J.D. Irving Ltd. launched a new push for more wood, working through the provincial forest industry association to persuade the PC government of Bernard Lord to help pay a

Finnish consulting firm, Jaakko Pöyry, to study the Crown lands system. Not surprisingly, the report recommended the province double the wood supply over fifty years by allowing more plantations and by loosening the rules for special management areas, sections of Crown forest where logging was restricted to preserve wildlife habitat.

Environmentalists argued more plantations would accelerate erosion and soil loss and overwhelm the forest ecosystem—though Irving insists its management practices minimize these effects. "We've got a good story on the wood, you know," J.K. says. "We're the only outfit east of Montreal that has a wildlife biologist, who's been with us for years. His sole job is to make sure everybody in the company is doing things right as far as the environment goes. Things change. People are getting more information and do things today differently than they did it twenty years ago. We change."

Environmentalists weren't alone in pushing back against Jaakko Pöyry: small-scale contractors and private woodlot owners felt threatened by greater industrialization on public land. And on an internal government website, foresters, biologists, and forest rangers—the very people who monitored and regulated Crown land use—called the report's doubling scenario "biased," "misleading," "a travesty" and "a big roll of the dice" that did not account for climate change. "Give your head a shake," wrote one.

The industry had counted on Premier Lord to endorse the report, but Lord, elected on a promise of a more consultative style of government, sensed the strong current of opinion against Jaakko Pöyry. "Outside the cities, it was in their face," says environmentalist David Coon. "So many people had livelihoods based on the woods, and they were losing that." Lord asked a special committee of the legislature to hold hearings, which only underscored the document's unpopularity: the committee was forced to schedule six extra meetings on top of the original seven, and more than two hundred witnesses appeared, most of them denouncing the doubling scenario. Coverage of the hearings by the pre–Jamie Irving Brunswick News was even-handed, treating critics of Jaakko Pöyry as serious and sincere. "I'm asking the committee for a forest management system that is people-oriented, not industry-oriented," Stephanie Coburn, a farmer and woodlot owner, told the committee at one hearing. The committee report, released a year later, called the response "overwhelming.… The management of New Brunswick's Crown lands is obviously of great significance and consequence to the people of New Brunswick."

The PC, Liberal, and NDP members unanimously rejected the doubling scenario and the additional harvesting in conservation areas, and called for a reduction in clear-cutting—surely not the outcome Jim Irving had hoped for. While the committee called for some kind of guaranteed long-term wood supply for industry, it also implicitly repudiated Irving's endless-growth philosophy: technological advances in mills, the report said, put "continuous upward pressure on the demand for wood," creating "an insatiable industrial appetite for fibre which is unlikely to diminish over time." And while market forces require companies to keep expanding, it said, "there are biological limits to the amount of wood that can be grown in New Brunswick."

Doug Tyler says the conclusions show how Irving's supposed influence is actually an albatross. "They are seen as being big and powerful," he says. "There's always a fear of government doing anything that's seen in any way to be favouring the Irvings, so it becomes very challenging for them. They have a much steeper hill to climb than most people do. They have to work much harder at it than other people would have to."

Lord commissioned more studies, delaying a decision on wood supply until after the 2006 election, which he lost to Shawn Graham's Liberals. Within weeks of taking office, Graham appointed Francis McGuire, another former McKenna advisor, to co-chair a study on how New Brunswick might end its dependence on federal equalization payments. Under McKenna, McGuire had orchestrated the subsidies that convinced Mary Jean Irving to move two Master Packaging production lines from Prince Edward Island to New Brunswick; now he revived Jaakko Pöyry's proposals for more plantations on Crown land and more harvesting in special management areas. The committee that rejected those ideas had included three Liberal members, but McGuire argued they "didn't understand exactly the debate." Despite ninety hours of testimony from two hundred witnesses, McGuire said, "a lot of people didn't understand the issue … there was a lot of misunderstanding."

A more accurate measure of public opinion, McGuire argued, were five thousand letters his task force had received—all but twenty-three supporting an increase in industrial harvesting. It later emerged that thirty-three hundred of the postcards came from Irving employees or employees of their contractors; many were generated by clicking on an Irving website called "More Trees Are the Answer." Of the remaining letters, all but nine were form letters from employees of other forestry companies. Almost two thousand postcards, pre-printed with the same "More Trees Are the Answer" slogan, also flooded in. McGuire argued that the response, though orchestrated by the industry, was nonetheless genuine, given the downturn in the forestry industry. "The person said, 'Yeah, I am worried about my job, so

I'm going to sign this card.' They're much more afraid now than they were in 2004."

Jeannot Volpé, the acting PC leader, accused Graham of using McGuire's study to find another route to cater to Jim Irving. "The McGuire report was the Irving report," he said. Today, Graham says McGuire tilted too far toward industrialization of the forest—"it was my job to counterbalance that a little bit"—but the day the report was released, he promised "to do my best to attempt to reach the recommendations in this report."

Despite one of the most extensive public consultations in New Brunswick history, despite a clear repudiation of its assumptions and its proposals, Jaakko Pöyry was still alive—in altered form, but alive. "The thing with the Irvings," says environmentalist David Coon, "is they never give up. If they don't get what they want they just keep plugging away."

Francis McGuire's report also called for a study on "properly allocating" the cost of electricity "between domestic and industrial users"—an innocuous little phrase that would soon dovetail with an extraordinary editorial crusade by the *Telegraph-Journal.*

The price of electricity was another preoccupation of Jim Irving's. Early in 2006, when Bernard Lord was still premier, NB Power, the provincial utility, applied to regulators for a 13 percent increase in the rates it charged both industrial and residential customers. The *Telegraph*'s previous position had been that rates should reflect the real cost of generating and transmitting electricity, but in 2006 it suddenly changed its view, supporting industrial rates below cost. "Jamie Irving made it clear to the editorial board there would be no room for argument on this one," said Mark Tunney, who had not yet been fired when the paper published three editorials, including one on the front page—a placement normally reserved for the gravest of subjects—calling for Lord to use his legal power to cap rate increases at 3 percent. Lord split the difference, capping it at 8 percent.

By January 2008, Shawn Graham was premier and Jim Irving was arguing that even a cap was no longer enough. UPM Kymmene, a Finnish company, had closed its mill in Miramichi and announced plans to build one in Russia. "These companies are not leaving the business, they're just leaving New Brunswick," Jim told the *Telegraph*'s editorial board, flanked by the CEOs of two other forestry companies operating in the province. They wanted Graham to order a *reduction* in their rates: true, the province would forgo $44 million in lost NB Power revenue, but that could be made up, they argued, by raising residential rates 4.5 percent, more than a hundred dollars a year for the average home—in effect, a subsidy paid by citizens. "We know that's a controversial approach to this," Jim said, but the *Telegraph* front-page headline shouted, "LET'S BE AGGRESSIVE." A second story ran on the front page of the business section; neither contained comments from anyone other than the three executives.

Daniel McHardie, who wrote one of the stories, blames the lack of reaction or context on the timing of the editorial board: the mid-afternoon session was followed by an hour-long meeting in Jamie's office to discuss the coverage plan. "I wrote the story based on an ed board, on tight deadline," McHardie says. "You look back and say, 'I should have done it differently.' ... Yes, I was an Irving employee sitting across, essentially, from my boss. And yes, his son was there and all that. There's obviously a way to see a million different conspiracies. I viewed my role as reporting that story straight as I heard it."

The stories also contained no disclaimer that Jim Irving's father owned the newspaper; McHardie explains that when he started working at the *Times-Transcript*, he would insert that kind of line—a token bit of transparency common in serious newspapers—into any Irving story he wrote. "They kept taking it out," he says. "After a couple of times, I asked why. They said everybody in New Brunswick knows it, and so why would we needlessly point it out?" At the Senate hearings in 2005, Victor Mlodecki had argued, absurdly, that such disclaimers would mean "dealing with Irving businesses differently from any other, which would be against our philosophy."

Nor did the coverage examine an important facet of Irving corporate culture: Jim Irving was right when he noted that the companies that had closed mills in New Brunswick had shifted operations elsewhere. But J.D. Irving Ltd.—though present in Nova Scotia, Quebec, and Maine—had never expanded globally to low-cost countries like Russia or Brazil to give itself similar flexibility during tough times. "We've looked at it and I don't think it's for us," J.K. reportedly said once. Overseas, of course, the Irvings might have a harder time influencing government policy, but Shawn Graham says there's a simpler reason they've eschewed foreign expansion: "They like to invest in things they can touch and feel."

As the power-rate campaign continued, however, Mark Mosher, a vice-president at Irving Paper, floated the idea of a relocation. "If we were to move our paper mill to Quebec," he said, "we would have a significant advantage over our operation here in New Brunswick, quite frankly." Mosher clarified his comments in a *Telegraph-Journal* story the next day: the comparison was a benchmarking exercise, not a threat to relocate.

The *Telegraph* didn't quash all dissent on the power-rates

story. There were critical opinion pieces by, among others, regular environmental columnist Janice Harvey and Troy Lifford, who worked for the New Brunswick Federation of Woodlot Owners. News stories quoted economists who opposed the idea. But Jim Irving's message got through where it mattered. "Our government's number one priority is to stop the loss of jobs in the province of New Brunswick in this industry," Premier Graham said. "And that's why we are looking at a number of the options quite seriously."

Mark Tunney, despite having been fired, was still watching the *Telegraph* closely, and considered the power-rates crusade the nadir of Jamie's tenure as publisher, a return to the same old dilemma: "How can the paper be authoritative, a newspaper that readers consider thoughtful and trustworthy," he asked, "and at the same time be so obviously on so many occasions the political organ of a family with vast economic interests in the province?"

Shawn Graham's dealings with Jim Irving on power rates and wood supply were complicated by his discussions with Jim's cousin Kenneth about the second refinery. The premier knew the family empire was coming apart, that lawyers were negotiating how the Irvings could separate their respective companies by buying out each other's stakes. He realized he was talking to Jim and to Kenneth more often than the two cousins spoke to each other. "You just have to look at the airport in Saint John, where two separate hangars were constructed," Graham says, "where the airplanes for the two companies are kept in two separate hangars." More profoundly, the interests of the companies could be at odds: while high energy prices were hurting J.D. Irving Ltd., they were a boon to Irving Oil, helping the business case for the new refinery.

Jim and Kenneth had both been schooled by their grand-father, but Graham found them very different businessmen. Jim, attuned to the life cycle of the forest, always thought of the long term, Graham says, while Kenneth's decisions "seemed to be made in a more immediate fashion." After meeting Jim, he knew what the company was asking for. If Jim could offer something in return, like the creation of jobs, the answer might be yes, Graham says, but sometimes it had to be no. Either way, "we knew where we stood." Kenneth was harder to read. "It was very difficult after a meeting with Kenneth to determine what role government needed to play in seeing a project come to fruition," Graham says. Often, the premier and his advisors might spend another hour "trying to decipher what needed to come out of that meeting." Sometimes, staffers had to place follow-up calls to Irving Oil to sort it out.

What Jim Irving wanted as 2008 drew to a close was more wood supply and lower power rates. Graham knew he would be criticized regardless of his decision. A study by Don Roberts, a bank economist, showed the province was actually losing money on the Crown lands it leased to forestry companies. A survey commissioned by the Department of Natural Resources and carried out by Tom Beckley, a University of New Brunswick forestry professor, found only 21 percent of respondents wanted big industry managing the forests; 56 percent said environmental organizations should do it. And in the legislature, Jeannot Volpé, the PC member, was still railing against special favours for the Irvings.

On January 30, 2009, Graham announced his decision: Jaakko Pöyry was back, in substance if not in name. The province would allow larger tree plantations on Crown land, increase subsidies for tree planting, and shrink conservation areas. "As premier, I can assure you that I am committed to this industry," he said to the forestry executives attending his news conference in Fredericton. The package, designed to increase the Crown wood supply by 75 percent over five decades, wasn't everything Irving wanted—environmentalist David Coon called it "Jaakko Pöyry lite"—but Jim Irving applauded. "The government's done a good job today to respond on some difficult subjects and help move the industry forward," he said. A headline in the *Telegraph-Journal* would declare that Graham's plan "falls short" of industry demands but was still an "improvement to status quo."

No wonder that, the previous evening, at his *Telegraph-Journal*–sponsored state of the province speech, Graham was introduced at the podium by Jamie Irving—who surely knew the contents of the forestry plan by then—as "the man whose leadership and vision has put New Brunswick on the path to self-sufficiency."

To Jeannot Volpé, Shawn Graham's alliance with the Irvings was now fully realized: Jamie Irving was praising Graham at the podium and in print; Graham was giving his father's forestry company most of what it sought; Jim Irving was offering his own thumbs-up. Five days later, Graham announced $14 million in government loans for two J.D. Irving Ltd. sawmills in northwest New Brunswick. "I think it's well-known by now," Volpé said, "that Shawn Graham is on the side of big business."

The two mills were in the provincial constituency of Restigouche-la-Vallée, where a by-election was scheduled for early March. The riding, held by the Progressive Conservatives for sixteen years, was adjacent to Volpé's, and his criticisms of Graham's Irving-friendly policies were well-known—and not popular among the mill employees. "They're trying to help, anyway," Marcel Cyr, a veteran mill worker, said of the Liberals. "At least they're doing something." The PC by-election candidate, Jean-Paul Soucy, distanced himself from his fellow Conservative: "Just because Mr. Volpé has an opinion doesn't mean I share it," he said. "Irving is putting food on the tables of people in this riding, so I need to work with them."

When the votes were counted, Graham's Liberal candidate won by a wide margin—an endorsement not just of Shawn Graham, but of the relationship he had forged with J.D. Irving Ltd. Now, Graham could move on to the next item on his, and Jim Irving's, to-do list: a reduction in industrial power rates.

And with the *Telegraph-Journal* enthusiastically on board, encouraging everyone to keep the wheels turning, it was hard to imagine anything getting in their way.

13

WHEELS WITHIN WHEELS

▼

The phones wouldn't stop ringing. Cellphones chimed and beeped. Devices set to vibrate twitched on desks, as if the newsroom were being shaken by an earthquake.

On a good day, there's a frantic buzz in a newspaper office. Reporters swap the latest gossip, pore over documents looking for a story, dash out the door when the police scanner squawks, pick up the phone and make calls in the hope of finding some news. But July 28, 2009, was not a good day in the *Telegraph-Journal* newsroom. The calls weren't going out—they were coming in. The newspaper was the story.

"My memory of that day is the amount of phone calls," one staffer remembers, "and what we were told to say." Reporters who made a virtue of getting others to talk were now instructed to say nothing and to refer all calls to David Stonehouse, one of the editors. "Everything seemed really tense," the reporter says. "It was the same conversation everyone was having outside the newsroom. 'Could this have happened? Is this true?'" And those calls kept coming: "It was everything from current staff working later in the day, to past colleagues, to other media outlets, just wondering," says another reporter.

No front page of the *Telegraph-Journal* had provoked such a reaction since the day in 1993 when Neil Reynolds had splashed K.C. Irving's will across several columns. Today the excitement was not the kind any reporter would wish for: in the middle of the page, just below the fold, was a short, four-paragraph item with a headline in capital letters: "TELEGRAPH-JOURNAL APOLO-GIZES TO PRIME MINISTER."

It wasn't a story. It didn't explain what had happened. It was, rather, an official statement on behalf of the newspaper, and—to use an old newspaper cliché—it raised more questions than it answered. It acknowledged that a story three weeks earlier "was inaccurate and should not have been published." It said the paper had not followed "high standards of journalism and ethical reporting." It withdrew the story's key assertion: that Prime Minister Stephen Harper, at the Roman Catholic funeral mass for former Governor General Roméo LeBlanc, had slipped the Communion wafer into his pocket rather than place it in his mouth. It admitted there was "no credible support" for publishing that.

Then the apology took an unusual turn: the two reporters whose bylines had appeared on the story, Rob Linke and Adam Huras, "did not include these statements in the version of the story that they wrote," the statement revealed. "In the editing process, these statements were added without the knowledge of the reporters and without any credible support for them." This was extraordinary: the *Telegraph* was apologizing not only to Stephen Harper but also to two of its own reporters. Around New Brunswick, journalists, business people, and the political crowd wondered: how could such a disaster have occurred? What of the Irvings' reputation for control?

Then the reporters in the newsroom noticed one of the nearby desks was unoccupied. Shawna Richer, the *Telegraph*'s top editor, was nowhere to be seen.

In the early nineties, Richer had edited the weekend magazine, the *New Brunswick Reader,* before leaving to work for the *London Free Press* and later *The Globe and Mail.* After publishing a book about Sidney Crosby in 2006, she returned to the *Telegraph.* Now, with the newsroom in crisis, she was missing. "It hadn't dawned on me to look at the masthead," says one journalist, referring to the list of senior staff at the top of the editorial page. Richer's name was gone. This now became the focus of the phone calls. "I got a call from a CBC reporter," one staffer recalls, "who said, 'Can you just tell me if she's at her desk?'"

David Shipley swears he foresaw the whole episode. "I knew it was only a matter of time," he says. The previous fall, in 2008, Shipley quit the *Telegraph-Journal* over a story edited without a reporter's knowledge—not one of his own, but one that touched him personally.

The paper was covering another of Kenneth Irving's grand plans for Irving Oil: the company wanted to move its corporate headquarters from its long-time home in the Golden Ball Building on Union Street, next door to the J.D. Irving Ltd. building, to a modern showpiece facility it would build at Long Wharf, on the waterfront. Irving Oil wanted to acquire the wharf from the Port Authority by giving it a former sugar refinery site in a trade—but first Irving had to buy the sugar site from the city, and that required council approval. As an incentive, Irving would let the wharf be a secondary berth for Saint John's growing cruise ship business. The city's business leaders, including the *Telegraph-Journal*'s publisher and its editorial page, embraced the idea, but the longshoremen's union argued the deal would hurt the port. The sugar site was of no use to the port, the union said, because it was not suitable for large ocean freighters. During a union news conference, its former president, Abel LeBlanc, a Liberal member of the legislature, suggested the Irvings would be "better off" on Partridge Island, a chunk of rock in the harbour once used to quarantine immigrants.

LeBlanc was well-known for his colourful talk, and this latest burst of hyperbole was quickly condemned by Liberal colleagues and Tory opposition members. But then Mayor Ivan Court, a friend of LeBlanc's, said he wouldn't be rushed into approving the land swap. The *Telegraph* published leaked documents in which Court called two business groups in the city "elitist." The ensuing debate prompted more stories: there was "inarguable support" for Long Wharf, one headline stated. City columnist John Chilibeck wrote after a public meeting that opponents "made some good points." When council finally approved the deal, LeBlanc blew up again, vowing organized labour would reclaim the power it once held in the city, perhaps with "protest and violence."

Reid Southwick, a junior reporter at the *Telegraph*, was assigned to write a profile of LeBlanc. The published piece began with an anecdote about LeBlanc that it called "an eyebrow-raising story of workplace thuggery," alleging a threat he made to punch the province's health minister in the face. The minister, the story claimed, had refused LeBlanc's demand that an unnamed Saint John woman with cancer be "fast-tracked past every other sick person in the province" waiting for a PET scan. But that wasn't true, and David Shipley knew it—because the woman LeBlanc had been trying to help was Shipley's mother.

Shipley says he saw Southwick's original story. "It was honest. It was fair and it was balanced." It reported what Shipley knew was true: LeBlanc had lobbied for more funding for the PET scan lab in Saint John so the machine could run more often and clear out a waiting list of patients. LeBlanc never suggested, as the edited version claimed, that Shipley's mother be allowed to jump the line.

Shipley, whose mother had since died, was convinced the story was twisted to punish LeBlanc for his anti-Irving statements. "You always heard the legend of stories being edited, and you work within the box of an Irving newspaper, and maybe there were stories we didn't cover, like the family feuding," Shipley says, "but it was the first time I'd ever seen anything like *this*. It was blatant." He says he and Southwick complained to Shawna Richer and David Stonehouse about how the story was edited; when nothing was done, Shipley quit. A year later, when he saw the apology to Stephen Harper *and* the two reporters, he said, "I was not surprised in the least."

Richer had returned to the *Telegraph* to run *Salon*, the weekend arts section Jamie Irving launched to replace the *Reader*, but everyone assumed "she was the boss-in-waiting," says one reporter. She became Saturday editor in 2006, after Tunney's firing, and pushed for more colourful, people-oriented pieces on the front page, a refreshing change from the dry, policy-heavy opuses favoured by Stonehouse. "Shawna liked big, flashy stories," says Daniel McHardie. In 2008, she became editor. "She knew a good story and she loved a good story," says one reporter. "Any time she worked with a reporter on their copy, it would always improve the story." Still, some were careful what they said about the publisher in her presence. "I could tell right off the top that she was very loyal to Jamie. She couldn't say enough good things about him."

Jamie, meanwhile, was gaining new authority: despite his lineage, he had been reporting to Victor Mlodecki, the vice-president of Brunswick News. But in November 2008, Mlodecki was removed. According to documents filed in a civil lawsuit against the company by his son, Daniel Mlodecki, who also worked there, Jamie was ousting several of the elder Mlodecki's recruits—including Daniel himself—"as part of an ordered re-organization" so Jamie could take over as vice-president. Daniel, running Web operations from Moncton, claimed Jamie "did not wish to have the then Vice-President, Victor Mlodecki, or any of his closest employees remaining in the employ" of Brunswick News. Jim Irving told Daniel he had "a poor way with people" and offered him a job at Midland Transport, Irving's trucking company. In court filings, Brunswick News accused him of planning to launch a competing online classified advertising site.

Daniel Mlodecki and Brunswick News eventually settled the lawsuit, with none of the allegations ever proven; still, by the end of 2008, the Mlodeckis were gone, Richer's flashier front-page style was gaining traction, and Jamie no longer answered to anyone aside from his father, who was focused on other J.D. Irving Ltd. operations.

Jamie and Richer were soon drawn into a public spat with Mayor Court, who was elected in 2008 in part because he had opposed the LNG tax break as a city councillor. The paper was running stories and columns critical of Terry Totten, the city manager, alleging that his wife, a city employee, planned to travel with her husband to a conference in Florida, despite being on sick leave. The issue, potential nepotism at City Hall, was legitimate, but the volume of coverage seemed excessive to some; the paper appeared to blame Totten for myriad problems. "The sense in the community was they were on a witch-hunt against Totten," says one *Telegraph* reporter. "I heard that from people socially."

City Hall reporter John Mazerolle said editors "never go into my stories after they're written and try to torque them up"—because the torque was applied beforehand: "It's the way the story is pitched to you," he told Mark Tunney, who wrote his master's thesis on Jamie's reign. "The angle is already decided." John Chilibeck, the city columnist, told Tunney he agreed with Jamie on "key things" and had never been told not to write something. "I've danced around it, I guess," he said. "There's a bit of self-censorship involved. I'm giving them what they want."

Totten suggested to Tunney that even Jim Irving's cousins Kenneth and John—the sons of Arthur and Jack, respectively, who had no role in the paper—had let him know they disapproved of the coverage. But the *Telegraph*'s monopoly gave Totten few outlets to respond. "Where does someone turn when they have issues and concerns such as I have had?" he said.

In December of 2008, Totten met with Richer, Jamie Irving, and the managing editor, Ron Barry, to plead his case. Mayor Court arrived unannounced, and later accused the *Telegraph* trio of offering him a deal: the paper would ease up if Court cut taxes and fired Totten. "Why is Jamie Irving hell-bent on the destruction of City Hall, its mayor and its management staff?" Court asked in a public council meeting. Richer would not confirm the demand for Totten's firing, but in a column, she acknowledged telling Court and Totten that if they cut taxes and addressed problems like poor roads and an employee pension deficit, "the stories we wrote would reflect that reality." It was highly unusual for senior journalists to privately lobby public officials for specific policies, though Richer equated it with publishing editorials. "I am proud of that meeting," she wrote after Court went public. The mayor also cancelled his office's subscription to the *Telegraph-Journal* and challenged the publisher to a public debate. "It's not Jamie Irving's job to debate Ivan Court in public," Richer responded in a CBC interview.*

Richer defended the newspaper again in May 2009 after she fired Matt McCann, a journalism student just starting his second summer at the paper. McCann filed a story about a petition signed by about a hundred professors at the University of New Brunswick, objecting to the granting of an honorary degree to Premier Shawn Graham. The assignment desk, he says, "got so excited by it that they made me go back and get a picture" of one of the professors. But after the story ran, Richer called him, "questioning whether it was balanced." McCann also made two minor errors in the story, misspelling a name and misstating Graham's degree from UNB. The next day, Richer fired him, a decision that drew national attention. "It was a decision based strictly on professional issues," she told the *Toronto Star*. In her dismissal letter to McCann, Richer wrote that the newspaper had "worked very hard to establish good communication with the university to facilitate news coverage and this story has placed that relationship in jeopardy." Graham's office and UNB both said they didn't ask for McCann's firing. "It was a very, very odd turn of events and I felt awful for that young guy," says one advisor to Graham. "It was just horrible."

---

* Shawna Richer did not respond to my requests for an interview.

Now, in late July 2009, the *Telegraph* was caught in yet another public controversy—and this time, Richer was gone in the wake of an extraordinary front-page apology to Stephen Harper.

Then it dawned on the staff that *another* name had vanished from the top of the editorial page. Jamie Irving had been the first member of his family listed on the *Telegraph-Journal* masthead. Now he became the first member of his family *removed* from the masthead.

It is protocol for prime ministers to attend the state funerals of governors general. Roméo LeBlanc, an Acadian, was an old-fashioned Liberal, an MP, a minister, and a senator, and a close political ally of Pierre Trudeau and Jean Chrétien. Chrétien's appointment of his friend as governor general—the representative of the monarchy under whose authority the Acadians were deported in 1755—struck a chord with New Brunswickers. The funeral mass in Memramcook, the little village where LeBlanc grew up, drew mourners from across the political spectrum, including Stephen Harper. The mass was held July 3 in the imposing nineteenth-century stone church that dominates the village and the surrounding landscape of the Memramcook Valley. Harper was seated, along with other dignitaries, in the front pew. Like all New Brunswick media organizations, the *Telegraph-Journal* covered the funeral extensively.

The story that will forever be associated with the event, however, appeared five days later. "IT'S A SCANDAL" screamed a large, all-caps, front-page headline. Under a byline shared by Moncton reporter Adam Huras and Ottawa correspondent Rob Linke, the story stated as fact, without attribution, that Harper, after taking the Communion host from the archbishop of Moncton, André Richard, "slipped the thin wafer … into his jacket pocket." To Catholics, the wafer represents the body of Christ, and Monsignor Brian Henneberry, the vicar-general of the Saint John diocese, was quoted saying that *if* Harper did not consume the wafer—a vital *if*, as it turned out—"it's worse than a faux pas, it's a scandal from the Catholic point of view." Harper, he said, should "at least offer an explanation." Henneberry's use of the word *scandal* gave the *Telegraph* a dynamite headline—though his caveat, *if*, was lost along the way.

The evidence, in retrospect, was thin: the TV feed captured New Brunswick's lieutenant-governor consuming the host, but "Harper does not consume the wafer before the camera cuts away several seconds later," the story said. It quoted "one official" anonymously: "You could see he was, 'Uh-oh, I don't know what to do with this.'" Archbishop Richard told the newspaper he didn't see what Harper did with the host "because I was busy doing something else." And that was it for sourcing. After reading the story, some reporters in the Saint John newsroom had gone online to see the footage themselves. "A bunch of us watched it, in some cases, over and over again, and couldn't really say conclusively one way or another," says one. "And we thought, 'Hmmm. Bizarre.'" Harper and his officials, travelling to Italy for an economic summit, had not been available to comment, the story said. "We weren't going to hold this to get the prime minister of Canada's comment?" asks the same newsroom reporter. "*Really?*"

National media picked up on the *Telegraph-Journal* report the day it ran. Doctrinal debates broke out: should a Catholic priest even offer Communion to a non-Catholic? Was Harper, an evangelical Protestant, permitted by his faith to accept it? The prime minister's press secretary, Dimitri Soudas, said the TV camera hadn't lingered long enough to record that Harper "accepted it and consumed it as well." The Speaker of the Senate, Noel Kinsella, a New Brunswick Tory, said he personally saw Harper place it in his mouth. That moment of confusion on the prime minister's face was because Harper knew Catholics normally line up for Communion, and had been briefed that the mass would follow that practice. He hadn't expected the archbishop to approach him. "That wasn't supposed to happen," his chief of staff, Guy Giorno, says now.

Harper had arrived in Italy and was preparing for an audience with the Pope. "I think somebody running a story— and I don't know where the responsibility lies—that I would stick Communion bread in my pocket is really absurd," he said, clearly angry. "First of all, as a Christian, I've never refused Communion when offered to me. That is actually pretty important to me. And I think it's really, frankly, a low point. This is a low moment in journalism, whoever is responsible for this. It's just a terrible story and a ridiculous story, and not based on anything, near as I can tell."

Harper's comments, in retrospect, are intriguing. He went out of his way, twice, to leave open the question of who was responsible for the story. Back in Ottawa, one of his staffers had already called Rob Linke, the *Telegraph*'s parliamentary correspondent, to angrily denounce the piece. Perhaps word had already got back to Harper that Linke swore the published story was not what he had filed—that the key allegations had been added later. *

Lloyd Mackey, a writer for several religious newspapers who sat near Linke in the Ottawa press gallery, says the story Linke filed reflected that there was chatter about what Harper *might*

---

* Rob Linke declined my request for an interview.

have done, then went on to soberly analyze the theological implications. "I don't recall it ever entering [Linke's] mind that Harper
did anything with the host other than consume it," Mackey says.
Mackey had published a book on Harper's religious views, so
Linke picked his brain while working on the story. "There wasn't
anything in his copy that indicated as a fact that he had pocketed
the host," Mackey says. After publication, "Rob was not too happy
that the lede had been changed based on some other information
that the editor had."

In the Saint John newsroom, "the word was Linke was just
wildly furious that his name was on it, and wondering where
this came from," says one employee. Linke assumed he would be
blacklisted in Harper's Ottawa, unable to do his job. His byline
vanished from the paper. "No one would say what he was up to,"
says an editor. After the apology, Linke returned to work, but he
soon resigned from the *Telegraph-Journal* to take a communications job at Canada Post's head office. "The man was totally
destroyed by that whole situation," says a former government
official who dealt with him often. "I could not believe that that
had happened."

For Jim Irving, there was another potential consequence to
the fiasco: one of the companies he ran, Halifax Shipyards, was
bidding for a federal contract for billions of dollars' worth of naval
frigates, supply ships, patrol boats, and icebreakers. It was the
largest government procurement in the history of Canada, and
would create thousands of jobs and a secure revenue stream for
the winner—so it was not the time to anger the prime minister.
"When I saw the front-page apology," says one newsroom staffer,
"I was just blown away. And a lot of us thought, 'They sure got
lucky. They just dodged the bullet on that thing.' The PMO
turned the other cheek. Unbelievable. Wow."

The Irvings understood the potential of the frigate contract better than most: though K.C. Irving acquired the Saint John shipyard in 1958 to build and service vessels for his own Kent Lines, the yard's most lucrative work—and one of J.K. Irving's greatest triumphs—was an earlier $9 billion federal contract in the 1980s for a previous batch of a dozen naval frigates. The 1983 tender for the first six ships was split for political reasons: Saint John Shipbuilding would lead the project, but was forced to subcontract three boats to the MIL shipyard in Sorel, Quebec. In 1987, the second tender, for six more ships, went entirely to Saint John. "Now, for the first time," J.K. exulted at the announcement, "we can see years of work and stability ahead." Not everything ran smoothly: Irving sued MIL for delays at its Quebec yard, and dropped the suit only when Ottawa paid $323 million in compensation to Saint John Shipbuilding. But in the end, the frigate program came in on time and under budget, a testament to Irving efficiency and quality. At its peak, it employed four thousand people.

By 1995, the project was winding down, and layoffs were accelerating. Rather than give up, J.K. bought up other shipyards around the Maritimes, including the Halifax yard in 1994, to create economies of scale. "Anybody who says you're a sunset industry, you're going down—we've got no time for that," J.K. said. Facing competition from low-cost yards overseas, however, the Irvings eventually decided one of their two largest shipyards had to close—and they chose Saint John. There was one last subsidy: in 2003, the federal government gave the company $55 million—matched by Irving—to convert the yard, by then idle for three years, to other industrial uses. It became the site of J.D. Irving Ltd.'s Atlantic Wallboard, a drywall manufacturer. A scandal erupted when it was revealed that the federal industry minister, Allan Rock, whose depart-ment provided the money, was among several Liberal ministers who accepted free trips to the Irving family's private fishing lodge on the Restigouche River. The *Telegraph-Journal*, not yet run by Jamie Irving, called Rock's trip a "fly-fishing junket" and a visit to "the corporate trough." Among the opposition MPs critical of Rock was the new leader of the Canadian Alliance, Stephen Harper. "We're going to want to look over the record and some of his answers and question him on the veracity of some of his claims," Harper said.

As Harper fumed over the Communion story in 2009, then, he was well aware of the Irvings and the importance of their shipyards. And he was known to carry a grudge. There is no evidence whatsoever that the prime minister would even contemplate depriving Halifax Shipyards of the contract because of the wafer article—or even that he *could*: the tender was to be awarded under a unique new arm's-length process, isolating elected politicians completely from the decision. In July of 2009, though, no one, not even the Irvings, could be sure of that.

"I handled it, and it was bad," Jim Irving says. "The paper was offside, and Jamie had to be responsible for that. It was bad judgment, all around. If we're wrong on something, we own up to it, and deal with it head-on. But that was just bad."

J.K., sitting across from me, appears pained by the subject. "That was terrible, just terrible, as far as I'm concerned," he says. "You know, you're going through the world, you're young, and there's a learning curve, eh? Sometimes you learn from your mistakes. I just hope to hell that we learned from our mistakes. But that was not very good. That was terrible."

"As soon as we found out what was afoot," Jim says, "then we moved in to make sure we understood all the components and dealt with it forthwith. And that didn't take very long.... Everybody got dealt with in one form or another."

But, I ask, who exactly was responsible? What happened? No one from Brunswick News has ever answered those questions. "I'm not going to get into the details of it," Jim says, "but it was public information."

J.K. speaks up again: "There were wheels within wheels," he says.

It was definitely *not* public information. The apology clearly exonerated Rob Linke and Adam Huras, the two reporters, but it was a corporate statement, not a work of journalism. "They were half-atoning for what happened," says Chelsea Murray, a 2009 summer intern at the *Telegraph* who later wrote about the affair for the *Ryerson Review of Journalism*. Even the staff was offered no explanation, only the confirmation that Richer was fired and Jamie was suspended for thirty days, leading to the logical conclusion that they were responsible.

CTV's Robert Fife reported that unnamed Liberals had made the claim about the wafer to Jamie, and that he passed it on to Richer. The people in the front rows of the church in Memramcook were well-connected players, some of whom had Jamie's ear, so Fife's report seemed plausible. Guy Giorno, Harper's chief of staff at the time, who assured Catholic leaders in the wake of the story that the prime minister hadn't sought Communion, believes the source had to be Catholic: "It takes a Catholic mind to have seen the opportunity there" to damage Harper's standing among Catholic voters, he says. But there were no answers.

The *Telegraph-Journal*'s opacity was not unusual: with few

exceptions, media organizations do a lousy job investigating themselves. *The New York Times* assigned teams of reporters to diagnose how Jayson Blair was able to make up stories and how Judith Miller became part of the Pentagon's Iraq hype. But such transparency is rare, and when the actions of a newspaper intersect with the industrial holdings of its proprietors, the instinct for secrecy is that much stronger. As extraordinary as the apology was, it was typically Irving, not a full airing of "Wafergate," as it became known, but the minimum required acknowledgment of what had happened—the family's trademark lack of introspection. "If they really cared about their readers," says Murray, "I thought they'd give them more details or tell them more of the truth about what happened."

The humiliation was far-reaching. *The New York Times* took note. "The affair has again drawn attention to the Irving family's extraordinary control over not just New Brunswick's news media," it reported, "but also its political and economic power." Craig Silverman, a journalist who blogs about media errors and corrections, labelled it Error of the Year for 2009. Inside the newsroom, reporters were embarrassed. One journalist, seeking an interview for a routine story weeks later, was reminded of Wafergate: "The guy said, 'Do I get to read it before it goes to print?' And I said, 'That's not a policy we have.' And he said, 'Yeah, but you guys are known for making some mistakes.' And he said, 'I guess I'm not going to do the story.' It felt horrible."

Morale was sinking fast; reporters grumbled that Matt McCann had been fired for a considerably milder offence than Wafergate, which earned the publisher a mere suspension. "People were wondering how fair that was, and whether it would really be thirty days or, because he was an Irving, they'd quietly ship him off to Kent Homes in Bouctouche," says one editor.

In September, Jim Irving announced on the front page that Jamie would "return to his responsibilities" as vice-president of Brunswick News, but that Neil Reynolds was also coming back, this time as editor-at-large of all the Brunswick News newspapers. "Mr. Reynolds's focus will be on the development and oversight of the editorial policies, standards and journalistic practices of the newspapers," the announcement said. Jamie, it explained, would handle "the day-to-day operations of the newspapers" but would report to Reynolds "on matters related to editorial policies, standards, and journalistic practices."

The news was greeted with relief and even excitement. "It was like, 'Oh, is this place going to rock and roll again,'" says one reporter familiar with Reynolds's earlier tenure. Younger staffers were buoyed. "My perception was he had a pretty good history at the paper," says one.

Reynolds moved quickly to close the books on Wafergate. A second apology appeared in the *Telegraph-Journal*, this time to Monsignor Henneberry, whose supposed demand for a prime ministerial explanation was the heart of the original story. "The newspaper has determined that Monsignor Henneberry said no such thing," the apology said. "The sensational manner" in which he was quoted "resulted in a serious distortion of his actual remarks." The same day, Reynolds addressed readers in a column: "The *Telegraph-Journal* is not a runaway train," he wrote, "though it did go flamboyantly off the rails in one regrettable instance." He promised a new code of ethics to win back the trust of readers, including a ban on anonymous sources "under any circumstances" and a vow to remain neutral and "play fair" on all stories. The code was posted on the lunchroom door and distributed to all reporters: balance, fairness, accuracy, civility, and resistance to spin would be the hallmarks of the *Telegraph-Journal* again. The paper would also avoid engaging in politics "as a protagonist," Reynolds said. He elaborated to the *Ryerson Review*: "Just given the ownership of these papers, it's really important they play it safe in terms of politics."

Reynolds nonetheless rejected the conventional wisdom about the Irvings. He told readers he looked forward to "working again with the irrepressible Jamie Irving" and his father and grandfather. "I find it highly ironic that people frequently attribute the sins and omissions of journalists to proprietors rather than to the professional writers and editors who commit them," Reynolds wrote. "I can assure the readers of the *Telegraph-Journal*, based upon my own personal observations, that the proprietors of these newspapers are determined, fairly and impartially, to publish the truth and nothing but the truth." Implicitly, this blamed Richer, not Jamie, for what had happened—though Reynolds would not elaborate. "I'm not going to go back and focus on the past," he told the CBC. "I think it's obvious that there was a problem, and I think that's enough said about that." The man who put K.C. Irving's will on page one would not investigate what happened in the pages of the *Telegraph-Journal*. "It was like it never happened," one editor said.

Less than three weeks after Reynolds's return, Stephen Harper was in New Brunswick again, visiting Saint John to promote the infrastructure spending his government had launched after the global market crash. It included $9 million to Irving's New Brunswick Southern Railway for upgrades, a sum that had been announced the day before the wafer story. For news photographers, Harper climbed onto the front of one of the company's train engines and stood smiling next to Jim Irving as it crawled slowly along the tracks.

The image amazed those who had watched the Wafergate scandal: the prime minister, widely seen as the unforgiving type, had moved on with astonishing speed. The wheels were turning once more, and the *Telegraph-Journal* coverage made no mention of the significance of the two men appearing in public together.

It was a chilly night in late October, and Quentin Casey, a reporter for the *Telegraph-Journal* in Fredericton, was struggling with the no-anonymous-sources decree Neil Reynolds had issued weeks earlier. Casey, who was leaving the job within days to work in Halifax, snuck away from his own going-away party at the bar of the Crowne Plaza hotel to try to nail down one last story. The worst-kept secret in the capital was that Premier Shawn Graham's government was about to announce it was selling NB Power, the provincial electricity utility, to Hydro-Québec. There was talk that *The Globe and Mail* had the story confirmed—through anonymous sources—and might run it the next morning, a Friday. Casey was desperately trying to at least match the scoop, but no one from the Graham government would go on the record.

Reynolds himself got involved. Casey walked across the street to his desk in the press gallery of the legislature to write what he knew; Reynolds called staffers in Graham's office, begging for something on the record. "He pleaded for ten or twelve minutes," says one, but to no avail. The story in the *Telegraph* the next morning said only that energy discussions between New Brunswick and Quebec, announced in the vaguest terms the previous June, were continuing.

The *Globe and Mail* story appeared on Saturday, scooping the *Telegraph* on a story from its own backyard: NB Power would indeed be sold to Hydro-Québec, for $5 billion, enough to eliminate the New Brunswick utility's debt. Hydro-Québec would acquire New Brunswick's hydroelectric dams, its nuclear generating station, and its cross-border transmission connection to the New England power grid. In return it would supply electricity to New Brunswick at reduced rates, the *Globe* said. "Sources say the Irving family, which owns much of New Brunswick's industry, is keen for a deal with Hydro-Québec to reduce electricity rates," the paper reported. That factor would hang over the *Telegraph-Journal*'s coverage of the sale.

When Graham announced the deal five days later, he promised "lower power rates for New Brunswick residents and New Brunswick businesses, in every corner of the province." On closer examination, however, only large industry would see rates cut, by 30 percent; residential rates would merely be frozen—"lower" only in comparison to what they would be otherwise. The CEO of Hydro-Québec, Thierry Vandal, later confirmed the two-tier structure was Graham's idea, reinforcing the view of the sale as a gift to the Irvings and other big industry. "They're giving rebates to McCains, Irving, all these mills," said the owner of a convenience store in the village of Nackawic. "What about us lower-class people or middle-class people?" The perception of corporate favouritism, along with other factors—Graham blames anti-Quebec sentiment—made the deal unpopular and put the Liberals on the defensive from the beginning.

And the cynicism was made worse by the perception that the newspapers, particularly the *Telegraph-Journal*, were helping sell the deal. "I see editorial support in the Irving papers," David Alward, the PC opposition leader, said in the legislature, "but I think most New Brunswickers understand where that's coming from." A typical online comment said that "if the TJ was serving its public, the people of NB would not have to go through the stress of the NB Power fiasco." Doug Tyler, who worked on the Hydro-Québec deal, says the paper's editorial-page endorsement—"The Deal of the Century"—was consistent with its support for industrial power-rate cuts since early 2008. "You could have a hundred examples of where public policy issues do not align with an Irving paper and Irving businesses," he says, "but the one where they do align, everybody's saying there's a big conspiracy here."

Premier Graham, one advisor says, was counting on the newspapers: "He assumed that it was such a good deal for the Irvings that they would use everything at their disposal to sell it." But inside the post-Wafergate *Telegraph*, Jamie was playing less of a role in decisions about the news pages than when his father began lobbying for power-rate cuts. "The story meetings were no longer held in his office," an editor says. "There was a lot less day-to-day involvement with story placement and that kind of thing." Internally, and on the editorial pages, "we were way in favour of it," he says. But the message was sent back to Graham's office that the *Telegraph* would tread carefully, striving for balance in the news pages. The paper did not want to be, to use Reynolds's term, "a protagonist" in the debate, as it had been on rate cuts in 2008. Wafergate had perhaps deprived Shawn Graham of a full-on Jamie Irving editorial crusade on NB Power.

It's not even clear whether such a crusade would have helped. By 2009, Jamie's romance with the golden age of print journalism was becoming a liability. The paper's website was updated once a day and was difficult to navigate, while critics of the Irvings and the NB Power sale were using social media to deliver their own "coverage." For a family genetically disposed to consider news to be what you printed on the pulp from your mill, it must have been baffling to see critiques, conspiracy theories, and nasty attacks play out on blogs and on Twitter. It was far from a scientific measure of public opinion, but a Facebook page opposing the sale quickly gained almost thirty thousand members, a number hard to ignore. "Social media was driving the debate," Shawn Graham says. "I had my cabinet colleagues more frustrated every day with what was on Twitter and in the blogosphere than what was in the newspapers."

Despite this shift, "there was an overemphasis in the communications shop on print media," says Kelly Lamrock, one of Graham's ministers. "You would frequently hear people say, 'We're handling this well. We were above the fold today.' I don't think we were aware how many people were getting their news without a fold." With Facebook and Twitter, any clever or compelling take on the issue could spread to thousands of people within an hour, yet the communications advisors were consumed with winning over the *Telegraph*. Graham, too, recognized that the Frank McKenna model—persuade the *Telegraph* and you shape the agenda—was a thing of the past. "That was a different time, when the papers actually mattered," he says. "How many people literally get up and read the newspaper every morning?" Jamie Irving, who had longed to be a player in policy debates, was being marginalized.

The debate over the *Telegraph*'s role was a persistent subplot in the Hydro-Québec saga. Neil Reynolds, rebutting a critique in an academic journal in 2010, cited several examples of balanced coverage, as well as numerous opinion pieces by critics of the deal. Certainly the paper was more even-handed than in the 2008 power-rates coverage—yet in tone it was often condescending toward the deal's critics. An editorial denounced politicians who built their arguments on "a foundation of fear," implying opponents were irrational. Another editorial, on demands for a referendum, said, "The status quo isn't a scenario worth voting for"—taking for granted the premise for the sale. A third editorial praised a critique of the deal by a twenty-two-year-old business student "for leaving emotion out of the debate.... From the start his goal was to seek the truth rather than to impose a fixed opinion." These were legitimate editorial opinions, but cumulatively the subtext was clear. The paper treated the expert, elite debate fairly, but failed to reflect—and respect—the remarkable populist movement against the sale.

This was also the tenor of what Reynolds considered the jewel of the *Telegraph*'s coverage, a multi-part freelance series he commissioned by Philip Lee examining Hydro-Québec's history and NB Power's massive debt. Lee's otherwise intelligent and insightful series didn't capture the unprecedented grassroots revolt. "It didn't have that," Lee says, "but it also didn't have a single voice from the political side talking about why the deal was good. I tried to avoid the rhetoric and tried to deal with it strictly on facts." Lee, who says he personally supported the deal, attended several public meetings organized by opponents, "and they really weren't dealing with anything that was factual," he says. "I tried to stay away from emotional things." And, he adds, "that was definitely not a corporate-driven project. There was no direction. That was Neil and me, just doing what we do."

The series was published in late February 2010, then repackaged as a special tabloid insert in all Brunswick News newspapers. Lee's investigation "got a lot of it right," says a government official, "but I think it was too late. I don't think any amount of support or elucidation or illumination at that point would have done anything." By then, two of Graham's cabinet ministers had resigned over the sale, and the province had renegotiated the deal to retain ownership of NB Power's transmission lines and their valuable links to the New England grid. Industry's rate cut would be 23 percent instead of 30, a change that did little to soothe public opinion. Regardless, Jamie Irving decided to have Lee's series translated and published in the province-wide edition of *L'Étoile*, which had absorbed the various local French weeklies acquired by Brunswick News.

The stories were being readied for publication when Graham rose in the legislature on March 24 with a dramatic announcement: because of unexpected complications in the final negotiations with Quebec over the cost of looming upgrades to a New Brunswick hydro dam, he said, the deal was dead.

It was a humiliating defeat for the Liberal premier, and for the big industrial owners, whose rate cuts evaporated. More pressing was the future of a Norwegian solar company that had been lured to New Brunswick on the explicit promise of power costs that matched Quebec's. "We're going to have to look at other innovative solutions on how we can help this company attain those competitive rates with Quebec, and we're in those discussions as we speak," Graham told reporters. The premier knew Jim Irving would demand the same for his mills. Irving, who had been aware of the promise to the Norwegians, "wanted to be treated fairly and equally like any new company coming in," Graham says now. "I respected that."

Graham never got the chance to deliver. Six months later, his government became the first since Confederation to lose an election after a single term. But premiers come and go; the Irvings endure. Despite PC leader David Alward's attacks on industry favouritism in the NB Power sale, as premier he forced industrial power rates down. In 2011, his government ordered the utility to buy, at a legislated high price, "renewable" power—generated, for example, by wood waste burned at cogeneration plants at forestry mills—and then sell it back to those industries at a lower price. "What we're trying to do with that program is make sure that intensive users of energy have competitive prices," said Alward's energy minister, Craig Leonard, sounding not unlike the Graham Liberals.

So Jim Irving's forestry business finally got the break on power costs it was looking for. His son's newspaper business, however, did not emerge unscathed. In 2003, journalism professor Kim Kierans asked Jamie Irving what she would be reading or hearing about him in five years. "Not much, probably," he answered. "Chugging along." But for the young publisher, 2009 had been a horrific year in the spotlight. It would take all his efforts to salvage his newspaper's damaged credibility.

14

DEAD TREE EDITION

▼

It was a special moment: K.C.'s boys, the three Irving brothers, J.K., Arthur, and Jack, in their late seventies and early eighties now, gathered for a rare public appearance together. Dressed in tuxedos, J.K. and Jack with black bow ties and Arthur in a pewter-grey necktie, they smiled shyly on the stage of the Metro Toronto Convention Centre as the former premier of New Brunswick, Frank McKenna, inducted them into the Canadian Business Hall of Fame.

This induction in May 2008 had been announced the previous November, at that press conference atop the TD Tower where J.K. confirmed to Gordon Pitts of *The Globe and Mail* that the brothers were splitting their companies. Six months had passed without a further word about it. The *Telegraph-Journal* hadn't pursued the story. There was plenty of gossip in Saint John, but no one knew for sure what was happening, and the tycoons onstage were as discreet as ever. "There was no visible animosity between the three brothers," Donald Savoie, a Université de

Moncton economist who attended the gala, would recall. The *Telegraph-Journal*'s Marty Klinkenberg was there, too. He wrote, as he had the previous fall, about the guests, the fancy surroundings, and the meal—beef Wellington, "a meal fit for a king, or at least a business titan." He did not mention the fracturing of the empire.

Arthur Irving was keeping another secret that night. Two days later, Irving Oil announced it was partially withdrawing from the gas station business, the family's most tangible symbol in Eastern Canada and New England. Couche-Tard, the Montreal-based convenience-store chain, would lease and run 252 Irving stations; Irving Oil would remain the owner and supply the gasoline, and would still operate the larger Big Stop highway locations. There was speculation the deal was driven by the looming family breakup. "It's to raise cash," Dave Wilson, the owner of a rival chain of gas stations in the Maritimes, told the Canadian Press. "It's a great way to raise money to buy out various cousins and uncles." Others said Arthur's son Kenneth, Irving Oil's CEO, didn't see selling coffee and snacks as a core business and wanted to focus more on Canaport LNG, the second refinery, and his green-energy expansion into the United States. For months, Premier Shawn Graham had been working with Kenneth to promote an "energy corridor" into New England: electricity from the gas-fired Bayside Power station would move south on transmission cables mounted on poles, while refined oil and natural gas would travel the same route in a pipeline beneath the ground.

To reflect his vision, in early 2009, Kenneth gave Irving Oil's holding company a new name, Fort Reliance Co. Ltd. (Its operating subsidiary would remain Irving Oil Ltd.) No branding consultants were involved; the name, Kenneth told *The Globe and Mail*, had a personal meaning. Fort Reliance was an old exploration post in the Northwest Territories that he and his father had visited during a canoe trip on Great Slave Lake. "We just like the name for itself," Kenneth said. But *fort*, the *Globe* said, also denoted "strength and protecting values," while *reliance* conveyed trust and confidence. The company opened an office on King Street in Toronto, in the heart of the Canadian financial industry. Split or no split, Kenneth was on the move.

Then, just as dramatically, came a series of setbacks. Just two days after that interview with the *Globe*, Irving Oil announced it was selling Bayside Power to Emera Inc., a Halifax-based energy company. The business case for electricity exports was not what Kenneth had hoped. A month later came a more shocking announcement: the second refinery had been cancelled, sending a shudder across Saint John. Housing prices had risen in anticipation of a coming boom and the province had committed $65 million to build the highway interchange to accommodate increased traffic. But BP, which had joined the project as a partner, had looked at the falling demand for gasoline in North America and pulled out.

"It's not the end of the world," said the provincial energy minister, Jack Keir, who had predicted the refinery would bring "growth and prosperity" to the city. The *Telegraph-Journal* published a story in which economists, political scientists, and opposition politicians admonished Premier Shawn Graham for overhyping the project—though the story made no mention of the paper's large and enthusiastic headlines, such as "OUR BLACK GOLD." "The *Telegraph-Journal* was more of a cheerleader than the government was," Graham told me. For Kenneth, the sale of Bayside and the cancellation of the refinery were personal blows: together, they sounded the death knell for his dreams of turning Irving Oil into a regional energy giant.

Early in 2010, Kenneth made what looked like a desperate lunge in the midst of Graham's effort to sell NB Power to Hydro-Québec. While his cousin Jim's mills stood to benefit from the deal's lower power rates, Kenneth was leery, suspecting the Quebec utility would compete with him to sell New Brunswick energy into the U.S. But during a conversation with Thierry Vandal, Hydro-Québec's CEO, Kenneth gleaned that what Vandal really coveted was the province's hydro- and nuclear-generating stations; NB Power's Transco subsidiary, which owned the transmission cables linked to the New England grid, was peripheral. So Kenneth contacted Graham's office, offering to buy Transco himself. "He was emphatic that he needed Transco for his business operations," Graham says. The hefty fees Transco charged other regional utilities moving electricity into the United States represented a guaranteed revenue stream for Kenneth. But Graham, already mired in controversy over Hydro-Québec, turned him down. "There's going to be no public appetite for saying we're keeping it to sell it to the Irvings," Graham remembers saying. If Hydro-Québec didn't want Transco, he decided, NB Power would keep it. Kenneth, says a government insider, "wasn't happy," but his role—as the catalyst for Graham's first, partial retreat from the Quebec agreement—remained a secret.

Around the same time, Kenneth also cancelled the grand, new Fort Reliance corporate headquarters planned for Long Wharf on the Saint John waterfront. There was talk in Saint John that the design had grown too grandiose and too expensive for Arthur's liking, though a company spokesman blamed the decision on the recession.

Another plausible theory is that the breakup of the Irving empire left Kenneth short of the cash needed to build it. Irving-watchers around Saint John were piecing together the story of the split: Kenneth's father, Arthur, and Arthur's brothers, J.K. and Jack, had agreed to conduct a valuation of all the Irving assets, it was said, then divide the total by three to establish the value to which each brother was entitled. They would then transfer and sell assets and make cash payments to achieve that equal split. Arthur's assets turned out to be worth far more than one-third, requiring him to hand over companies or cash to his brothers. But the agreement held that the valuation would be made on September 1, 2008. Two weeks later, global markets crashed, the price of oil tumbled, and Arthur's assets "weren't worth nearly as much," says one informed observer. Arthur, says another Irving-watcher, "couldn't come up with the cash to equalize the payments." He gave Jack and his family a stake in Irving Oil, and probably had to borrow money to pay off J.K.—which may have deprived Fort Reliance of the liquidity to go ahead with Long Wharf. It may also explain why Kenneth grasped for the guaranteed revenue stream of Transco.

Whatever the reason, Irving Oil, so recently rebranded to project strength and confidence, suddenly looked vulnerable.

In a rare public speech in 2006, Kenneth Irving alluded to the average CEO of a publicly traded energy company holding the position for about five years; he lightheartedly thanked his father, who was in the audience, for keeping him around as long as he had.

But in mid-July 2010, a decade after Arthur had handed him the top job, Kenneth's time was suddenly up.

In a memo emailed to employees, Arthur told Irving Oil employees his son was taking a leave of absence for "personal reasons." A week later, Kenneth himself announced by email that he was departing for good. He thanked everyone for their concern. "I appreciate the thoughtfulness and would like everyone to know I am doing well and expect to fully recover from my health setback." There were no details of his illness, but there was a thank-you to "my father and the board for their support and understanding while I continue to recover." Kenneth was succeeded by Mike Ashar, a Mumbai-born chemical engineer and former Suncor executive who came to Irving Oil in 2008. Kenneth, meanwhile, relocated to New Hampshire, near his wife's native Vermont, and later became a director of Kinross Gold Corp., a Toronto-based mining company. He would not be heard from in public again.*

For many in Saint John, the story of Kenneth's illness didn't add up. In the popular imagination, bloodlines were paramount for the Irvings, the departure of a key family member unthinkable. One *Telegraph-Journal* reporter had seen Kenneth address a meeting of Atlantic premiers and New England governors a few months before, where he seemed healthy, at ease, and in command. "I don't think he even had a note." The prevailing theory was that Arthur fired Kenneth over Irving Oil's various setbacks. Arthur was said to consider the gas station deal a mistake that damaged the brand and deprived Irving Oil of reliable cash flow. Arthur once explained to author John DeMont how little things—larger napkins, clean washrooms—gave the Irving gas stations and restaurants their pristine reputations. Under Couche-Tard, says one Irving-watcher, "the standard of

---

* I requested an interview with Kenneth Irving through a Kinross spokesperson. I was told that while he appreciated the offer, "it has not been his practice to entertain such requests."

service declined. The washrooms weren't quite as clean as they were before." And Arthur knew it.

In fact, Kenneth left because of a fight over money, sparked by the family split. In 2009, the trustees of K.C. Irving's will, including his widow, Winnifred, filed an application to a court in Bermuda. The file is sealed, but it's believed they sought to dissolve the trust established by K.C.'s will and to distribute its assets as part of the corporate breakup—a process that generated legal bills "in the region of $100 million," according to a subsequent court ruling. Arthur would use his share, worth $1 billion or "roughly one-third of the global estate" left by K.C., to set up his own trust, with Irving Oil its principal asset.

A problem arose when Arthur declared he would give his five children equal shares in the trust. A 2012 ruling by Chief Justice Ian Kawaley of the Supreme Court of Bermuda reveals that Kenneth expected "his unique contribution to the value of the Onshore Operating Company"—Irving Oil—"which he worked for at a senior level for several years should be recognized" with a greater share of his father's wealth. "When he discovered that his father intended to treat [him] and his siblings equally, his relationship with his father broke down," Kawaley wrote. Kenneth "suffered a mental breakdown and his relationship with both the Company and his family was severed." So Arthur hadn't fired his son after all: Kenneth's original explanation, a "health setback," was somewhat closer to the truth—but was still far from the whole story.

The falling-out between father and son belies, of course, what Irving company spokespeople told the *Telegraph-Journal* in 2007: that succession planning was normal and that it was "business as usual" for the companies. Instead, the split between K.C.'s three boys—and the ambitions and emotions it roused—had cost the energy company its CEO, and Arthur Irving his relationship with his son.

And its blight was spreading. On July 22, 2010, just hours after Kenneth announced his departure from his father's company, Arthur's brother Jack Irving died—a sad event that would also bring some of the same family divisions to the surface.

"When Jack was dying and [his brother J.K.] went into the hospital to see Jack, he was refused" by Jack's family, Joan Carlisle Irving says. J.K. "was turned away at the door, which I thought was appalling." The day before his funeral, hundreds of people lined up in the summer heat at the Gothic-style stone Trinity Church, built in 1784, for the viewing. People waited ninety minutes to get in; among them was J.K., "standing in line to give his condolences with everyone else," according to another mourner. J.K., in his eighties now, was "standing out in the sun," Joan Carlisle Irving says, "standing in line for an hour and a half to go in and see his brother's body, his brother who he'd taken care of as a little boy." At the funeral the next day, J.K. and his family were seated several rows back from Jack's and Arthur's families.

Joan Carlisle Irving says despite her contentious divorce from Arthur decades ago, she remained friends with J.K. and his wife, Jean. During a visit with them in Bouctouche in 2012, she remembers, they hashed over "this horrible wrenching apart of the empire." She says Jean pointed, as an explanation, to "the way their father treated them." There's Joan's story of K.C. leaving a misbehaving, five-year-old Arthur on the side of the road on that drive to Nova Scotia, and her theory that it marked Arthur for life. Joan also remembers K.C.'s childhood friend Leigh Stevenson recounting a conversation with the industrialist: "Why don't you just split it up, let them go their own way, cut them loose and let each of the boys run their own?" Stevenson asked.

"No, no, no, it has to stay together," K.C. reportedly answered. "It's the only way it will work. It has to stay together." Hence the tangled ownership structure that forced them to work in unison. Now the very qualities that allowed K.C. Irving to construct his empire—ruthlessness, determination, an unwillingness to ever surrender—were, in his progeny, causing the whole edifice to come apart.

"This terrible business of succession," Joan says, "seems to have devastating effects."

Jack's death and funeral received fulsome coverage from Marty Klinkenberg in the *Telegraph-Journal*, though he steered clear of any Kremlinology on where J.K. was sitting in the church. Kenneth's departure was dutifully reported, but the real story of Arthur's trust never appeared—even though Jamie Irving must have known of the court filings in Bermuda: he was named, along with dozens of his relatives, in the 2009 application to dissolve K.C.'s trust.

Amid the turmoil rattling the empire, Jamie was busy reshaping his own corner of it. The rest of the newspaper industry was scrambling to adapt to the online news revolution, but the Brunswick News website looked like it came from the late nineties—a bygone era in media terms. The day's stories were posted at dawn, as the print edition hit the streets, and stayed there, unmoving, unchanging, until the same time the next morning, regardless of breaking news. "People could see what everybody else was doing, and as reporters, they were frustrated," says one *Telegraph* journalist. The younger reporters "wanted to adapt, they wanted to take charge, and they saw they were being halted by this static site."

The Irvings are rarely first to embrace untested new methods: "You show me a group of pioneers and I'll show you a ditch full of people with arrows in their backs," Jamie once said, quoting his grandfather J.K. But now the young vice-president persuaded his forebears they could not afford to wait. Across Canada, print circulation dropped 8.5 percent between 1996 and 2006; at Brunswick News, a similar drop—from a combined hundred thousand copies of the three dailies to less than ninety-three thousand—happened in just three years. Fewer readers meant less business from advertisers. Stripped of the romance of journalism, newspapers were a delivery platform for ads—ads that traditionally provided a much larger share of revenue than subscriptions. But in the United States, ad revenue fell 18 percent from the third quarter of 2007 to the same period a year later. The market crash of 2008 was accelerating an existing trend; the Irvings had to saddle up. A company headhunter went looking for a new editor-in-chief to steer Brunswick News into the online age.

The search produced the name of Rob Warner, the managing editor of the *Ottawa Citizen*. Warner grew up in the capital, and, after working at the *Windsor Star* and the *National Post*, came home to run the *Citizen* newsroom. When Brunswick News called, "I wasn't particularly interested," he says. "I was working at a newspaper I loved." But the chance to work with Neil Reynolds "captured my imagination," he says. As a journalism student at Carleton University, Warner had heard Reynolds speak about the Kingston *Whig-Standard*'s Afghanistan caper. Reynolds arranged for him to come to Saint John to meet Jamie in person. "He impressed me as an exceptionally bright young man," Warner says, "and I believe today he's an exceptionally bright young man—but I know today more than I knew then."

Jamie was attending conferences, consulting experts, studying how to shift the existing model—gathering news and selling it to an audience advertisers want—online, but without cannibalizing the print edition. To Warner, Jamie sketched a *Telegraph-Journal* website "that can be tracked and measured in a way they had never measured the business." It sounded like Big Brother, but it made good business sense. Warner was intrigued, but he knew the reputation of the Irving newspapers. "I didn't want to put myself in a situation where I would have to quit because I didn't agree with something," he says. Jamie reassured him. The young vice-president "always understood the newsroom and what the role of a newspaper is. He always had a firm grasp of that." It was on other commitments—to spend the money required on new staff, hardware, and software to produce proper online news—that Warner says he was disappointed.

On a second trip to Saint John, Warner joined Reynolds and Jamie at 300 Union Street so Jamie's father, Jim Irving, could sign off on his hiring. "There were very few questions that he asked," Warner says. "It was more a talking-to, a setting of the ground rules at the front end." He liked that Jim was colloquial, comfortable in his own skin, and candid. "You have to understand that this is a small province," Warner remembers him saying. "When things go wrong, my phone rings, not yours." Then—echoing the "spicy, but not hot" admonition he once gave Philip Lee—Jim told Warner, "I don't want any mavericks here. I don't want a cowboy." Warner took it as a reference to Wafergate. "Look, you've got to cover what you have to cover as a newsman," Jim continued. "My only concern is that you get it right." That was what Warner wanted to hear. He took the job, and says Jim Irving lived up to the promise, never interfering on Irving stories.

Many of the journalists liked Warner; they enjoyed his newsroom war stories and his beer-and-wings demeanour. "He's one of those good old boys, but he's very polished as well," says one of the staff. "Rob was the newsman that the journalists wanted to see in a high position. ... People were excited that this kind of a guy was here." And he would need that popularity, that social capital, to effect an enormous cultural change. In the old newspaper world of a single evening press deadline, reporters could spend the entire day researching and writing stories—not a lot of time, but a leisurely pace compared to feeding a constantly updated website. Warner caused a stir when he wrote in his internal newsletter that "newspapers are dying." In a subsequent issue, he tried to soothe feelings by casting the change in a positive light: circulation trends suggested a time would come when there would be no printed newspapers, but by then, he promised, "we'll be in a position to carry on as a news and information company that has mastered online and mobile."

Warner also had to oversee the newsroom's adoption of J.D. Irving Ltd.'s "metrics-based system for measuring productivity, quality and output," as he described it in a newsletter. Bylines, local photos, corrections—all would be tabulated along with subscriptions and single-copy sales. "No one will be measured on any one metric in isolation," he wrote. "But newsroom staff will be held accountable." He began planning for the centralization of copyediting and pagination—the computerized design and layout of newspaper pages—in a single editing hub for all the Brunswick News English newspapers. (The French papers would have their own hub in Moncton.) There would be centralized budgeting for newsrooms. And Warner was drawn into the Irving Way: interminable meetings, tedious PowerPoint presentations, and the development of measurable benchmarks—a constant re-evaluation designed to wring out inefficiencies. Jim Irving may not have grasped newsroom culture but he would at least be able to measure its productivity.

As the September 2011 internal launch approached, the newsroom software, designed to move content effortlessly between printed pages and the Web, was plagued with problems. Staff felt "eternal frustration," Warner says, when a promised batch of new laptops and video cameras didn't arrive. And rather than hire new staff, the editor-in-chief had to eliminate vacant positions and shift others to the online team.

Jamie's most controversial decision was to charge customers to read the site. This in itself reflected a growing recognition in the industry that online news had to be monetized, but the Irvings would go about it differently. *The New York Times*, one of the first papers to erect a paywall, allowed a quota of free stories each month to non-subscribers, and Google searches and links from Facebook and Twitter didn't count against the total. The Brunswick News paywall, however, would be absolute, with no free passes via Google or social media. Irving reporters were banned from using Twitter: it gave away news for free. "If anyone wants anything, they've got to spend money," Jim Irving says. "That's how most things work in life. It takes money to pay the reporters and pay the rent, and nothing's for free. Our job is to have a valuable product."

Jamie told a staff meeting the paywall would work because Brunswick News was in the enviable position of not facing competition—though no one recalls him using the word *monopoly*. He was right, but only to a point: the CBC New Brunswick website was a temptingly free alternative for frugal news consumers. And the pricing scheme was telling: $19.95 per month for a Web-only subscription, but $16.95—a *lower* price—for Web access plus the print edition of one daily paper. "The print still pays the bill," says a staffer. "They really do want you to get both, and it's priced that way." David Shipley, a former reporter, says that, fundamentally, Brunswick News "is still a flyer-delivery mechanism."

Industry-wide, publishers feared that charging for content would drive readers to free competitors; everyone wanted someone else to make the first move. The revenue would be paltry, said the skeptics, while proponents countered that some revenue was better than none. There were predictions that well-known brands would make it work but that the average smaller-market paper might not be essential enough to attract online subscribers. As the debate raged, the Irvings made their leap of faith: all the Brunswick News sites went behind the wall, with little fanfare, on Monday, December 5, 2011. For once, Brunswick News would be a pioneer.

Other journalists watched the experiment with fascination. "One of the things I remember Neil [Reynolds] saying is that editorial content is worth money," says Mark Leger. "I get why they want to charge for it." But the paywall short-circuits conversations between papers and readers, he says: a Brunswick News story that might engage non-subscribers and encourage them to start reading will never reach them via Twitter or Facebook unless they subscribe, for example. Leger knows "really, really engaged community members in Saint John" who are not reading. Philip Lee says the papers "have disappeared from the Internet, which seems like a strange business model. If you're not on Google, you're not really in the game."

At first—to extend J.K.'s vivid pioneer metaphor—it appeared Brunswick News might well end up in the ditch. There was no free trial period to hook people, and no story in the papers explaining the move. In the early weeks, the log-in system had all kinds of problems. The launch "was botched so badly it's a wonder anybody has bothered to subscribe at all," one employee complained in an internal company survey.

The shaky paywall rollout worsened already poor morale. Staffers complained about the looming creation of the centralized editing hub, faulty equipment, and the paper's poor reputation among journalism-school graduates. At one point Jamie Irving called a meeting in the lunchroom to address complaints first-hand. "People say I don't talk," he told them. "People say I'm representing my father." He vowed to be more approachable, says one staffer, "but it was like this bad skit on *Saturday Night Live*.... His fists are clenched, his arms are crossed, his legs are crossed and he's looking about as uncomfortable as he can be.... His body language was saying *I have to do this and that's the only reason I'm doing this*." The surveys held cold comfort for the editor-in-chief: "Rob Warner is the best boss I've had in a long time," someone wrote, "but the man is going to have a heart attack trying to plug all the holes and deal with staff shortages."

No wonder Warner leapt at the first chance to do what he loved most: quarterback a big story. In March 2012, three months after the website launch, an unusual heat wave melted large amounts of snow and ice in the Saint John River watershed, flooding the village of Perth-Andover. Late on a Friday afternoon, the village's hospital was evacuated. Warner, driving home from work, called the office to learn *The Daily Gleaner* in Fredericton, the closest daily paper, had no reporter available to file that night, and only one assigned to cover the flood on the weekend. "I blew a gasket," he says. "We have dynamic online news and we can provide updates every five minutes, and we've got one person covering an entire region?" He assigned six journalists. "Let's stop acting like a newspaper chain that doesn't have any competition," he remembers thinking. "Let's start acting like newspeople." The flood coverage was comprehensive and impressive, and it showed the *Telegraph-Journal* could produce excellent journalism.

A month later, Warner was gone. Jamie sent out a memo on May 14 announcing his departure. All along, Warner had been uneasy because his name was never put on the masthead; he had also learned his salary came not from the editorial budget but from a special J.D. Irving Ltd. fund. His hiring, he concluded, "was a contract job disguised as a full-time job, and my dismissal had nothing to do with me."

Warner left New Brunswick unsure how the paywall experiment would turn out. "What Jamie is doing is valuing what we as journalists do," he says. "Content costs. He's telling the reader it costs. He has taken a stand, a bold and courageous stand. God love him for that." But Warner also realized that his broader ambitions had been doomed from the start. He wanted to create a journalistic "centre of excellence" to lure the best young journalists to New Brunswick. "In the end it was never going to happen." Brunswick News, he says, "doesn't aspire to greatness. It's a business. I get it, but I wanted something more. You can make money and still be great."

Instead, the editorial operation felt increasingly like a factory, spewing out content indifferently. A decade earlier, Jamie had promised local flair, not "a Walmart thing." Now deskers in an office blocks away from Crown Street pounded out pages for the weeklies and the dailies, cookie-cutter style. Reporters were required to file fifteen hundred words a day—and managers were counting. Quality didn't matter as long as they hit the quota; if they didn't, they were called in for a chat. The newspaper's most unique commodity—news—was being treated like wood pulp, just another product.

"It's really hard for the Irvings," one editor said. "They have all these solid managers and good performance indicators in all these other sectors. It's easy to evaluate whether we've sold more toilet paper or delivered more oil. In journalism that's hard to do." Philip Lee says the 2013 *Telegraph-Journal* reminds him of early 1993, just before Neil Reynolds arrived. "I was shovelling those pages out the front door. We'll do everything but good journalism first. I think there's a lot of that going on right now in journalism and that's going on at the TJ, too. I think the salvation of the business is just to do really good journalism.... That's the hardest thing to do in many ways."

The Irving Way was the road not travelled for the *Portland Press Herald*, the largest and most influential newspaper across the border in the state of Maine. In the fall of 2008, when the Seattle Times Company put the paper and its two sister dailies in Maine up for sale, Brunswick News came calling. Global markets had crashed, and prospects for the newspaper business were dim, but "we heard that the Irvings were interested," says Tom Bell, president of the Portland Newspaper Guild, the union representing *Press Herald* employees. "At one point a team of managers from Irving walked through the building. They were all men. They were all in suits. Maybe as many as ten guys walked the building." Jim Irving confirms Bell's account. "We looked at it," he says. "We turned over the stones."

The *Press Herald* owners wanted to unload the company in an asset sale, which meant selling the physical plant alone, freeing new owners to lay off the employees, tear up their union contract, and rehire from scratch. "We determined after some research that Irving was unfriendly to unions and would likely take that route,"

Bell says. The mood was bleak among employees. "The attitude was, 'We'll have a job but they won't be very good to work for,'" says Mary Ann Kelley, the company's human resources director. "No one was looking forward to it."

Bell was also alarmed by the reputation the Irving newspapers had for not covering their owners' business interests independently. For the largest newspaper in Maine, the Irvings were undeniably newsworthy—a controversial and increasingly dominant force in the state's forestry and oil sectors.

K.C. Irving made his first cross-border incursion in 1946. His purchase of the pulp mill in Saint John from Edouard Lacroix, a Maine lumber baron, also included two hundred thousand acres of forest land along the state's Allagash River and Lacroix's sawmill in Van Buren, Maine, an American town overlooking the international border on the Saint John River. A decade later, he began trucking industrial fuel oil into the state. When major U.S. gas retailers started pulling out of the state because it was too remote from their refineries and thus too expensive to supply, Irving Oil swooped in. He picked up service stations and home-heating oil retailers, all of them based only a few hours' drive from the Saint John refinery.

By the late seventies, a U.S. government survey found Maine had the most foreign-owned land, 17 percent, of any state, and the Irvings owned most of it. In 1992, when K.C. died, Irving Oil had 25 percent of the state's gas business and 60 percent of its industrial fuel market. And Maine provided the empire with an ideal jumping-off point for expansion farther south. "The Maritimes are closer to New York and Boston than to Toronto," Arthur Irving told author John DeMont. "The richest market in the world is in the northeastern seaboard of the United States. That is the natural way for us to go."

Mainers, like other Americans, admire self-made entrepreneurs, but many have a libertarian streak that makes them leery
of anything *big*—big government, big labour, big oil companies that appear to compete unfairly. In some towns, Irving Oil
would buy up several gas stations to squeeze out established
retailers. Urged on by citizens, state legislators sought legal
means to block them, or at least slow them down. In the vast
forested northern reaches of the state, meanwhile, there was
anger over clear-cutting by Irving Woodlands, J.D. Irving Ltd.'s
U.S. subsidiary. The company was accused of violating federal
health and safety rules and timber-harvesting standards. Some
towns passed local ordinances to block tree plantations. "I hate
to see Canadians control my country," one local businessman
grumbled to John DeMont.

Being portrayed as foreign invaders was new to the Irvings,
who in New Brunswick could always rely on their "This is home"
message. In Maine they responded with a range of tactics, from
writing cheques for charitable causes to hiring well-connected
lobbyists in the state capital, Augusta. Even Premier Frank
McKenna called state legislators to urge them to defeat a bill to
force Irving Oil to publicly report its sales figures. (The bill passed
regardless.) Over time, however, the legendary cleanliness and
friendly service of Irving service stations won over customers;
their red, white, and blue motif didn't hurt, either.

In forestry, however, their logging practices still rankled,
particularly around Portland, Maine's largest population centre
and a bastion of Boston-style liberalism. In 1996, environmental activists gathered enough signatures under the state's
ballot-initiative law to force a plebiscite to ban clear-cutting and
regulate large forestry companies. Early polls indicated it would
pass, but when the industry estimated the passage would cost

the state fifteen thousand jobs, Angus King, the governor, intervened. "The fine print would have killed commercial forestry, in my view, which was why it was so dangerous," he said. King negotiated a more moderate package of logging regulations with forestry companies, called the Compact for Maine's Forests, and convinced the legislature to add it to the ballot, creating a three-way choice for voters.

This was something new for J.D. Irving Ltd.: a direct vote on how it and other forestry companies ran their businesses, something that has never occurred in New Brunswick. The industry created a political action committee, or PAC, Citizens for a Healthy Forest and Economy, to campaign for the compact; records filed with the Maine Ethics Commission, which supervises campaign spending, show Irving companies donated the equivalent of $125,000 to the PAC, including a cash donation of $100,000. It was a small part of the overall $5.7 million campaign budget, but far more than the Irvings were allowed to spend in a New Brunswick election. By July 1996, slick television ads were telling voters the ban would devastate the state economy, and support for the measure began to erode.

On election day, only 29 percent of voters supported the ban. The industry-approved compromise, the Compact for Maine's Forests, got 47 percent, while 33 percent voted against both options. Without a majority, the compact was placed back on the ballot, in a straight yes-no choice, during local elections the following year; it was defeated outright, leaving Maine with no new logging rules at all. Yet Angus King argued the threat of a crackdown led to improvements. "There's much less clear-cutting in Maine than there was when this started," he said. "There's a more rigorous Forest Practices Act. There's a significant part of the forests that come under certification."

Still, manifestations of Irving's power continued. In 2009, Irving Woodlands began laying off workers in northern Maine. The company cited a five-year-old law that let independent logging contractors use collective bargaining with any corporation controlling more than four hundred thousand acres of forest—a designation that applied to just one company. "There is a significant cost to managing our operations under this punitive law that targets our company," Irving spokesperson Mary Keith told the *Bangor Daily News*. "We can no longer afford to pay this price." State senator Troy Jackson, an Allagash Democrat who sponsored the law in 2004, called the Irving layoffs "blackmail." But Governor John Baldacci, once a supporter of regulating the Irvings, moved to repeal the law, and Jackson, after consulting logging contractors in his district, reluctantly agreed. "I guess I'll just sit down now and will let the boss man have what he wants," he said during the debate in the legislature. The law was no more.

Jackson, a logger by trade, sounded a kinder note four years later. The *Portland Press Herald* broke a story that J.D. Irving Ltd. had won an exemption from state clear-cutting regulations and other harvesting standards under an experimental program called Outcome Based Forestry. Conservationists denounced the decision, but Irving argued the increased wood supply helped justify a $30 million upgrade to a sawmill it owned in northern Maine—an announcement applauded by Jackson. "This is a good example of how in Maine we should be doing everything we can to capitalize on our natural resources, process our resources here and buy our made-in-Maine products," he told the *Bangor Daily News*. "There's nothing more American than buying what you or your neighbor makes." To hear Jackson speak, you would never have known he was praising a Canadian company. "As far as we're concerned," Jim Irving told the newspaper, "we consider Maine to be home, in a lot of respects."

And the Irving presence is deep in the state: J.D. Irving Ltd. is one of the largest employers in hard-luck northern Maine, and has poured money into worker training and into forestry research at the University of Maine. Other Irving companies, including Cavendish Farms and Maine Northern Railway, are vital parts of the state economy. In 2012, *The Land Report*, a magazine for wealthy landowners, listed "the Irving family," with its 1.2 million acres of forest, as the biggest private landowner in the state and the fifth-largest in the United States.

In one part of Maine life, however, the Irvings have failed to embed themselves the way they have in New Brunswick. Facing the Brunswick News bid for the *Press Herald* in 2008, Tom Bell, the union president, "used fiery union language to say that we were going to fight to protect our contract," he recalls. That included threats to go to court to block the asset sale, which would force a buyer to honour union contracts. "That's not really the way I usually speak or the way I am. I'm a fairly moderate union leader. But I employed scary union language to try to scare them away, apparently successfully, because we never saw them again."

Instead, the paper was sold to a group of investors who, Bell says, nearly bankrupted the company. "I hope the Irvings appreciate what I did for them, because the newspapers were in much worse shape than would have been apparent to them," he says. "It was just a mess, an absolute mess. They were very lucky they didn't buy the papers."

Jim Irving agrees: "Thank God we didn't buy it," he says. "It was a lucky day. You only have to know what happened down there. Newspaper valuations—you talk to the financial people—have gone down appreciably."

In 2012, wealthy financier Donald Sussman bought the *Press Herald* from the group of investors, and invested in upgrades and new hirings. Sussman, Bell says, is a dream owner, committed to quality journalism with no corporate agenda. "He doesn't necessarily need to make a profit," Bell says. "He sees owning a newspaper as a community service."

15

A FAMILY ACTIVITY

▼

On a May morning in 2013, I walked in a light drizzle across uptown Saint John and through the Loyalist Burial Ground, restored by the Irving brothers, to 300 Union Street, the J.D. Irving Ltd. building, to interview J.K. and Jim Irving for this book. I was early, and there was no security person at the desk in the ground-floor lobby. I studied a large brass plaque near the elevators that reproduced a full-page *Telegraph-Journal* ad from October 1925 announcing K.C. Irving as the new dealer of Ford automobiles in Saint John. "Our policy is better and more satisfactory service, to be honest in our relations with our customers," it said. As if on cue, a bespectacled mid-level-manager type who happened to be exiting an elevator asked me, "Have you been looked after?" He insisted on calling upstairs to let them know I had arrived.

The J.D. Irving Ltd. offices were the colour of the forest: wood door frames, beige-brown paint, green carpets. This maze of offices and cubicles offers a silent rebuttal to those who argue New

Brunswick would do just fine without the Irvings. True, another timber company would be out in the woods, cutting down trees and turning them to pulp. And some other oil company would eagerly operate gas stations and distribute heating oil. But the head offices of those companies would not be in New Brunswick, and the hundreds of white-collar jobs at 300 Union Street and next door at Irving Oil—accountants, engineers, lawyers, marketers, and vice-presidents—would not exist here. The province would be different; the story of the province, told through its newspapers, would surely be different as well.

Father and son sat down with me in the boardroom, along with Mary Keith, their vice-president of communications. "That makes me nervous," J.K. said, pointing to my digital recorder, "but okay." Sitting across from me, he asked me to remind him who ran the *Telegraph-Journal* when I worked there. Twice, the eighty-five-year-old billionaire played interviewer: "You're a journalist. You've worked for the company. You're in the province here. How do you perceive it, our position in the newspapers? I'd be interested." A while later he tried again: "The newspapers, what should they be doing that they're not doing? We've got to get something out of this." Caught by surprise, I sputtered something about wanting more long, in-depth feature stories, like the ones I wrote in the nineties.

Jim sat at the head of the table. "This is not something we do, interviews on this subject," he said, "but it's important to New Brunswick." His father, though, soon warmed to the topic, offering that familiar Irving refrain: local ownership is important. The papers wouldn't know how to properly serve New Brunswick, he said, if they fell into the hands of outsiders— the same argument *his* father, K.C. Irving, made to the Davey committee in 1969.

Jim told me that what I'd heard, that he saw owning news-papers as an irritation, was wrong. "We don't find them a nuisance at all, but it's a business that's got to be run properly," he said. "We get all the criticism over the newspapers, so we decided a few years ago, if we're going to get criticism, we better be right, and we better work at getting the management so it's right, try to train journalists, invest capital, upgrade the technology, whatever it was."

This was typical Irving talk—he might as well have been describing the pulp mill—and it explains the counting of words and bylines, the integration of the newspapers into the family's results-based corporate culture. Similarly lacking in nuance was Jim Irving's view of how the papers should cover other Irving companies: "If we're right, you should support it," he said. "And if we're wrong, by geez, we should get a kick in the backside, too, because we're no different than anybody else." And what about investigative journalism—digging deeper? His mind went immediately to a negative connotation. "We've had more than one instance where somebody from the paper didn't get the facts right on something we were doing. They've done a poor job on it. It's about getting the facts right. If we're wrong on something, that's the facts, too."

Then Jim Irving said something that echoed his "spicy, but not hot" complaint to Philip Lee, and his "I don't want a cowboy" warning to Rob Warner. "We're not interested in fellas raising hell," he said, "just for the sake of raising hell." *Don't rock the boat,* he seemed to imply. *Don't stir the pot.* "Every once in a while," Jim explained, management at the papers gets "off track. And we've got to have management that's smart enough to understand what's going on, and be for New Brunswick, and try and make the place better.... We work hard at our business, our employees work hard at our business, a lot of communities depend on it, and it's our reputation. We want to be proud of it."

"For New Brunswick." "Make the place better." "Keep the wheels turning." "Not interested in fellas raising hell." These are the slogans, simple and blunt, that define the Irvings, including how Jim Irving sees his newspapers. And in a province where his family plays a ubiquitous role in the economy, that philosophy has daily implications, in story after story.

When the new PC government of Premier David Alward put the brakes on Shawn Graham's wood-harvesting rules, J.D. Irving Ltd. helped organize another ostensibly grassroots lobbying campaign. This time, three thousand employees working for Irving and other forestry companies signed petitions asking for the province to maintain the existing cut. The petitions were tabled in the New Brunswick Legislature in 2011; there was no acknowledgment of the company's role until the CBC revealed it. The *Telegraph-Journal*, meanwhile, hosted Jim at another editorial board, giving prominent coverage to his case for more wood.

In Nova Scotia, Jim Irving was scoring a major triumph: in 2011, Ottawa awarded Halifax Shipyards the largest part of the new navy contract, a $25 billion tender for twenty-one combat ships. It meant thousands of jobs for Halifax for years to come, and plenty of regional spinoffs. The selection process was, as promised, non-political: an independent consultant monitored the process, and elected politicians were told of the choice only minutes before the announcement, which was made by a non-partisan bureaucrat. "What a great day for Halifax!" Jim shouted at a ceremony at the Halifax yard in what author Harvey Sawler called "a rare state of unbridled enthusiasm."

The announcement took up the entire front page and the

full front of the business section in the *Telegraph-Journal*, on a day when big stories on rural health care, French immersion, and power rates—three hot-button New Brunswick issues—were shoved inside. "The ownership had absolutely zero, and I mean nothing, to do with the placement of those stories," says Rob Warner. In fact, he remembers Jamie staying out of the newsroom, probably deliberately. Warner says it was his call: "There was nothing bigger on this day in my humble opinion than that story." Inevitable controversies—a $260 million loan to Irving from Nova Scotia's NDP government to help modernize the shipyard, and the outsourcing of some architectural and engineering work to Denmark—did not get similar exposure in the *Telegraph-Journal*.

Nor did the most contentious of all Irving stories, the quiet breakup of the family empire. Throughout 2011 and 2012, it remained a non-topic in the pages of Brunswick News.

"How much of an answer are you looking for?" J.K. asked, after a long pause, when I asked him about it. "It's a big, big subject, but we're all happily going on our ways now. Art's looking after the oil company, and Jack is no longer with us, which I feel very badly about. We're working our end of the business and going about it our way. It's our business, and we've never talked about it."

"The short answer is, everything's moving on," Jim said. "Everything's reorganized, and we're moving on." A short answer indeed: for these questions, the slogans did not come as easily.

"That's in the past," J.K. said.

"That's right." Jim nodded. "It's done."

"Everything's humming around here," J.K. said, trying to sound upbeat.

I asked about the status of K.C. Irving's trust in Bermuda—a subject that was fair game for the *Telegraph-Journal* run by Neil Reynolds in 1993.

"Oh, I tell you, we're not going to get into all that," J.K. said. "You asked the question, and everything's tidied up."

It's a big story, I said, a big topic of speculation in the city and the province.

"Let me tell you," J.K. said, showing impatience now, "it's nobody's damned business, okay?"

"We're doing well," Jim said more gently, but his tone indicated this would be their last word on the subject. He nodded in the direction of the Irving Oil building down the block. "That fella's across the street, selling gasoline, just like he always sold it.... We're over here, sawing lumber, chasing everything else. So we're busy, they're busy, and everybody's moving on, which is a good thing."

They made a good team, father and son, finishing each other's thoughts, reinforcing each other's message. Their basic logic was the same—but they kept returning to that hint of a difference between them, between emotion and the hard logic of finance. Jamie "appreciated journalism," J.K. said; "Yeah," Jim added, "but basically, we had a business." The pattern repeated several times: Jim would huff impatiently about how he couldn't afford to wait much longer for a more conducive provincial policy—then J.K. would wax philosophical about the irreplaceable joys of visiting the mills, poking around, meeting workers.

"No, I'm sentimental about it," Jim said when I put this to them. "But you want to find out how much sentimentality the Royal Bank's got if you don't pay them. You'll find out in a damn hurry. Fredericton's been trying to fix things, Christ, for way too long.... You fix it or you won't have it. That's my view." He glanced at his father. "You might have a different view."

"The best place to have a plant is right here in New Brunswick," J.K. replied. "I can go out to see, Jim. I can go see what's going on and there's some enjoyment in that."

It was also possible that what I was witnessing was an act, a well-rehearsed good cop–bad cop routine, because, fundamentally, father and son share the same goal: to persuade whoever they are dealing with that they are mere stewards of this vast machine, this great venture tied to the province so intimately that it can never be allowed to falter, this sprawling entity that they have nonetheless chosen to keep rooted here—not for the billions, but for the benefit of all.

They apply this logic to the newspapers as well. One consequence of outside ownership, J.K. said, would be the loss of the various distinctly local dailies and weeklies. "If we sold the newspapers, we'd end up with one newspaper. That's what would happen."

You must have thought about merging them yourselves, I said, angling for confirmation of the rumour that resurfaces regularly in New Brunswick media circles.

"The accountants will tell you that's what you do," J.K. said. "But we really feel we have an obligation to the province. And *you don't do that.*"

"You certainly don't do it *today,*" Jim said. "I don't know what the thing is going to look like down the road."

"Oh, Jim," his father said, with mild exasperation.

"The world's changing awful fast," Jim answered.

Here again was the same routine as before. But perhaps on this point, there is a genuine distinction between father and son: J.K., after all, told Valerie Millen to publish a newspaper that would "stir things up," while Jim insists that editors not "raise hell." And J.K. seemed to grasp that the newspaper business is not like other Irving companies. "At all our businesses over the years, if the manager left," he said to Jim, "you or I would know enough about it to go in and run it and feel comfortable with it. The media business—I know I couldn't." Jim wasn't quite as diffident: "It's a revenue business—on the commercial side," he said with a shrug. "Then you've got writing stories, editorial," he conceded. "That's a bit more of an art. But it's a business, too. You've got to have something that sells."

J.K.'s time was passing, of course, and he had decisions to make about Brunswick News—whether to bequeath the newspaper company he owned to his son Jim, or directly to his grandson Jamie. Would that give Jamie a measure of independence? He once seemed to share his grandfather's desire to "stir things up" but has since adopted his father's reluctance to "raise hell." What might he do with a little more freedom? What stories would he tell?

"Good newspapers should be a service to the people of the province," J.K. continued. "You've got the *Telegraph-Journal* carted all around the province"—at considerable cost, he was suggesting—"but it's one of the few vehicles in the province that ties the province together a little bit. And that's quite important. Financially you're a hell of a lot better off to bring it in. But the mandate of the newspaper is to be a good newspaper for the province."

And here I wondered if this canny billionaire was thinking of his own family and his own brothers—the decades they spent together building an empire, the history that had passed between them, and, more recently, the pain of seeing it torn apart.

"The province requires something to bind it together, you

know?" J.K. said. "You can get separated so damn fast in a lot of things."

Three and a half months after J.K. spoke those words, his brother Arthur Irving stepped into the bright, midday August sun to be heralded as a nation-builder. TransCanada Corp., the Calgary-based oil company, was officially launching a bid to build a pipeline to carry crude oil from the oil fields of Alberta across Canada to the Irving Oil refinery in Saint John. "The pipeline is as important today … as the railway was in the past," the premier, David Alward, had told the legislature. Now, with Alward at his side at a podium outside the refinery, Arthur invoked not a grand vision but a familiar Irving trope: a thank-you to employees and customers for supporting the pipeline proposal. "All of you helped out," he said, his voice crackling with energy. "You're our friends, you're our neighbours, you're proud Maritimers. We believed in it, we were successful, and we did it with you."

Arthur was triumphant after years of setbacks. Kenneth, his son and heir, was gone, along with his plans for a second refinery and a new corporate headquarters. Kenneth's dreams of a new, rebranded, diversified energy company were gone, too. The energy corridor had been shelved, as had a pilot project to harness tidal power in the Bay of Fundy. Canaport LNG's volume had dropped by half in 2012; Repsol, the Spanish oil company and co-owner of the plant, was unable to sell it when it unloaded the rest of its global natural gas assets earlier in the year. Irving Oil was back to basics, buying crude oil, refining it, and selling it as fuel.

Alward liked the parallel to Sir John A. Macdonald's CNR, but it overstated Irving Oil's motives. When Ottawa was looking, in 1958, to give Alberta's oil exclusive access to eastern markets, K.C. wanted no part of pan-Canadian nation-building schemes. Prairie crude was more expensive than what he could import from the Middle East. He argued for the freedom to buy wherever he liked, and got his way: the new federal rules were not applied east of the Ottawa River. Half a century later, Alberta's price was more appealing, offering Irving Oil potential savings of as much as $1.2 billion a year, one report estimated. Political opposition had stalled pipelines through British Columbia and the United States; western crude, stranded inland and heavily discounted, could sell at the premium world price if it could reach the ocean—and the most viable route in 2013 was across Canada, through a converted three-thousand-kilometre line to Quebec and an extension to be built the rest of the way to the Saint John refinery.

And there was a new impetus for the pipeline in the summer of 2013, when, on the night of July 6, a train of more than seventy tanker cars carrying crude oil to the Irving refinery derailed and exploded in the town of Lac-Mégantic, Quebec, killing forty-seven people and destroying thirty downtown buildings.

With the Bakken fields of North Dakota producing oil more quickly than it could be sent to refineries, sellers and buyers had opted for long trains of tanker cars to carry the discounted crude where it needed to go. Starting in 2012, trains bound for Saint John would snake through the American Midwest, into Canada at Windsor, and on to Montreal, where the Montreal, Maine and Atlantic Railway picked up the tanker cars and carried them back across the border into Maine. At a small railway hub, Brownville Junction, the MMA would hand off the shipments to the Eastern Maine Railway, which then hauled the crude to the Canadian border and to the New Brunswick Southern Railway, which carried it on to the Irving refinery.

Bakken rail shipments grew fiftyfold between 2009 and 2013; by July, Irving Oil had received more than three thousand eight hundred tanker cars of crude. This revolution in the transportation of oil went largely unnoticed, however, until the MMA train exploded in Lac-Mégantic. The disaster shocked Canada, and would haunt Irving Oil: in the months to come, federal investigators would raid the Saint John refinery offices for evidence that shipping labels had misstated their risk of exploding. With trademark speed and decisiveness, Irving announced in early 2014 it would voluntarily upgrade or withdraw from service the older, riskier class of tanker car in its fleet. In the immediate wake of the conflagration, though, the horrific images of destruction transformed the debate over pipelines, building the political case for Energy East.

Lac-Mégantic had implications for Jim Irving as well. The two railways that hauled the Bakken crude from Brownville Junction to Saint John, the Eastern Maine and the New Brunswick Southern, are owned by J.D. Irving Ltd. When the MMA declared bankruptcy in the wake of the accident, Jim's rail operations were one of its largest unsecured creditors, owed $2 million. Jim began planning a classic K.C.-style move, a buyout of the Maine sections of the MMA on the cheap to expand the Irving rail network in the state.

Such were the implications swirling in the salty Bay of Fundy air that August morning at the refinery. And at almost precisely the same time as the pipeline announcement, Jack's son John Irving was enjoying his own moment—more modest and local—in the heart of the city. John helped unveil a century-old bandstand in King's Square, restored in part with his money; the gesture lent credence to the rumour that John became a much wealthier man as the empire was carved up. He is widely believed to have inherited a large stake in Irving Oil that his father received during the settling of accounts from the breakup: in early 2011, John was listed, along with his uncle Arthur and his cousin Arthur Jr., as a director of a new company called IOC Oil Holdings Ltd., which indirectly owns a majority of Irving Oil. John also took over his father's construction and real estate companies and was expanding the Acadia Broadcasting chain of radio stations, which he co-owned with his sister, Anne. And now he was establishing his own civic profile as a builder and philanthropist.

In one day, then, all the branches of K.C. Irving's family were demonstrating they were still players. Despite Saint John's ongoing efforts to rebrand itself with a high-tech gloss, it was still a blue-collar city that *made* things—and the Irvings were still the biggest makers by far.

As he stood at the podium, Arthur Irving declared that he wanted to "wind the clock back a bit." He paid tribute to K.C. Irving, "a great man, a great father, and a great believer in New Brunswick and the Maritimes and Canada." He recalled the doubters who questioned K.C.'s vision of the original Canaport, built to accommodate freighters on a scale that did not yet exist. "My father said, 'We can do it,'" Arthur boasted. "The first large tanker in the world to ever cross the Atlantic Ocean came to Saint John, New Brunswick!"

Mike Ashar, who became CEO of Irving Oil after Kenneth's departure, retired a few weeks before the pipeline announcement. He told *The Globe and Mail* in an interview to mark his exit that his tenure at a family company taught him how "family members are deeply aware of the history and look at it as a business that will pass through generations." But as Arthur basked in the applause, it was not clear to which Irving it would pass next: his nephew John, though a director of the company, had no executive role, while his son Arthur Jr. was in a low-profile job running the property management division; the senior jobs were held by non-family managers. And Kenneth was still nowhere to be seen: the quarrel with his father, precipitated by the breakup of the empire, had grown even more fractious.

After his abrupt departure from Irving Oil in 2010 over his father's trust money, Kenneth—showing the same tenacity as his father and grandfather—had refused to forsake his claim. Supported by his sister Emily, he continued to insist on a larger-than-equal share of Arthur's fortune in Bermuda; his siblings Arthur Jr. and Jennifer, and his half-sister Sarah from Arthur's second marriage, sided with their father in resisting him. In November 2011, they agreed on a settlement. It included extra money for Kenneth—though not all he'd demanded—and an elaborate governance structure for the trust, designed to isolate father and son from each other. As described in the 2012 court ruling by Bermuda's chief justice, Ian Kawaley, the money from K.C.'s trust would flow between Arthur's trust and several "children's family account" holding companies; these companies were, Kawaley wrote, "tax efficient vehicles" for distributing profits from Irving Oil to Arthur's children and grandchildren. Kenneth, while a director of two family holding companies, would have no role in the trust itself and therefore not in Irving Oil; Arthur, a director of the trust and chairman of the oil company, would be "excluded" from the family holding companies, which would have the power to invest their trust money.

Almost immediately after receiving his payment, Kenneth had second thoughts. The settlement required that an accounting firm assess the dollar value of Irving Oil's operations and laid out "contingencies" for if it gained or lost value. When Kenneth asked for financial information about Irving Oil and suggested he might be able to help, the trust's directors, wary that he coveted a greater role in the company than the settlement permitted, turned him down. This convinced Kenneth that the trust directors, who under the settlement were also directors of his family's holding companies, were in the "thrall" of his father, unable to act independently. He hinted he might challenge the governance structure of Arthur's trust—and even the dissolution of the K.C. trust—in a Canadian court. "I wished I didn't have to intimate that that is a possible step, to force people to come to the table," he would explain. "It unfortunately is a long-standing pattern of negotiating with my father. Unless he knows that I have the resolve to go the whole way, I'll be stonewalled."

Arthur was furious. Kenneth couldn't sue in Canada because the terms of the settlement, which both men had agreed to, held that the trust was subject to the laws of Bermuda. In a pre-emptive strike, Arthur filed an application in Bermuda for an order blocking his son from going to court in Canada. He also asked the judge to penalize his son by removing him as a director of the family holding companies and ordering him to return what he'd been paid in the settlement. "It was obvious," Justice Kawaley later wrote in his ruling, "that the motivations of the main protagonists, a strong patriarch and an equally strong-willed son for whom family and business connections are closely intertwined, were heavily infused with deep-seated emotions of an intensity rarely seen outside of familial relationships."

During his two days of testimony in the dispute, Kenneth was "overcome emotionally on more than one occasion," the judge wrote, lamenting the loss of his link to Irving Oil and "the ruination of his once close relationship with his father and the consequences of this for his children's relationship with the wider family." Kenneth, "honest and straightforward," was "least convincing," the judge said, when he claimed "he was not nurturing lingering discontent" over the 2011 settlement. Kenneth, Kawaley concluded, wasn't really seeking to challenge the trust structure, but was hoping to force open a line of communication with his siblings. "Everyone trying to play a role in continuing to isolate me from information … is leaving a terrible track record," Kenneth said. "I want to be recognized at some point by my siblings that I did good."

Justice Kawaley ruled Kenneth would indeed breach the terms of the Bermuda settlement if he sued in Canada, and issued a permanent injunction to prevent him from doing so. But he turned down Arthur's request to oust Kenneth as a director and revoke his payment. Kenneth's threats, Kawaley explained sympathetically, were "emotionally motivated … to a significant extent based on legitimate feelings of hurt" over his estrangement from his father and his siblings. "He was, it seems to me, seeking to recover a lost extended family and lost working relationships nurtured in a cherished family business which had been brought to an abrupt end."

Kawaley pointed out Kenneth had offered to drop the matter entirely if four conditions were met: a family meeting of all of Arthur's children "assisted by a professional facilitator," a retirement dinner honouring Kenneth's contribution to Irving Oil, a commitment to not discourage Irving Oil employees from dealing with Kenneth, and—most poignantly—a promise from Arthur that he would attend "a family activity" with his son. But Arthur had rejected the offer, so angry at his son's disobedience, Justice Kawaley surmised, and so determined to preserve the trust structure, that he was blind to the possibility of repairing his relationship with Kenneth and to "the emotional harm that the current estrangement may be inflicting by way of collateral damage on other family members including his own grandchildren."

Instead, Arthur stood fast, and pressed for victory over his oldest son and erstwhile heir—and won, as he always did.

Now in the summer of 2013, with another of his family's industrial visions poised to become reality, Arthur, in his eighties, was surrounded by admirers, yet alone. His refinery loomed in the background, soon to be linked to the rest of the country, but his family was torn asunder, the split with his brother having led to the break with his son. If the Alberta pipeline was one legacy of the legendary single-mindedness passed down from K.C. Irving, this bitter schism—likely to reverberate in the family for generations—was surely another.

Only Arthur knows whether he considers it too costly a bargain.

In their 1973 book, *K.C. Irving: The Art of the Industrialist*, Russell Hunt and Robert Campbell compared the Irving empire to a dinosaur that was too large and ungainly to survive changing times. "As with the dinosaur, history is clearly against the Irving monster," they predicted. "It cannot adapt to change." Yet four decades on, the family was still building, never resting, always moving forward. Arthur was holding Irving Oil together despite a Shakespearean break with his son Kenneth. John, Jack's son once seen as the odd man out, was ascendant. Yes, Jim, the eldest of K.C.'s grandchildren, failed in his bid to acquire sections of the Montreal, Maine and Atlantic Railway. Yes, New Brunswick's

PC government finally moved to impose a higher natural gas fee on his companies, closer to the market price. But in March 2014, Premier David Alward handed Jim Irving the biggest prize of all, the one he'd been seeking for a decade.

Two years after rolling back the Liberals' pro-industry policies by reducing logging on Crown land and expanding conservation zones off-limits to industry, Alward's government announced a near-complete reversal. Harvesting would be allowed to increase by 21 percent, while conservation areas would shrink. And this time, the wood-supply numbers would be entrenched in contracts between the province and logging companies, tying the hands of future governments. Irving's twenty-five-year-agreement stated explicitly that its intent was "to ensure the ongoing global competitiveness of Irving's forestry operations." Environmentalists, retired government foresters, and former provincial cabinet ministers all sounded the alarm; one activist said the contract "set a record for caving into one company's demands."

New Brunswick's political leaders may privately chafe at the Irvings' power, but the new policy underscored that the family remains integral to the province's economy: Jim immediately announced upgrades to the company's largest mills, including a $450 million modernization of the Saint John pulp mill. Maybe, as they will claim, the Irvings don't get everything they ask for—"I don't think we have the influence that some people perceive that we have," Jim said after Alward's timber announcement—but they always get enough to keep growing. If they are dinosaurs, it's because they toil in old-economy industries: chopping trees, cutting steel into boats, turning carbon into energy. But those old ways still make the wheels turn.

Only one among them, however, is transforming the

fundamentals of his business for the twenty-first century. Jamie Irving understands that the newspaper, as a printed object, may cease to exist, and he is ready, his father says, to replace it with an entirely new product. "We could run the paper fully digital without any difficulty," Jim asserts; Jamie "has done a good job overall—better than most papers in North America.... Our circulation is now increasing, which is a good thing at a time when everybody else's is decreasing. It's not huge numbers, but it's going the right way." Profits, he says, are "coming. We spent a lot of money. But it's helping drive the circulation.... I'd say we're very much in the game." This forestry man, once a maker and seller of newsprint, foresees a day when there is no print edition at all—yet won't rule out more acquisitions for Brunswick News. J.K. agrees: "You never say never."

J.K. acknowledges that Jamie's 2004 appointment as publisher—the first time a family member crossed that psychological barrier to sit in the newspaper office every day—was controversial. "Was that a mistake on our part?" he asks me. Before I can formulate an answer, he continues: "He's down there and he's running it and that's fine. But his name showed up on the top of the paper, just what you said there, and there's a reaction to it."

Now it's starting to look like Jamie was the right Irving at the right time. "You look at what he's done to give the papers some chance of survival and it's pretty impressive," says Michael Camp, the former *Telegraph-Journal* reporter now teaching journalism. The centralized editing and pagination hub, though it rubbed many staffers the wrong way, has reduced costs and kept the papers afloat, Camp says. "I think his goal is to save them. You hate to say that your choices are the Irving press or nothing, but at the moment that's our choice."

Rob Warner, too, despite his own frustrations, gives Jamie credit: the word from inside Brunswick News is that online subscriptions reached twenty-five thousand in 2013; if so, it may have eclipsed the *Telegraph-Journal*'s print circulation, which would be a remarkable milestone. Subscription revenue was increasing, the vast majority of the growth from the website. "I think it was a tremendous success and I think that success was driven largely by Jamie's vision in the beginning," Warner says. Though he chafed at the Irving Way, Warner says Jamie now appears to have built a large enough audience to sell to advertisers. "He's made it work behind a hard paywall where no one else in Canada has," Warner says. "Good on him."

Other larger Canadian newspapers, including *The Globe and Mail* and the *Toronto Star*, installed paywalls after the Brunswick News move. It is still not clear whether they will save the industry: subscribers tend to stick around a site longer, a selling point for advertisers, but many newspaper sites remain worrisomely ad-free. One bright spot for the business came in 2012, when *The New York Times* revealed that, for the first time, paid circulation, including online subscriptions, brought in more revenue than advertising, the traditional cash cow of the business.

The New York Times, of course, is a premium product, arguably the finest newspaper in the world. In an online market of infinite choices, most of them still free, mediocre content won't sell. And this is where Brunswick News still faces a challenge: it won't give readers premium coverage—essential coverage, *probing* coverage—of one vital subject: the province's largest industrial family. In December 2013, the *Telegraph* reported, laudably, on the Lac-Mégantic search warrants at Irving Oil and the Irving bid for the MMA railway assets. But the biggest Irving story of all remains off-limits: "What we would be reading now if we had a more diversified ownership in New Brunswick," says Camp, "would be about the breaking up of the Irving empire. It's happening completely in the dark."

Rob Warner says he didn't assign reporters to the split during his tenure because "I don't even know about the story." He researched the Irvings before taking the job in 2011, but "that's one that doesn't ring a bell for me.... I know nothing about the brothers' relationships with each other. That's just something that never came up." He adds: "I wasn't close enough to it, I was too damned busy, and quite frankly there are certain things better left alone."

But when a family's forestry operations employ fifteen thousand people, and its oil refinery generates more than half the exports of an entire province—and when it has argued that the growth and success of its businesses benefit that province as a whole—its tragedies, its divisions, its struggles over succession are part of the province's story. In March 2014, citing "better information," the *Forbes* billionaires list stopped treating the Irvings as a single company, and for the first time gave J.K. and Arthur separate rankings: J.K., worth an estimated $6 billion U.S., was 234th globally, while Arthur, at $5.5 billion, was 256th. Saint John was now a two-company town, with each company bearing the name Irving, but the local newspaper, the *Telegraph-Journal*—with its supposedly business-focused coverage—has not acknowledged or analyzed this vital fact.

And the Irving story never ends. J.D. Irving Ltd. press releases have been referring to brothers Jim and Robert as co-CEOs, a sign J.K. is also planning for the future by binding his sons together—as his father K.C. did with his three boys. One of Jamie's younger brothers, David, is reportedly being groomed to take over J.D. Irving Ltd. Jim and John, so long estranged, were seen chatting civilly at a recent public event. And at a ceremony in December 2012 where Saint John city council conferred the rare Freedom of the City honour on the Irving brothers, J.K. and Arthur, the two survivors, reportedly treated each other warmly.

It is impossible, of course, to know what they were thinking—but a serious newspaper would try to find out. The Irvings "have been the backbone of industry and commerce in New Brunswick," Michael Camp says, "and considering the implications of this, it's amazing not to see it reflected in the paper. So that's a sign of the fact that we have an Irving press."

The signs have been there for decades. From the cautious approach to Irving stories dating back to the forties, to the generous reporting on Jim's lobbying for lower power rates, readers have always had to wonder if there was more to the story. When Neil Reynolds died in 2013, the *Telegraph-Journal* obituary mentioned his return in 2009 but didn't explain the scandal that prompted it.

Later that year, however, Brunswick News hired its first ombudsman, Patricia Graham, a former editor-in-chief of *The Vancouver Sun*, to fill the void left by Reynolds—a recognition, perhaps, that Brunswick News still needed an ethical compass. Though Graham says she believes perceptions of the Irving ownership are "simply not accurate and not based in fact," she has also said the company is "sensitive" to the concerns "and won't shy away from considering or addressing them." Around the same time, the *Telegraph-Journal* conceded, in a 2014 editorial endorsing Alward's forestry plan, "that a major player in the provincial forestry industry also has family ties to this newspaper"—a rare but laudable acknowledgment.

These steps may reflect the reality that the Irvings can no longer be complacent about Brunswick News. "You don't need to read the *Telegraph-Journal*," Jim Irving says. "There's so many other sources. It's on Facebook and Twitter. It's a low barrier to entry now. If somebody wants to start a virtual newspaper today, I guess you could do it. Today, never before has New Brunswick had such a breadth of media." The diversity of choices that many New Brunswickers longed for over the years has arrived, says former *Telegraph* reporter David Shipley, a student of online news. "Technology is going to do what Senate committees couldn't do.... It's going to end that information dominance."

Shipley points to Charles LeBlanc, a civic gadfly and activist who prowls the streets of Fredericton, confronting politicians with impudent questions and posting videos of their answers to YouTube. "In the pre-Internet days, Charles LeBlanc's only outlet was to write a letter to the editor," Shipley says. The internet has also allowed environmentalist Charles Thériault to upload documentaries criticizing industrial forestry. In Moncton, a group of young Acadians, including a former employee of *L'Étoile*, launched an online commentary magazine, *Asteure*. A Saint John tech enthusiast aggregated the province's public property-tax data on an easily searchable website. Alternate sources of information are flourishing in New Brunswick.

But none of this replaces good reporting. When LeBlanc encountered J.K. Irving on the streets of Fredericton in 2011, the normally irascible blogger giggled like a star-struck fan and didn't ask a single tough question. Erin Steuter, the Mount Allison professor and Irving critic, says independent media in the Maritimes "is kind of an awkward teenager," still unable to deliver professional-level coverage of alternative viewpoints. "I would like to see professional journalism—standard techniques and abilities—in the indie media," she says. "We need that." David Coon, the leader of the New Brunswick Green Party, says the growth of alternative media online "has provided more opportunity, definitely," but says the "counterpoint" is the Irving acquisition of the weeklies. In the past, a maverick editor—what Jim Irving might call a "cowboy"—could decide to stir the pot. Coon cites the *Miramichi Leader* breaking stories about mill contamination, the *Kings County Record* editorializing against insecticide spraying by forestry companies, *The Woodstock Bugle* playing a "pivotal role" in a campaign to clean up the Saint John River.

Now, stirring the pot is officially discouraged at those newspapers, too. This doesn't preclude good journalism—the *Telegraph-Journal*'s 2013 coverage of the murder of a prominent New Brunswick businessman earned it a National Newspaper Award—but admonitions about not "raising hell" can only make editors reluctant to tackle certain stories.

And that includes the Irving story, an epic of our times: a tale of ambition and achievement, of a family that built an industrial economy where few others believed one could be built—and also a tale of ruthlessness, jealousy, and loss, of power amassed and exercised. Any media company that purports to reflect New Brunswick—that claims to be "about New Brunswick, for New Brunswick"—has to contend with that story, fully and completely, with all its complexities and contradictions.

These newspapers, and the remarkable entrepreneurs who own them, can't tell the story of their province if they won't tell the story of themselves.

NOTES

Throughout various chapters of this book, I rely frequently on four volumes that, in different ways, provide valuable insights into the Irving family: *K.C. Irving: The Art of the Industrialist* by Russell Hunt and Robert Campbell (Toronto: McClelland & Stewart, 1973), *Citizens Irving: K.C. Irving and His Legacy* by John DeMont (Toronto: Doubleday Canada, 1991), *K.C.: The Biography of K.C. Irving* by Douglas How and Ralph Costello (Toronto: Key Porter Books, 1993) and *Twenty-First-Century Irvings* by Harvey Sawler (Halifax: Nimbus Publishing, 2007). I owe a considerable debt to these authors. I also draw a considerable amount of information, particularly revealing comments by the Irvings themselves, from *The Irvings: Unlocking the Mystery*, a CBC Television documentary series broadcast in March 1998. Jamie Irving's comments are from an interview that Kim Kierans conducted with him in January 2003; Kierans provided me with a copy of the original recording. I also consulted hundreds of articles from the Irving newspapers. The most significant ones are cited in these notes.

The following people gave me on-the-record interviews that I quote throughout the narrative: Harry Bagley, Elaine Bateman, Tom Bell, Michael Bembridge, Conrad Black, Peter Boisseau, Amy Cameron, Michael Camp, Andrew Cochran, Pat Darrah, Gary Dimmock, Charles Enman, Richard Foot, Jonathan Franklin, Guy Giorno, Shawn Graham, Fred Hazel, Scott Honeyman, William Hoyt, James D. (Jim) Irving, Joan Carlisle Irving, James K. (J.K.) Irving, Mary Ann Kelly, Kelly Lamrock, Abel LeBlanc, Philip Lee, Mark Leger, Lloyd Mackey, Jill Mahoney, Matt McCann, Daniel McHardie, Steve McKinley, Doug Milander, Jim Morrison, Chelsea Murray, Gordon Pitts, Bob Rupert, Carolyn Ryan, David Shipley, Peter Simpson, Erin Steuter, Mark Tunney, Doug Tyler, André Veniot, Rino Volpé, Julian Walker, Rob Warner, Jackie Webster, and Paul Willcocks. A number of other people agreed to speak to me on condition of anonymity.

I have generally used the present tense to indicate when I am quoting from the interviews I conducted; attribution using the past tense usually indicates the quotation comes from a secondary, contemporaneous source such as a newspaper article.

Twelve days after I contacted Jamie Irving to seek his cooperation for this book—a request he turned down—he sent a memo to journalists working at the Irving newspapers to tell them they were "prohibited from granting interviews to external sources if the content of those interviews may involve discussion about Brunswick News Inc."

Mary Keith, the vice-president of communications at J.D. Irving Ltd., arranged my interviews with J.K. Irving and Jim Irving in May 2013. In October 2013, I contacted her by email with additional questions and a request that she clarify several points and help me check some facts. On January 2, 2014, Mary Keith responded that the company would no longer cooperate with my research.

PROLOGUE: BEHAVE YOURSELVES

Coverage of K.C. Irving's will in the *Telegraph-Journal* was published on August 18, 19, and 20, 1993.

1: BECOMING K.C. IRVING

In addition to the Hunt and Campbell, Costello, and DeMont books, this chapter relies on *I Like to See Wheels Turn*, a 1981 National Film Board documentary by Giles Walker; Gordon Pitts, "A Generational Divide," *The Globe and Mail*, Dec. 27, 2007; and Ralph Allen, "K.C. Irving: The Unknown Giant," *Maclean's*, April 18, 1964.

2: A LOCAL OIL COMPANY

Alden Nowlan's essay "What About the Irvings?" appeared in Walter Stewart (ed.), *Canadian Newspapers: The Inside Story* (Edmonton: Hurtig Publishers, 1980). For references to Howard Robinson, see Don Nerbas, *The Changing World of the Bourgeoisie in Saint John, New Brunswick in the 1920s* (MA thesis, University of Winnipeg, 2003) and "Howard Robinson and the British Method: A Case Study of Britishness in Canada in the 1930s and 1940s," *Journal of the Canadian Historical Association*, vol. 20, no. 1, 2009, pp. 139–160. See also Douglas Fetherling, *The Rise of the Canadian Newspaper* (Toronto: Oxford University Press, 1990). The three articles that appeared in the March 1959 issue of the *Atlantic Advocate* were Michael Wardell, "K.C. Irving: The Amazing Creator of Millions"; H. Herlof Smith, "The St. Lawrence River and the Chignecto Canal"; and D.A. Young,

"Report on Chignecto." Charles Lynch's description of the Saint John *Citizen* is from his memoir *You Can't Print That* (Edmonton: Hurtig Publishers, 1983).

Accounts of Michael Wardell's life are from Anne Chisholm and Michael Davie, *Beaverbrook: A Life* (London: Hutchinson, 1992); Jacques Poitras, *Beaverbrook: A Shattered Legacy* (Fredericton: Goose Lane Editions, 2007); and Bill Hagerty, "The Real Crusader," *British Journalism Review*, vol. 13, no. 1, 2002, pp. 19–31. Wendell Fulton's paper for the University of New Brunswick (1993), "Michael Wardell, Lord Beaverbrook and the Fredericton, New Brunswick *Daily Gleaner*," is an invaluable summary of Wardell's correspondence with Beaverbrook about his dealings with K.C. Irving.

3: HIS PRESENCE IS THERE

Two valuable accounts of Louis Robichaud's battle with K.C. Irving are J.E. Belliveau, *Little Louis and the Giant K.C.* (Hantsport, N.S.: Lancelot Press, 1980) and Michel Cormer, *Louis Robichaud: A Not So Quiet Revolution* (Moncton: Faye Editions, 2004). The *Telegraph-Journal*'s editorial recanting its opposition to Equal Opportunity, "Little Louis Was a True Statesman," appeared Jan. 7, 2005. Kenneth Bagnell's article "Does the News Belong to K.C. Irving?" appeared in *The Globe Magazine* (Toronto), June 14, 1969.

For coverage of the Combines investigation and media ownership, see Robert Campbell, "Other Mergers Probed, but Irving Trial First for Canadian Newspapers," *The Globe and Mail*, Nov. 10, 1972; John Porteous, "Another Try at Irving Case for William Hoyt," *Financial Post*, Nov. 29, 1975; James Rusk, "Press Bill Proposes New Limits on Chains," *The Globe and Mail*, July 7, 1983; and Murray Campbell, "Requiem for the Kent Report on Ownership," *The Globe and Mail*, Nov. 15, 1984. See also Joseph

Jackson, "Newspaper Ownership in Canada: An Overview of the Davey Committee and Kent Commission Studies" (Library of Parliament, 1999, PRB 99-35E); and Keith Davey, *The Rainmaker* (Toronto: Stoddart, 1986).

4: STRAIGHT ROADS

Ralph Costello's farewell memo was published in the *Telegraph-Journal* after his death as "A Publisher's Last Message: 'That's all, folks,' on April 20, 2001. See also "Costello: Saying Goodbye Was the Hard Part," *Telegraph-Journal*, March 19, 1988; and Edward Larracey, "Irving Was 'ever a gentleman,' Says Former Publisher," *Times-Transcript* (Moncton), Dec. 14, 1992. Elaine Bateman's series "Endangered Bay" was reprinted as an undated special supplement to the *Telegraph-Journal* in the fall of 1990. Bateman lent me a copy of the supplement for my research.

5: STIRRING THE POT

The *Telegraph-Journal*'s extensive coverage of K.C. Irving's death was published on Dec. 14, 1992, and his funeral was covered on Dec. 17, 1992. The Neil Reynolds era at the Kingston *Whig-Standard* is recounted in Douglas Fetherling, *A Little Bit of Thunder: The Strange Inner Life of the Kingston* Whig-Standard (Toronto: Stoddart, 1993); David Prosser, *Out of Afghanistan* (Montreal: Eden Press, 1987); and Charlene Yarrow, "Hail and Farewell to the *Whig*, at Least as We Knew It," *Ryerson Review of Journalism*, June 1993. Reynolds's own writings on journalism and literature include "Journalism: The Literature of the People," the *Whig-Standard Magazine*, June 10, 1989, and "The Word and the Book," the *Whig-Standard Magazine*, July 11, 1992.

Accounts of Reynolds's early tenure at the *Telegraph-Journal* include Merle MacIsaac, "Stop the Presses, I Want to Get Off,"

Canadian Business, Nov. 1994; Harvey Enchin, "Irving Takes New Paper Route," *The Globe and Mail*, Nov. 27, 1993; and Mark Leger, "He's Hired. He's Fired. He's Hired. He's ..." *Ryerson Review of Journalism*, Spring 1995. Philip Lee's story on *The Daily Gleaner* publishing hints about Karl Toft's abuse in 1971, "Kingsclear Problem Written of in '71," appeared in the *Telegraph-Journal*, Aug. 14, 1993, p. A3. Neil Reynolds's essay launching the *New Brunswick Reader*, "A Good Read," was published Nov. 20, 1993.

6: REYNOLDS, REFINED

Michael Woloschuk's contentious story on the firing of Neil Reynolds, "Editor Dismissed from Post," ran in the *Telegraph-Journal*, Aug. 25, 1994, p. A3; the announcement of Reynolds's return, "Neil Reynolds Renamed Editor-in-Chief, Assumes Role of Publisher," appeared in the *Telegraph-Journal*, Oct. 22, 1994, p. A2.

Erin Steuter's writings on the Irvings and their media holdings include "The Myth of the Competitive Challenge: The Irving Oil Refinery Strike, 1994–96, and the Canadian Petroleum Industry," (with Geoff Martin), *Studies in Political Economy*, Autumn 2000; "The Irvings Cover Themselves: Media Representations of the Irving Oil Refinery Strike, 1994–96," *Canadian Journal of Communication*, vol. 24, no. 4, 1999; and "He Who Pays the Piper Calls the Tune: Investigation of a Canadian Media Monopoly," *Web Journal of Mass Communications Research*, vol. 7, no. 4, 2004. Richard Foot's feature on labour relations in New Brunswick, "The State of Our Unions," was published in the *Telegraph-Journal*, Nov. 2, 1996, p. E1.

The account of Jill Mahoney's work on the refinery story is based on John White, "Woman Fought for Clean Air," *Telegraph-Journal*, May 30, 1995; and Campbell Morrison, "Refinery's

'Secret' Data Revealed," *Telegraph-Journal*, June 3, 1995. Jill Mahoney provided me with a rough draft of her unpublished story and her interview notes with Christie Marino from June 7, 1995.

7: OUT OF HIS SYSTEM

Jim Irving's reference to "those bastards" is from Geoffrey Stevens, *The Player: The Life and Times of Dalton Camp* (Toronto: Key Porter Books, 2003). For the account of J.K. Irving installing his son Robert to run the potato business on Prince Edward Island, see Alan Freeman and John Urquhart, "All in the Family: Hard-Working Irvings Maintain Tight Control in a Canadian Province," *The Wall Street Journal*, Nov. 1, 1983, p. 1. One of Jamie Irving's early bylines was "'Green Giant' Gardener off to Gagetown Fair with 200-Pound Pumpkin," *Evening Times-Globe*, Aug. 23, 1995, p. B1.

Philip Lee's series "Watershed Down" ran for several weeks in the fall of 1995 and was published in book form as *Home Pool: The Fight to Save the Atlantic Salmon* (Fredericton: Goose Lane Editions, 1996). Richard Foot's series "Timber Land" ran over three Saturdays in the *New Brunswick Reader* beginning on Feb. 17, 1996; his story on the argument that Irving Crown licences were subsidized by taxpayers was "'I'd Make Them Pay,'" *Telegraph-Journal*, Feb. 19, 1996.

Besides interviews and newspaper stories, the account of the *Irving Whale* salvage is based on several documents lent to me by Barry Murray. They include Government of Canada, "The Further Assessment of the Recovery of the *Irving Whale* in Light of the Presence of PCBs," March 1996; Searle and Associates Ltd. International Marine Consultants, "Technical Review: PCBs on the *Irving Whale*," 1996; Sawyer EnviroEconomic Consulting,

"Economic Assessment of the Options Related to the Salvage of the Barge *Irving Whale* with an Emphasis on the Release of PCBs: Final Report," March 1996; Government of Canada, "*Irving Whale* Recovery Project Scoping Sessions: Summary of Issues," January 1996; and R.J. Dutch Ritter (managing director), Marex International Ltd., "The *Irving Whale* Memorandum," May 16, 1994.

Newspaper articles include Campbell Morrison, "Copps calls in Mounties to investigate *Irving Whale*," *Telegraph-Journal*, Nov. 18, 1995; Steve McKinley, "And the Countdown Continues," *Telegraph-Journal*, July 27, 1996; and Steve McKinley, "'This Is the *Irving Whale* Calling,'" *Telegraph-Journal*, July 31, 1996. The 2012 ruling in the insurance case is *Universal Sales, Limited, Atlantic Towing Limited, J.D. Irving, Limited, Irving Oil Company, Limited and Irving Oil Limited vs. Edinburgh Assurance Co. Ltd. et. al.*, Reasons for Judgment: Federal Court of Canada, 2012 FC 418. See also Adrian Humphreys, "*Irving Whale*'s Insurers on the Hook for Millions, 40 Years After Barge Sank," *National Post*, May 14, 2012.

Neil Reynolds's parting essay, "A Watershed Moment for Our Province," was published in the *Telegraph-Journal* Nov. 2, 1996, p. E1.

8: STOP THE PRESSES

The editorial endorsing the federal PC party was "The Tories Are the Best Bet for a Prosperous, United Canada," *Telegraph-Journal*, May 31, 1997, p. E2. The proprietor's response was J.K. Irving, "Irving Says *Telegraph Journal* Is Wrong," *Telegraph-Journal*, June 2, 1997, p. 1.

9: SPICY, BUT NOT HOT

Bud Bird's comments on challenging the Irving bid for the natural gas franchise are from J.W. "Bud" Bird, *Sixty Seconds Run*, self-published memoir, 2011. Among the many *Telegraph-Journal* articles used in this chapter are Lisa Hrabluk, "A $-billion or Nothing, Says Irving," Sept. 3, 1998; Lisa Hrabluk, "'All Bets Are Off' If Rules Change," Sept. 3, 1998; André Veniot, "Gas NB Shrugs off Ultimatum," Sept. 4, 1998; Lisa Hrabluk, "Natural Gas 'Ultimatum' Just 'Facts,' says Irving," Sept. 5, 1998; and André Veniot, "'The People's Pipeline,'" Sept. 16, 1998. For Jim Irving's subsequent complaints about the natural gas rates, see Greg Weston, "Energy Costs Must Be Reined In, Session Told," *Telegraph-Journal*, Feb. 9, 2011.

The quotation from Rino Volpé about snapping chickens' necks is from Mark Tunney, *Cheap Power* (MA thesis, University of Western Ontario, 2008).

10: ROWING IN THE SAME DIRECTION

Quotations from Victor Mlodecki, David Cadogan, David Henley, John Steeves, Gilles Haché, and Marie-Linda Lord are from Parliament of Canada: Proceedings of the Standing Senate Committee on Transport and Communications, April 21–22, 2005. The change to *Le Journal* was reported in "New French Weekly Will Replace *Le Journal*," *Telegraph-Journal*, Feb. 14, 1998; the Brunswick News acquisition of a stake in Cadogan's weeklies is from Derwin Gowan, "Cadogan Gains Partner," *Telegraph-Journal*, Jan. 23, 2002. Mark Leger's comments about *here* are from Megan Wennberg, "Judging Democracy by Its Weakest Link: When *here* Became Their," Friends of Canadian Broadcasting, 2005. For Jamie Irving's attempt to prevent journalists from interviewing Paul Zed, see Mia Urquhart, Brian

Kemp, and Brad Janes, "Elsie Wayne Does It Again," *Telegraph-Journal*, Nov. 28, 2000.

11: BLUEBERRY MUFFINS

A vital source for this chapter is Mark Tunney, Cheap Power (MA thesis, University of Western Ontario, 2008), his first-hand account of working for Jamie Irving at the newspaper. The "blueberry muffin" scene from the film *Casino* is on YouTube at http://youtu.be/Yz_-k9qoYns.

For Kenneth Irving's New England ambitions, see, for example, David Shipley, "Large-Scale Projects Key to Feeding Energy Hungry U.S.: Irving Oil CEO," *Telegraph-Journal*, June 10, 2006; and Dean Jobb, "Irving Oil Tackles an Uncertain Energy Future," *Canadian Business*, Jan. 18, 2010. Coverage of the LNG tax concession included Rob Linke, "Tax Break for Proposed Irving Oil LNG Terminal Sparks Controversy"; and Marty Klinkenberg, "Kenneth Irving Steps out of the Shadows to Extol Project," both published in the *Telegraph-Journal*, March 16, 2005. Mayor McFarlane's "look into my eyes" comments are from "Mayor Defends Tax Deal with Irving," CBC News New Brunswick, March 16, 2005 (www.cbc.ca/news/canada/new-brunswick/mayor-defends-tax-deal-with-irving-1.565430).

The editorial "Tax Incentives Must Be Fair; the LNG Tax Break Must Be Revisited" was in the *Telegraph-Journal* on March 19, 2005. See also Gordon Pitts, "An Empire Looks to the Future," *The Globe and Mail*, March 26, 2005. For Canadaport LNG's 2013 tax assessment, see "LNG Terminal's Property Value Jumps, Taxes Frozen," CBC News New Brunswick, March 6, 2013 (http://www.cbc.ca/news/canada/new-brunswick/lng-terminal-s-property-value-jumps-taxes-frozen-1.1408973).

The description of the Senate hearings is based on Parliament of Canada: Proceedings of the Standing Senate Committee on Transport and Communications, April 21–22, 2005.

Coverage of the second refinery announcement included David Shipley, "Our Black Gold," *Telegraph-Journal*, Oct. 6, 2006. The account of the *Carleton Free Press* battle is drawn from *Brunswick News vs. Ken Langdon*, New Brunswick Court of Queen's Bench court file SJC-549-2007. Rod Allen's stories on the hearing that appeared in the *Telegraph-Journal* are "Court Fight Continues over Woodstock Newspapers," Oct. 26, 2007; "Newspaper Court Case Decision Expected Friday," Oct. 27, 2007; and "Paper Publisher Wins Partial Injunction," Nov. 3, 2007.

The scoop on the family split was Gordon Pitts and Jacquie McNish, "Irving Brothers Look to Break Up Empire," *The Globe and Mail*, Nov. 21, 2007. See also Marty Klinkenberg, "The Elite Fraternity: Irvings First Family with Four Members Recognized in Canadian Business Hall of Fame," *Telegraph-Journal*, Nov. 21, 2007, and Derwin Gowan, "It's Business as Usual, Irving says," *Telegraph-Journal*, Nov. 22, 2007.

12: MORE TREES ARE THE ANSWER
Daniel McHardie's story about Peter Hyslop appeared as "From Power Critic to Tory Candidate," *Times-Transcript* (Moncton), Sept. 1, 2006; then the same article appeared again three days later as "Tory Slams Lord on Energy," *Telegraph-Journal*, Sept. 4, 2006. For the full debate on Jeannot Volpé's media ownership motion, see *Journal of Debates*, Legislative Assembly of New Brunswick, June 5–6, 2008.

The information about the "More Trees Are the Answer" campaign is based on research by my CBC colleague Terry Seguin, which he kindly shared with me. It includes videotaped interviews and documents released under the Right to Information Act.

Coverage of Jim Irving's editorial board presentation on power rates appeared in the *Telegraph-Journal* on Jan. 25, 2008; Mark Mosher's comments are from "Irving Considers Moving Paper Mill to Quebec," CBC News New Brunswick, March 10, 2008 (www.cbc.ca/news/canada/new-brunswick/irving-considers -moving-paper-mill-to-quebec-1.721713).

The assertion by Don Roberts that the province loses money on Crown land forestry is from p. 19 of "Thoughts on Transforming the Forest Sector in New Brunswick," his presentation to the New Brunswick Forestry Summit, Nov. 18, 2010.

13: WHEELS WITHIN WHEELS

The initial story that led to the so-called Wafergate controversy is Adam Huras and Rob Linke, "It's a Scandal," *Telegraph-Journal*, July 8, 2009; the apology, "*Telegraph-Journal* Apologizes to Prime Minister," appeared on July 28, 2009. For a good account of the fallout see Chelsea Murray, "The Calm After the Storm," *Ryerson Review of Journalism*, Summer 2010. See also Ian Austen, "Newspaper Apologizes for Inventing a Scandal," *The New York Times*, Aug. 2, 2009.

Coverage of the Long Wharf debate in Saint John included Andrew McGilligan, "ILA Slams Long Wharf Deal," *Telegraph-Journal*, June 21, 2008; Dave MacLean, "Inarguable Support," *Telegraph-Journal*, Aug. 12, 2008; Marty Klinkenberg, "Land Swap Gets Nod," *Telegraph-Journal*, Aug. 19, 2008; and Reid Southwick, "We Will Take It Back," *Telegraph-Journal*, Aug. 20, 2008. Southwick's profile of Abel LeBlanc, "The Cain Inside Abel," appeared in the *Telegraph-Journal*, Aug. 23, 2008. The allegations by and against Daniel Mlodecki are from *Daniel Mlodecki vs. Brunswick News Inc.*, Court of Queen's Bench court file SJC-648-2008. Shawna Richer's responses to Mayor Ivan Court are from a CBC Maritime Noon interview on June 29, 2009, and her column, "We Are Doing Our Job. Are You, Your Worship?" was in the *Telegraph-Journal*, June 30, 2009. For the story of Matt McCann's firing, I relied on Richer's May 13, 2009, letter to McCann and Andrew Chung, "Hot Scoop Burns Reporter at Irving Paper," *Toronto Star*, June 17, 2009.

The account of the shipyard's history is based in part on John DeMont's account, as well as Erin Andersen, "Ottawa Payment Settles Frigate Fight with MIL Davie," *Evening Times-Globe*, July 27, 1994; Kim Honey, "No Work, No Jobs," *Evening Times-Globe*, July 10, 1995; Erin Andersen, "Hope Costs $25 Million," *Evening Times-Globe*, Aug. 25, 1995; Richard Roik, "Federal Ethics Commission Doubts Rock in Conflict over Irving Gift," *Telegraph-Journal*, Oct. 15, 2003; and Richard Roik, "Controversy Continues to Stalk Veteran Cabinet Minister," *Telegraph-Journal*, Oct. 18, 2003. An editorial critical of the fly-fishing trips was "Ethics System Needs Overhaul," *Telegraph-Journal*, Oct. 15, 2003.

Neil Reynolds's comments on his return are from his own column, "A Commitment to Excellence," *Telegraph-Journal*, Sept. 12, 2009, and from his interview with CBC Radio's *Information Morning* in Saint John on Sept. 13, 2009.

The account of the NB Power–Hydro Québec debate draws upon "Power Talks Continue Between Province, Quebec," *Telegraph-Journal*, Oct. 23, 2009; Shawn McCarthy and Rhéal Séguin, "Quebec, New Brunswick Nearing Power Pact," *The Globe and Mail*, Oct. 24, 2009; CBC News New Brunswick, "Hydro-Québec CEO Says Rate Structure not His Idea," Nov. 10, 2009 (www.cbc.ca/news/canada/new-brunswick/hydro-qu%C3%A9bec-ceo-says-rate-structure-not-his-idea-1.849673); Julian Walker, "The Once and Future New Brunswick Free Press," *Journal of New Brunswick Studies*, St. Thomas University, vol. 1, 2010; and Neil Reynolds, "Response to Julian Walker's 'The Once and Future New Brunswick Free Press,'"

Journal of New Brunswick Studies, St. Thomas University (appended to vol. 1, 2010). Two examples of Philip Lee's coverage are "Down by the Old Mill Stream," *Telegraph-Journal*, Feb. 20, 2010, and "How Quebec 'Cornered' Hydro Power," *Telegraph-Journal*, Feb. 22, 2010.

14: DEAD TREE EDITION

For the evolution of Irving Oil, see the Canadian Press, "Changes Coming to Irving Gas Stations on PEI," *The Guardian* (Charlottetown), May 9, 2008; Gordon Pitts, "Re-energizing a Dynasty, Irvings Gain a New Name," *The Globe and Mail*, June 25, 2009; Rebecca Penty, "Emera Buying Bayside Power from Irving Oil," *Telegraph-Journal*, June 27, 2009; Dave MacLean, "Refinery Plan Shelved," *Telegraph-Journal*, July 25, 2009; Reid Southwick, "HQ Project Halted," *Telegraph-Journal*, Feb. 3, 2010; Gordon Pitts, "Irving Empire Suffers Two Losses," *The Globe and Mail*, July 21, 2010; and Rebecca Penty, "Kenneth Irving Steps Aside," *Telegraph-Journal*, July 21, 2010.

The Bermuda ruling that reveals the feud between Arthur and Kenneth Irving over Arthur's trust is *In the Matter of A Trust*, [2012] SC (Bda) 72 Civ (12 Dec. 2012). It forms part of a larger court action relating to the K.C. Irving estate trust; the file number for the main action, which is sealed to the public, is 2009:361.

The account of Rob Warner's efforts to relaunch the Brunswick News website is based in part on *Newsroom News*, a daily newsletter Warner circulated to the staff. I obtained copies of the newsletters. Warner's remarks on the impending death of print journalism are from "A Case for Change," July 28, 2011; the *mea culpa* was by Matt Kilfoil, "Reports of Our Death Greatly Exaggerated," August 4, 2011. See also Jacqueline Nunes, "Going Down," *Ryerson Review of Journalism*, Summer 2006;

and James Surowiecki, "News You Can Lose," *The New Yorker*, December 22, 2008.

For coverage of the Irvings in Maine, see Phyllis Austin's stories in the *Maine Times*, including "Playing by Different Rules," Dec. 4, 1987; "Presto! The Forest's Gone," March 20, 1987; and "Irving Shoots Itself in Foot with Heavy-Handed Lobbying," April 10, 1992. Angus King's comments are from my interview with him for my previous book, *Imaginary Line: Life on an Unfinished Border* (Fredericton: Goose Lane Editions, 2011). The information on Irving donations to the 1996 plebiscite campaign is from political action committee reports for Citizens for a Healthy Forest and Economy of April 10, July 23, Oct. 10, Oct. 30, and Dec. 17, 1996, which I reviewed at the offices of the Maine Ethics Commission in Augusta. The ranking of J.D. Irving Ltd. as the fifth-largest private landowner in the United States is from "The 2013 Land Report 100," *Land Report* magazine (www.landreport.com/americas-100-largest-landowners/). Jim Irving's comment about considering Maine "to be home" is from a video that accompanied "Rare Interview Offers Insight into Irving, Maine's Largest Landowner," by Julia Bayly, *Bangor Daily News*, Feb. 7, 2014.

15: A FAMILY ACTIVITY

For J.D. Irving Ltd.'s activities during the 2010–13 period, see "Irving Defends Forestry Lobbying Campaign," CBC News New Brunswick, June 23, 2011 (www.cbc.ca/news/canada/new-brunswick/irving-defends-forestry-lobbying-campaign-1.1038354); Chris Morris, "Forestry Billed as Untapped Economic Engine," *Telegraph-Journal*, Jan. 28, 2012; "Bruce Northrup Unveils New Forestry Plan," CBC News New Brunswick, March 30, 2012 (www.cbc.ca/news/

canada/new-brunswick/bruce-northrup-unveils-new-forestry -plan-1.1184118); "Irving Endorses Plan to Reform Enbridge," CBC News New Brunswick, June 14, 2011 (www.cbc.ca/news/ canada/new-brunswick/irving-endorses-plan-to-reform -enbridge-1.1035487). Coverage of Halifax Shipyards winning the warship contract appeared in the *Telegraph-Journal*, Oct. 20, 2011.

Arthur Irving's comments are from a CBC audio recording of his remarks on Aug. 1, 2013. See also *Bloomberg News*, "Canaport 'A Big White Elephant': Analyst," *Telegraph-Journal*, Feb. 15, 2013; Jeff Lewis, "Repsol Writes Down Canaport by $1.3B After Failing to Sell LNG Terminal in Blockbuster Shell Deal," *Financial Post*, Feb. 26, 2013; and Adam Huras, "'Game-Changing' Day for Province," *Telegraph-Journal*, Aug. 2, 2013. Analysis of the Lac-Mégantic explosion's implications for the Irvings is based on Les Perreaux, "To the End of the Line," *The Globe and Mail*, July 27, 2013; the Canadian Press, "Irving Subsidiary Considering Acquisition of Insolvent MM&A rail line," Aug. 19, 2013; Grant Robertson and Jacquie McNish, "Inside the Oil-Shipping Free-for-All That Brought Disaster to Lac-Mégantic," *The Globe and Mail*, Dec. 2, 2013; Jacquie McNish and Grant Robertson, "How the Flames That Devastated Lac-Mégantic Were Lit in North Dakota," *The Globe and Mail*, Dec. 3, 2013; an Information to Obtain a Search Warrant filed by Transport Canada inspector Marc Grignon with the Provincial Court of New Brunswick, Saint John, on Dec. 11, 2013; Chalmers Hardenbergh, "MMA: Remarks During U.S. Hearing," *Atlantic Northeast Rails and Ports* e-bulletin, Dec. 20, 2013; and Adam Huras, "New Brunswick Company's Interest in Key Railway Revealed," *Telegraph-Journal*, Dec. 23, 2013.

The account of Kenneth Irving's legal battle with his father is based on the same 2012 Bermuda court ruling cited in Chapter 14.

This chapter also relies on Henry Blodget, "*New York Times and the Future of Journalism*," *Business Insider*, Aug. 1, 2013; and Gordon Pitts, "The First Non–family Member to Run Irving Oil Exits," *The Globe and Mail*, May 30, 2013.

Some information about the Energy East pipeline project, and Patricia Graham's comment about Brunswick News being "sensitive" to ownership concerns, are from Richard Valdmanis and Dave Sherwood, "A Family Plan to Pump Canada's Oil," Reuters, March 28, 2014.

ACKNOWLEDGMENTS

There is a certain type of New Brunswicker who makes a hobby of watching the Irvings. These people keep tabs on their activities, sift through their rare public utterances for hidden meanings, and swap gossip at every opportunity. They do not speak for attribution but they are exceedingly wise. I discovered during my research that they are also generous with their time and their observations. I thank these Irving-watchers sincerely. They know who they are.

I am very grateful to William Hoyt, who prosecuted the Irving Combines case and whom I met by chance at a book event in the summer of 2012. When I told him I was thinking of writing about the newspapers, he offered enthusiastic encouragement—and access to his files and recollections. I am in his debt for the gentle but decisive push he gave me.

This project might never have happened if not for a brief conversation at the 2012 Politics and the Pen gala in Ottawa, where Charlotte Gray offered to recommend me to her agent, Hilary

McMahon. I thank Charlotte for the recommendation and Hilary for accepting it. I am also very grateful to Diane Turbide at Penguin Canada for accepting the proposal that Hilary brought to her, for allowing me to be associated with such a venerable publisher, and for her judicious and diligent work on this manuscript, which has greatly improved it. Thanks to Chandra Wohleber for her meticulous and collaborative approach to the copyediting, Sandra Tooze for steering the book through production, and Erin Kelly for her work on the marketing and promotion.

Thanks as well are due to Mary-Pat Schutta and Dan Goodyear, my supervisors at CBC News in New Brunswick, for agreeing to accommodate my desire to write this book, and to Andrew Cochran, the regional director for CBC in Atlantic Canada, for granting me the permission to proceed without any constraints or conditions, and to draw on the CBC archives.

My CBC colleagues are the best journalists in Atlantic Canada and I thank all of them for their interest in this book. Special thanks to Robert Jones, Daniel McHardie, Terry Seguin, and Connell Smith for insights and feedback, and to Margaret Isaacs for pointing me to old archive tapes. I am also particularly grateful to my former *Telegraph-Journal* colleague Lisa Hrabluk, who generously shared with me her insights on power relationships in Saint John.

I was fortunate to be able to draw on the expertise and helpfulness of staffs at the Harriet Irving Library at the University of New Brunswick, the Library of the Legislative Assembly of New Brunswick, and the Provincial Archives of New Brunswick. In particular, Siobhan Hanratty at the HIL and Joanna Aiton Kerr at the archives made extra efforts on my behalf. And thanks to Jennifer Andrews, the catalyst to my becoming an honourary research associate at the UNB Department of English.

I am indebted to Josh O'Kane and Melanie Hopper for poking around in hard-to-reach places that I couldn't get to myself, and to Harry Bagley, Elaine Bateman, Wendell Fulton, Philip Lee, Jill Mahoney, Barry Murray, and Terry Seguin for providing materials I would not have been able to obtain anywhere else.

Special thanks go to Mary Keith, vice-president of communications at J.D. Irving Ltd., for arranging my interview with J.K. Irving and Jim Irving. I am also in the debt of Kim Kierans, from the University of King's College School of Journalism, for digging out the decade-old mini-disc of her interview with Jamie Irving and having it digitized for me.

I am grateful to the journalists who worked at the Irving newspapers during the time I was researching this book. They were explicitly prohibited from speaking to me, and I did not attempt to persuade them to violate this edict. But their interest in the project, and their own desire to understand the full story of their employer's media holdings, was a great encouragement. I respect their professionalism and appreciate their friendship.

My wife, Giselle Goguen, understood that if I were going to write non-fiction books about our home province of New Brunswick, this project was inevitable. She made it possible, however. When I needed time or space to work, she gave it to me, doing much more than her share at home. A recovering journalist herself, Giselle read the manuscript—twice—and improved it greatly with her suggestions. Mainly, though, it was her kindness and generosity that I needed most, and that she never hesitated to provide.

INDEX

335